Hear Our Truths

DISSIDENT FEMINISMS

HEAR OUR TRUTHS

The Creative Potential of Black Girlhood

Ruth Nicole Brown

UNIVERSITY OF ILLINOIS PRESS

URBANA, CHICAGO, AND SPRINGFIELD

For Maya Sanaa, Addis, and Kaleb

Contents

Acknowledgments

Thank you to everyone who has ever participated in Saving Our Lives Hear Our Truths. SOLHOT is such a small work with profound implications—I hope that everyone who has contributed to it is honored by this particular telling. To the girls of SOLHOT, I celebrate your genius and I thank you for making "the space" your own.

So much of the original shape of SOLHOT is inspired by the arts, particularly theater and poetry. My earliest training in social-issues theater came by way of Innervoices under the gifted direction of Ginny Sims. It was a powerful full-circle moment to have Innervoices, under the impeccable direction of Lisa Fay, perform *Endangered Black Girls* (EBG). To the original cast and crew of EBG, I thank you for elevation and freedom. EBG was a necessary bridge between what I thought I knew and what I know now about Black girlhood. To each of the sites SOLHOT has transgressed—and the waymakers, Regina Crider, Sara Powell, Angela Smith, Angela Evans, and Andrea Kirkland—I am humbled by your dedication and commitment to improving the community on behalf of Black girls. Thank you to Trudy Moore for sharing your greatest gift with me and making sure that as I taught, I was well.

SOLHOT gives me the honor and pleasure to work with some incredible individuals and emerging scholars. Sesali Bowen, Grenita Hall, Desiree McMillion, Porshe Garner, Dominique Hill, Durell Callier, Sheri Lewis, Pasha Trotter, and Blair Smith, you all require my best, and I am always inspired by your actions to give it. Thank you all for shining so brightly, each in your very own way with your very own style! Candy Taaffe, you've been such a constant source of all things SOLHOT, and the book is better because of our limitless conversations, texts, emails, and disagreements about it all. I am so very excited to read your SOLHOT dissertation, and I hope that this book provides a strong foundation for your own creation. Queen Jessica Robinson, you have a way of getting me together unlike any other. Your research assistance is just as fierce as your understanding and commitment to SOLHOT, and I thank you sincerely. Treva Ellison, your intellect and generosity are unparalleled. Thank you for your comments on internal SOLHOT documents as well as early drafts of chapter 1. Christina Carney-Anderson, it has been a gift to be in your presence and witness your power; I appreciate you always.

I would like to thank the University of Illinois College of Education's Charles Dunn Hardie Faculty Fellowship for supporting the early development of chapter 3. Also, this book has benefited greatly from the support of the University of Illinois Campus Research Board and the Civic Commitment Task Force of the Office of the Chancellor. Thank you to colleagues and staff in the departments of Gender and Women's Studies and Education Policy, Organization, and Leadership at the University of Illinois Urbana-Champaign for supporting my research agenda from the very beginning. A very special thank-you to Nancy Abelman and Craig Koslofsky for nurturing me as I conceptualized the book, developed a proposal, and sought publication.

The National Women's Studies Association and Imagining America have both been especially helpful as an academic home base from which to present and perform my research as an engaged artist-scholar. Thank you to Vivien Ng, Beverly Guy-Sheftall, Kevin Bott, Tim Eatman, David Scobey, Jan Cohen-Cruz, Bonnie Thornton-Dill, Nikol Alexander Floyd, Michele Berger, Allison Kimmich, Holly Blake, and Patti Provance for your vision, example, service, and dedication to creativity and interdisciplinary scholarship. My eternal gratitude to Tricia Lin for being a bright light and generous spirit. Thank you for your consistent encouragement and warmhearted support. The NWSA–Spelman Institute was a necessary intervention that greatly improved my professional life by introducing me to admirable master teachers and colleagues with whom I continue to stand in solidarity. I am particularly hopeful that traces of the best ways the institute profoundly influenced my thinking are legible to those who participated, particularly in chapter 2 and chapter 5.

To complete this book, I drew inspiration from lessons learned from mentors from quite some time ago up until very recently. Thank you to Dianne Pinderhughes, Todd Shaw, Greg Markus, Martha Feldman, Dominique Morriseau, Chernoh Sesay, Kyra Gaunt, Sarah Projansky, James Anderson, Anne Haas Dyson, Elaine Richardson, Adrienne Dixson, and Julia Jordan-Zachery. Thank you to Cynthia Dillard for instantaneous recognition, reading of drafts, and thoughtful suggestions. That I can work alongside sistafriendcolleagues who lift me higher is a gift unto itself. Quite seriously, I would not be as encouraged in the work if it were not for the abiding friendship of Chamara J. Kwakye, Zenzele Isoke, Robin Hayes, Aisha Durham, Melynda Price, Tiffany Davis, Lisa Cacho, Isabel Molina, Aimee Cox, Dana Edell, Jillian Hernandez, Mimi Nguyen, Fiona Ngô, Mariama Sesay, Soo Ah Kwon, Sharon Irish, Christina DeNicolo, Karen Flynn, and Michelle Tellez.

Thank you to the wonderful folks at the University of Illinois Press. Larin McLaughlin, it makes all the difference that you get me! I'd also like to thank Dawn Durante and the anonymous reviewers of my manuscript.

Christine Bryant Cohen, you are the very best! Two books down, more to go. I thank you for your clarity, candor, generosity, and patience. You make me want to write more, and I'm thankfully learning so much about writing and living in the process.

My family is the center of my strength, and you have all done something major to ensure this book's survival. Thank you to my parents, Lawrence and Evelyn. I am grateful to Denise, Byron, Anthony, Renee, Jasmine, Lauren, Jalen, Melody, Malik, Malayah, Karla, and TJ for the encouragement, support, and laughter. A very special thank-you goes to my mother, Evelyn, and sister, Denise, for being with the kids as I taught, conferenced, and wrote. I could not do this without you all! Getu, this book would not have seen the light of day if it were not for your consistent support and "on your feet" motivation. No doubt, your love grows me stronger, and I am beyond appreciative. I love you always! Maya Sanaa, thank you for being who you are and for naming and claiming me as an "author." Thank you, Addis, for typing on the keyboard as I attempted to write—it was always a welcome break. To the little one on the way, thank you for making me prove to myself on the daily just how much I wanted to share my truth about a work called SOLHOT that has also transformed me from the inside out.

Hear Our Truths

Introduction

The vision: Black girlhood is freedom, and Black girls are free. As an organizing construct, Black girlhood makes possible the affirmation of Black girls' lives and, if necessary, their liberation. Black girlhood as a spatial intervention is useful for making our daily lives better and therefore changing the world as we currently know it. Love guides our actions and permeates our beings. For those who do not know love, we create spaces to practice Black girlhood and sense love, to name it, claim it, and share it. What we know, what we say, our process, and what we make is of value, especially if it surfaces in unexpected forms. The space is specific enough that Black girls recognize it as theirs. The making of the space is collective and creative; uncertainty and complexity motivate, and revolutionary action is the goal.

To inspire greater visions of Black girlhood than I could dream of alone, I suggested Saving Our Lives Hear Our Truths, affectionately known throughout this book by the acronym SOLHOT. SOLHOT is a space to envision Black girlhood critically among and with Black girls, who, it seems to me, are often the people least guaranteed to be centered as valuable in collective work and social movements that they could very well lead and organize. This book is about SOLHOT as a particular methodology of creating spaces to practice and enact a visionary Black girlhood. Whether the vision is simply stated as the celebration of Black girlhood in all of its complexity, or revised and elongated as stated above in the opening paragraph, SOLHOT as utopia, SOLHOT as dismal failure, and SOLHOT as mostly everything in between is about foregrounding complexity in collective and creative work with Black girls and women.

SOLHOT is a small but important work that points to larger realizations about the artistic imaginations of Black girls and women, systemic violence and persistent inequality, and also the possibilities of social change ignited, for example, by a poem written by someone who claims not to be a poet, new organizing principles shaped by skeptics who have been Black women harmed by previous organizations, and, of course, a visionary Black girlhood that means freedom. More often than not, when SOLHOT shows up, they, we, have never seen anything like it, like us, being ourselves; and what we learn in and out of sacred time, practice, and relationship is that we are certainly worth our own liberation. SOLHOT reveals that our commitment to the practice of Black girlhood is incredibly imperative, and when we own our shine and feel compelled to share it, we feel free and affirmed. SOLHOT as a means of loving Black girls, loving ourselves, and valuing our interdependence embodies the very best principles of organizing, the very best principles of education, and the very best principles of living well.

The following questions guide my vision for Black girlhood as practiced in SOLHOT and also motivated me to write this book: What is necessary to imagine Black girlhood as a space of freedom? What would need to be abolished and created to enact such a vision of Black girlhood? Who would commit to such an idea? How do Black girls experience affirmation, and how does it feel, to them, to be free? How is this vision of Black girlhood useful for Black girls and women? What is so specific about practicing Black girlhood that the process is able to lead to something beyond the world as we currently know it? What does this vision of Black girlhood look like in practice, and what new knowledge emerges that may then be useful for and benefit everyone?

"At the end of the day" may be an overused cliché, except when spoken by a Black girl. In SOLHOT, I have learned that the words "at the end of the day" preface Black girls' truths, the kind of truth telling Audre Lorde (1984b) insisted is made possible when silence is transformed into language and action. At the end of the day, even as we toddle into another millennium, structural conditions shaped by sociohistorical forces continue to perpetuate injury, hurt, and harm in the lives of Black girls even as they continue to find practical ways to deal, cope, and resist (Ladner, 1995). Ask the beautiful Black girl in Minneapolis whose teacher turned the lie "You will never amount to anything" into a pedagogical practice; remember all of the Black women and girls who died prematurely with the circumstances of their deaths too often unknown and unresolved; know that quite a few girls, too many to be acceptable, are brilliant yet routinely disciplined into taking up less and less space. There are women afraid of working with other women and girls in collective projects because politics, labor, and movement work masquerading as justice have harmed them before. As Liberian peace activist and 2011 Nobel Peace Prize winner Leymeh Gbowee (2012) reminds us, too many African girls throughout the diaspora desire a space to be more than the expectations that others have for them. But for the space of SOLHOT, I would have to make do with singular celebrity-media-identified moments of Black girl praise, such as Willow Smith's "Whip My Hair," the Sesame Street video "I Love My Hair," and *Black Girls Rock* on BET. Thankfully, Janelle Monae and Issa Rae have influenced the public sphere so that Black girlhood is synonymous with time travel, being awkward, and receiving support from those who desire new images and sounds, presenting the full complexity of Black girlhood and womanhood. At the end of the day, while we have been injured, creating a space to practice visionary Black girlhood makes the creative potential possible.

In SOLHOT we have come to know the creative potential of Black girlhood as documented by Toni Cade Bambara. Bambara wrote of Black girls in her short stories and novels as the main protagonists and/or as critical plot co-conspirators. Her Black girl characters were memorable because they triumphed over less than ideal circumstances with resources such as humor, wisdom, and sharp tongues, often unrecognizable as tools that are completely capable of overturning structures, people, and frameworks once thought permanent (Holmes and Wall, 2008). These are the same Black girl resources necessary to make working with Black girls during after-school hours into no happy-go-lucky after-school special. Rather, creating spaces of emancipatory Black girlhood for the purpose of allowing each of us to hold the thought, as instructed by Bambara's character Minnie Ransom in *The Salt Eaters* (1992), that there is nothing that stands between us and perfect health, and therefore sets us up not so much to achieve freedom, but, as Bambara taught, to practice freedom and thereby improve on use. Avery Gordon (2008, p. 259) wrote that *usable* was a favorite word of Toni Cade Bambara's, and it is in Bambara's sense of the word that I offer this book as an examination of particular usable truths about Black girlhood that have emerged because of and through SOLHOT. At end of the day, the creative potential of Black girlhood is a useful framework from which to

1. Articulate visionary Black girlhood as a meaningful practice
2. Showcase Black girl inventiveness of form and content
3. Expand our vision of Black girlhood beyond identity
4. Sense radical courage and interdependence
5. Honor praxis, the analytical insight that comes only by way of consistent action and reflection

This book makes the case for a performative and creative methodology of a visionary Black-girlhood practice that does as SOLHOT suggests—saves our lives and facilitates the hearing of truths. However, I dismantle neoliberal and elitist normative assumptions typically associated with youth interventionist programming. Black girlhood as an organizing practice of resistance and wellness does not collude with white-supremacist sentimentalities of saving someone presumably less human for the purpose of conquest. SOLHOT, when thoughtfully engaged, has allowed us to save ourselves. The creation, documentation, meditation on, participation in, and analysis of particular SOLHOT practices and our productions all reveal the creative potential of Black girlhood to demonstrate and address the following: how creative work produces knowledge that Black girls are accountable to and relationships that hold them accountable; what is so problematic and patronizing about approaching Black girls as work to be worked over; how Black girlhood is an organizing construct unlike anything else; what is required of those who do the work to create the space; and the various media, artwork, and knowledges, individually and collectively produced, that innovate form and transform use.

Each chapter of this book shows through different archetypal evidence—a theatrical play, memories, photography, narrative, interviews, literary texts, ethnographic field notes, an anti-narrative photo-poem, poetry, and original music analysis of five songs made in SOLHOT—that Black girlhood as an emancipatory space depends on distance and difference to make recognizable the unfathomable truths of another's complexity. This project builds on women-of-color feminisms, hip-hop feminism, womanism, critical ethnic studies, and scholarship on Black girlhood and critical pedagogy to unearth radical interpretive sensibilities that allow for valuing Black girls even as they may be misunderstood and enacting a practice of Black girlhood contingent on creativity and imagination, collectivity and complexity, and unknowability and productive uncertainty. The aim of this book is to point at the fullness of a visionary Black girlhood embodied in SOLHOT and, as demonstrated through multiple exemplars of Black girl genius, the political necessity of redirecting our attention and effort away from blaming, shaming, and punishing Black girls, toward new articulations of age-old questions, organizing dilemmas, and sacred knowledge.

An interviewer once questioned Lorraine Hansberry, playwright, activist, and writer from Chicago's South Side, about her play *A Raisin in the Sun*: "Someone comes up to you and says: 'This is not really a Negro play; why, this could be about anybody! It's a play about people!' What is your reaction?"

Hansberry responded:

> Well, I hadn't noticed the contradiction because I'd always been under the impression that Negroes are people . . . In other words, I have told people that not only is this a Negro family, specifically and definitely culturally, but it's not even a New York family or a southern Negro family. It is specifically Southside Chicago . . . that kind of care, that kind of attention to detail. In other words, I think people, to the extent we accept them and believe them as who they're supposed to be, to that extent they can become everybody. So I would say it is definitely a Negro play before it is anything else . . . (1969, p. 114)

Black girlhood as practiced in Saving Our Lives Hear Our Truths is specific—it is very much about who we are and how we do it. All of us together in this very specific group of individuals are not all Black girls. Some of us are diasporically oriented and always foreground a homeland to intentionally decenter the United States as superpower or natural. We are also male. Sexuality is always of concern, particularly since so many in SOLHOT are attempting to know and claim all aspects of who they are. The collective work that is SOLHOT specifically exists in the Midwest of the United States. However, we carry SOLHOT with us wherever we go. We are all subject to compulsory schooling; many of us have continued on beyond our family's expectations, while some of us have been pushed out of school by the system itself. Two of us are white, one older and one younger. Christianity, Islam, and Ifa are specifically referenced spiritual practices in SOLHOT. We were once divided by ideology: there was the sex-positive crew and those that advocated abstinence only. Even as we do SOLHOT, some of us are against "females," and others are women-identified. We all enjoy food, snacks, and beverages when we gather. We use our cell phones even when having a face-to-face conversation, and many of us prefer to keep our coats on, even while indoors. Some of us drive to SOLHOT, some walk, others are dropped off, and some take the bus. Importantly, some of us are painfully shy, and others are proudly loud. I'm counting on the insight shared by Lorraine Hansberry that specificity can lead to a more general understanding of the human condition.

How SOLHOT happens, as the practice-based research site on which the evidence of this study is based, makes possible the exploration of highly complex entanglements of identity, power, and representations among Black women and girls, who range in age between eleven and fifty-five, in a particular community of practice. SOLHOT actively promotes self- and collective expression through culturally relevant activities that address the issues deemed important to participants. SOLHOT takes place in public schools and in community-based institutions. The process of SOLHOT is about a way of thinking about the world that foregrounds the full humanity of Black girlhood, rather than colluding with institutions, interpersonal interactions, and larger social and political systems that thrive on neglecting Black girls and depend on their disposability. In this way, SOLHOT transcends both the parameters of its physical location in a midwestern United States college town and the individuals who gather during a specific time and place in the name of SOLHOT. SOLHOT enables a critique of the social conditions that influence the most intimate aspects of Black girls' lives and relies on specificity to enable comparative understandings.

Drawing on the insight of Anita Harris (2003), who cautions that visibility for visibility's sake sometimes results in increased control and punishment of girls' bodies and interiorities, the public work we engage in SOLHOT is intentionally critical and unpredictable, and it varies from weekly sessions with the girls, to theatrical performances, photography exhibits, poetry, classes, conference presentations, and more. The more private conversations and decisions that circulate through texts, glances, side conversations, social media, and sista circles encourage us to promote a relational understanding of Black girlhood as the foundation for the public work we do. In this way, to introduce this book, for example, with profiles of individual Black girls would not be SOLHOT, as SOLHOT privileges a collective story about how we are together that is at all times negotiated. Sometimes positive, sometimes deviant, but mostly meaningful, the relationships created in SOLHOT because of SOLHOT may be thought of as its number-one production. SOLHOT enables the kinds of relationships that bring people together in ways that produce feelings of belonging—often referred to as *community*. In SOLHOT, we discuss diverse expressions of Black girlhood, critique the issues that are important to us, and create art that keeps Black girls' lived experiences at its center, even as some us do not identify as Black girls. For this reason, throughout this book you will notice that it is Black women, Black girls, and beyond whose stories make up this account and refute static and fixed assumptions of Black girlhood. But the problem of standard English remains, and therefore, to be consistent with the language used in SOLHOT, in this book I refer to *the girls* to signify those who assume and expect SOLHOT to permanently exist with or without their contributing efforts. I refer to *the homegirls* to mean those who consciously labor to meet the girls' expectations. I use these categories of distinction throughout the book, forgoing the usual fictionalized profiles of individual people. However, when particularities of the girls and homegirls were critical, I used pseudonyms, with the exception of those whose artistry informed my argument and those who gave me permission to credit them by name.

This book represents two years of data collection and a total of five years of working with Black girls in SOLHOT (2005–9), though I rely on the sum total of my experiences doing work with girls. According to Locke and Golden-Biddle (1994), post-positivist ethnographic studies that develop and convey authenticity, plausibility, and criticality as dimensions of convincing are key methodological assessments. Documentation of meeting these criteria—through prolonged participant observation, intensive relationship building with research participants and institutional gatekeepers, and my personal experiences as a Black woman traversing community and campus boundaries—becomes a specific type of index from which I build my ethnographic narrative. That my insider status in SOLHOT permeates all aspects of data collection, analysis, presentation, and writing is not so much unusual as it is intimate. I am the ethnographer, whose fieldnotes are documented; I am the SOLHOT visionary often mentioned and referenced by others; I am the artist who offers new poems based on the creative works made by girls and homegirls in SOLHOT; I am the theorist who analyzed our practices; and I am the researcher who is speaking to and building on the ideas of those who have helped me come to understand something more about Black girlhood.

Given current constraints on knowledge production as it relates to contemporary public-university life, to implement SOLHOT as a sustainable collective practice, create original art, transform academic scholarship by advocating for a more nuanced understanding of Black girlhood, and perform with SOLHOT participants to create dialogue about Black girls' issues in the communities they are most accountable to is a summertime privilege that too often feels like the dead of winter. It used to be plenty significant to do and write about any one of these things. It takes a certain skill set to pull off a SOLHOT session that everyone enjoys, and a different set of skills to write an academic paper about what we did that is personally and professionally satisfying. To create art requires certain resources and willfulness; to then publicly perform as a collective ensemble about the work we do in SOLHOT requires yet different gifts and talents. Certainly the idea of SOLHOT is highly improbable considering that university life is increasingly bureaucratic, privatized, and oriented toward the corporate. But SOLHOT as practiced, the process and productions of our labor as documented in this book, proves that we are more than possible, that Black girls are beyond what we now know and should never be underestimated. This is both a cautionary statement and testament to generations and generations of Black girls and women-of-color scholars to come.

If you are privileged to be in consistent relationship with Black girls and research on Black girlhood, then you will be immediately dissatisfied by literature that frames being Black and female as the problem. Academic research that defines Black girlhood as absence, or Black girls as always sexually immoral, a sum of bad choices, or as perpetual servants of other's happiness persists even in its incredulousness. Overly distant research accounts seem contrived and unbelievable. If you so happen to be, or have been, or still consider yourself to be a Black girl, looking for something recognizable, or at least an entrance into conversations that Black girls themselves have brought to your attention, you will probably become so dissatisfied by most of what you read, only one choice will seem worthwhile (though daunting): Write the story yourself. Writing the story is not as risky, I suppose, as doing so within current academic confines, which you will ultimately have to disrupt or transgress.

My first book, *Black Girlhood Celebration: Toward a Hip-Hop Feminist Pedagogy* (Brown, 2009), detailed the political context and my personal motivations for collaborating with Black girls in community spaces in Saving Our Lives Hear Our Truths, which at that time was exceptionally experimental. Writing within and against girls' studies and hip-hop feminism, I critiqued commonly sensed academic assumptions about programming Black girls for the purpose of controlling their bodies and producing white middle-class girl subjectivities, I documented why a space like SOLHOT was needed for Black girls and how it could engender disordered radicalness even as it was organized. In that book I described SOLHOT in very practical terms, giving the reader a sense of the content of SOLHOT (for example, what we do in the weekly sessions with the girls) and its promise. I knew then that what I developed and called hip-hop feminist pedagogy served as a necessary intervention to teach and learn through media, particularly hip hop as influenced by Black girls, because the girls I initially met in SOLHOT did not know life without it.

This book continues to theorize Black girlhood through representations, memories, and lived experiences of being and becoming in a body marked as youthful, Black, and female, while also playing with experimental interpretive methods. However, because Black girlhood rests sometimes so easily on the slippery slope of identity politics that now unfashionably conjures liberal rhetoric of a multiculturalism misunderstood, even I sometimes surprise myself with an insistence on using language so often misappropriated.

My continued use of *Black girlhood*, especially when coupled with *celebration*, may signal to some that I too am complicit in this misappropriation. However, what these terms mean and how they circulate in SOLHOT, I am aware, differs from how the most critically astute reader may assume. Black girlhood as a discursive category is boundless and should not be thought of in this book as a reductionist category of a fixed identity. In the same way that Susan Driver (2008, p. 2) maintains that the designation of queer youth is not meant to entrench a new label, so too do I deploy Black girlhood as a political articulation that intentionally points to Black girls, even as I mean for Black girlhood to direct our attention beyond those who identify and are identified as Black girls.

Explicitly organizing on behalf of Black girlhood and Black girls ensures that those who identify and are identified as Black girls know that the space is for them, which is important since many youth spaces do not mean well for girls, and many groups for girls do not intentionally or unintentionally engage girls of color. Moreover, the use of Black girlhood does not mean that for those who show up, race and gender are the most important or only significant categories of identity and difference. Simultaneously, the vision of Black girlhood as freedom is useful for providing direction and intent, so that in the practice of doing SOLHOT we do not forget that the more quotidian elements of Black girlhood and Black womanhood under current dominant and domineering structural formations would have us assemble only to take each other out. Importantly, this analysis as lived out and written about is meant to coalesce with studies related to critical transnationalism, abolitionist paradigms, queer-of-color critique, Afrocentric and diaspora orientations of Blackness, queer youth studies, and postcolonial politics and thought. Inherently interdisciplinary, this book intervenes in multiple and contested genealogies of feminism, girls' studies, cultural politics, and studies of performance, theater, and drama with the hope of making Black girlhood academically relevant on its own terms. The academic contribution of this book fully intends to transform the academy by insisting on Black girls' studies as critical to disrupting the disciplines, starting with gender and women's studies, African American and diaspora studies, performance studies, and education, and to positively influence stakeholders in service-provider positions that affect young people. My hope is that these movements, people in positions of power, and academic schemas so too intentionally remember Black girls by advancing analytics that increase our interdependence and thereby intensify opportunities for those similarly positioned to live more freely, with greater justice.

~◇~

The suggestion of SOLHOT, its implementation, its consistent practice, and its possibility are indebted to many scholarly traditions, and not least among them are the ideas, essays, poetry, scholarship, and theories advanced by women-of-color artist/scholars. My hope is that this book contributes to an intellectual-activist-artist tradition pioneered by Black feminist, women-of-color, Afrocentric, and queer radical thinkers that is sometimes celebrated but is not always recognized as *real* scholarship. I use "real" to connote authenticity because I am suggesting, not unlike many before me, that there is a mythical standard of authentic scholarship that anyone unapologetically creative does not meet, with the possible exception of those credentialed in a legitimate and hard science, *legitimate* and *hard* being similarly problematic and laden with value. In any case, it has become more and more important for me to specifically acknowledge the contributions of Black feminists, womanists, women of color, and those who call themselves by different names but whose art, words, published works, and actions have illumined a path that directs the work of SOLHOT and also informs the meaning and nonsense I attribute to the analysis presented in this book. I am able to think through our practice and write academically about it as a way to continue the legacy of women-of-color feminists, poets, dramatists, and essayists whose polemics were wise and scholarly, concerned with our collective survival and self-expression.

As a Black woman scholar, writing from the location of the academy, I find it inspiring and somewhat problematic that I have intimately personalized what other scholars recognize and call academic literatures. Consider the first example that comes to mind: June Jordan's *Poetry for the People* (Jordan and Mueller, 1995) motivated me to be right where I am in the academy and organize with others to write poems, perform, and co-create ideas that would then give rise to new dreams of Black girlhood. The way Jordan put words together in the form of poetry and essay catapults me always from the paralysis so often promoted in contemporary university life, to do SOLHOT, to act with others in order to collectively envision a Black girlhood that is accountable to my singular self and beyond. When I recite, for example, "Poem About My Rights," I really get into it, and if it's not the sound of my own voice that conjures change, then it is Jordan's voice that I hear holding me, though I have never met her. Furthermore, when I say I do SOLHOT and it is not new, I acknowledge that Jordan gave me a blueprint and that her prolific publication record traverses multiple academic literatures, including and extending beyond women-of-color feminisms, critical landscape and architecture, literary theory, politics and political education, and theories of childhood and youth culture. When I reference June Jordan, I am calling on diverse and extensive subject areas, currently called *transnationalism, diaspora, intersectionality and assemblages, critical disability, ethnic and gender and women's studies, Afrofuturism, queer theory,* and beyond. June Jordan has been there and done that. Sometimes the academy overthinks itself. For the sake of those who want to know the literatures I address, or what literatures I am speaking to, against, and within, I would reply: I am a student of June Jordan and many others, whom I emphasize and call by name throughout this book to build on their ideas, awesome works, and critical insights. I do not claim to get it as right as they have, but I do mean for you to know that their works have inspired my own. It is the conversations they initiated, building on conversations started before they arrived, that inform my inquiry and practice.

The creative is often lost to critics who dismiss arts methodologies as nonsystematic, feel-good fluff, having no substance. The creative, as epistemology, theory, method, analysis, and praxis, fuels the imaginative capacities needed to generate ideas, provide radical explanation, and forgo academic trends. To let go of the false divide between creative expression and theoretical analysis, and to hold on to the lessons of artist/scholars who fiercely assert that their work is theory or not theory, means to embrace the creative as an avenue to the unknown, to assert a kind of listening that demands particularity, and to always maintain a willingness to be surprised. Creative engagement means coming to terms with artistic genres as productive of (at least) knowledge that can do well what positivist approaches cannot do—embrace collectivity, dwell unapologetically in uncertainty so that it becomes productive, question even as it claims to know, and move people to act, inspired by a feeling, or lack of options, or to invite a Black-feminist poetic and communitarian politic centered in Black women's and girls' creativity renowned for generations and generations.

The process of writing this book has been enriched by the joys and tensions involved in theorizing, practicing, art making, organizing, and performing, and more theorizing, practicing, art making, organizing, and performing. I am a poet, and I often rely on poetry and poetic analysis in this book. I am a playwright, and I often rely on theater and dramatic techniques and assumptions in this book. I am an artist, and I advance poetry, photography, narrative, and music found in this book as theory and not theory. I am an organizer who loves working with people. I am a theorist, and so is my mother. I am a performer who has been trained informally by way of family functions, Black vernacular, "the church," and grassroots theater collectives. I am a practitioner of Black girlhood because of SOLHOT.

Creativity fuels the back, forth, and between, to enable this retelling. The need to call attention to creativity as a mode of knowledge production genuinely engaged in and perfected by many of women-of-color feminists-artists-scholars-activists-warriors-mothers is because while we love to cite them, we are also in a moment when they too are discredited, and by extension their tools and their literature—which are vital to do revolutionary work and research that means something beyond personal gain—are ignored. In this book, I have intentionally called on and relied on the wisdom, methodology, and literatures of creative women-of-color feminists-artists-scholars-activists and womanists by name to give attention to the necessity of creativity and creative engagement. Creativity as source, life force, and methodology fortifies women-of-color feminisms, particularly the works of artists-scholars-activists. Yet, in a university context that depends increasingly on capitalist formations of knowledge production as income revenue, beware the student who has studied their works and dissected their methodology with the intent of using it, practically and theoretically. Though programs and departments of study have been built on and because of their ideas . . . I wonder if they would they be able to grow their work, to nurture their bodies, to strengthen their hearts . . . in rooms named after them, in classes dedicated to them, and in departments that could no longer exist without them or their progenies. The need to call attention to creativity as a mode of knowledge production genuinely engaged in and perfected by many women of color feminists-artists-scholars is also a call to create and to encourage creativity.

It is typically and wrongly assumed that if you are a woman scholar and writing on gender, then all is well in a little academic corner of the institution dedicated to feminism. If in fact you are a woman of color who engages the creative as means to make art, your labor may be wrongly reduced to leisure and does not count, not because it is actually uncountable, but because the work is (or worse yet, you are) deemed unproductive. The too-often-unstated reality is that creative women-of-color scholars are rarely perceived as producers of knowledge in the academy, even in disciplines built on and indebted to the creativity of women of color. Through the naming of various departments and assigning of titles and appointments with too little regard for those who aspire to the arts, and as scholar-artists trained in the most traditional of disciplines or in interdisciplinarity, there is no security. Creative women-of-color artists-scholars-activists-theorists-writers-warriors-mothers, I celebrate the hyphenated identities even as I despise them. There are so many more binaries the hyphen seeks to undo: art/science, fact/fiction, theory/practice, intersection/assemblage, creative/same ol', traditional/innovative, woman of color/white, real/fraudulent, accessible/inaccessible, simple/complex, rigorous/easy, collective/individual, youthful/experienced, wise/ignorant, countable/intangible, written/oral, grown/growing, permanent/ephemeral, good/bad, objective/subjective, high/low, standards/willy-nilly, reliable/here today gone tomorrow, digital/analog, public/private, white/Black, queer/natural, silent/loud, rich/poor, transnational/local, secular/sacred, funky/rigid, trained/undisciplined, expert/novice, hobbyist/researcher, sung/staccato, bliss/depression, solidarity/singularity, selfish/narcissistic, engaged/aloof, shared/sequestered, mentor/tyrant, free/private, humility/arrogance, labor/leisure, call and response/didactic, homegirl/foe.

Thankfully, creativity thrives without permission. Permission-seeking behaviors work only to the detriment of creativity. For example, the creative as a means, mode, and source enables me to discuss, practice, and analyze Black girlhood and feminisms even though very few girls and older women who do SOLHOT identify as feminists—even as they do feminism. Creativity is the tension upholding the tightrope between those who insist on bringing feminism to girls, and a space like SOLHOT where we do not presume to know what our work is together until after some time (travel), relationship, dancing, and creating something that we collectively appreciate. The creative is wide enough to encompass the space between Black girls' lived experience and Black feminism already named and celebrated. The creative allows me to attend to the complexities of Black girlhood and affirm Black girls' lives, it motivates me to start something small like SOLHOT that makes big movements possible, and it has been absolutely critical to advancing the ideas in this book in a way that seemed most accountable to those in SOLHOT and also to scholars interested in ideas that transform how people commonly sense Black girls and work them over. But then again, if the artists/scholars/activists I'm speaking to and through and standing with, whose creativity I hope to emulate—if their work is discounted, then perhaps I have not done anything. Which may or not beg further consideration of a question I first heard provocatively posed in a performance by Robbie McCauley (2009):

Is this art?

And a few of my own . . .

Is this theory?
Is this academic?

～◇～

SOLHOT—the weekly sessions where the vision is refined—is for the girls. Conversely, this book is for scholars, artists, intellectuals, and activists interested in thinking through interactions, time/space, love, and relationships that have Black girls at their center. The analysis advanced in this book is very much dependent on what occurs in SOLHOT, but it is not meant to definitively describe SOLHOT, nor should it be interpreted as the work of SOLHOT. This book, written on a flat surface, consists of chapters that echo a few of the ideas made possible in SOLHOT that would not let me go. Those ideas continued to resound and resonate in my heart until I wrote them out, made more of them with a poem, or analyzed what I was learning in SOLHOT for the benefit of breaking it all the way down—with the hope of shedding some much-needed light on a different way of seeing Black girls that will hopefully influence the reader, challenge policies, and/or make possible arrangements of power and relationships currently not yet formed for the benefit of Black girls not yet overcoming. The analysis that follows in the forthcoming chapters helped us in SOLHOT to do the work better, to think again, and to continually revise our collective vision of Black girlhood. It is my hope that this book also contributes to conversations that direct our attention to the fullness of a visionary Black girlhood as a space of freedom.

The book begins with a performance about how an individual Black girl's story changed how I thought about the kinds of work that could honor the complexities of Black girlhood. Chapter 1, "Tiara: Endangered Black Girls Instruction 301," features a scene from a play I wrote titled *Endangered Black Girls (EBG)*, based on the lived experiences of Black girls I worked with in an after-school program (not SOLHOT) and learned about through news stories. Theorizing the process of writing and performing *EBG* on through to subsequent productions made possible only because of the show's original cast, I illustrate how creative means of expression make it possible to fully capture the complexities of Black girlhood and that attending to the complexities of Black girlhood is necessary to affirm Black girls' daily lives. Importantly, performances of *EBG* generated new ideas for ways Black women and girls could be present with each other, and the play was a primary catalyst for suggesting and co-organizing Saving Our Lives Hear Our Truths (SOLHOT) as transformative collective and creative work. *EBG* as a creative performance not only made it possible for those who were a part of the cast(s) and audiences to revel in the complexities of Black girlhood, but it changed how I related to Black girls and guided the setup of a material space that could thrive on the performative ways Black girls dared to express themselves among each other, in relation to those who loved them, and express their sense of the world.

Giving attention to sacred work and spirituality in relation to time, chapter 2, "Black Women Remember Black Girls: A Collective and Creative Memory," shows how first, before any such thing experienced as freedom can be claimed, Black girlhood must be made, and in SOLHOT the space of Black girlhood is made through time, a timing that is infused with the sacred and spirit. In SOLHOT, to "homegirl" means engaging Black girls in the name of Black girlhood as sacred work that implicates time. Sacred work acknowledges the ways spirit moves one to act, often beyond the material conditions of one's immediate circumstance. The primary question guiding this chapter's analysis is, How do homegirls remember SOLHOT as a sacred experience that makes Black girlhood possible? In response, this chapter features a creative and collective memory constructed from the interview transcripts of eight SOLHOT homegirls and M. Jacqui Alexander's (2005) *Pedagogies of Crossing: Mediations on Feminism, Sexual Politics, Memory, and the Sacred*. The memory shows how homegirls' labor constructs SOLHOT as a methodology and cosmology that makes Black girlhood possible, affirms Black girls' lives, and enables personal and collective transformation. Homegirls do the sacred work of making time and mastering several kinds of knowledge, of the body, interior and personal, and the body collective, extending beyond oneself, to make Black girlhood possible as a matter of life and death.

Chapter 3, "When Black Girls Look at You: An Anti-Narrative Photo-Poem," considers what it means to be seen and looked at as a Black girl. Building on the visual-poetic analysis of June Jordan's (1969) *Who Look at Me* and M. NourbeSe Philip's (2008) *Zong!*, I offer an "anti-narrative photo-poem" that couples photography, poetry, and intersubjective insights of Black girlhood to specifically address the institutional norms and interpersonal dynamics that govern their lives and promote a limited knowing of Black girls premised on sight alone. The primary purpose of this chapter is to show that Black girls actively decide who and what is worthy of their presence and attention. The anti-narrative photo-poem invites those who dare to look to answer with action, as June Jordan suggested, but to do so while giving attention to the kinds of nuanced intersubjective interactions that hinge on the particular usable truth that Black girls are looking at you, watching them.

Chapter 4, "Bad Days: 'If You Hit Me, I'm Gonna Hit You Back,'" foregrounds girls' stories about fighting against a critical literary backdrop of Black girlhood as recounted in June Jordan's (2000) *Soldier: A Poet's Childhood*, Toni Cade

Bambara's (1992) "A Girl's Story," and performance poems written by four SOL-HOT homegirls. This analysis of girls' narratives about fighting and violence in their daily schooled lives does three things: (1) validates girls' stories about fighting within a larger context of structural and interpersonal violence; (2) describes the kind of power Jordan argues is necessary to address both adults' complicity in violence (against youth) and the systemic nature of violence; and (3) demonstrates how and why the performance of homegirls' poetry enables girls in SOLHOT to practice freedom as Bambara instructed. In response to girls' stories, a performance of listening, courage, and interdependence as exemplified by SOLHOT homegirls is advocated as a visionary solution to the popular-policy problem so often constructed as girlfighting, mean girls, and/or bullying. Rather than making state-centered appeals for justice within a flawed system that depends on the further criminalization of Black youth, this chapter speculates on what freedom and justice may mean between Black girls and women beyond the United States prison-industrial complex.

Chapter 5, "More than Sass or Silence: The Creative Potential of Black Girlhood," presents a soundtrack of Black girls' expressive culture as ethnographically documented in SOLHOT in the form of original music. To think through the more dominant categorizations of how Black girls are heard, as both sassy and silent, this chapter samples Andrea Smith's (2006) "Heteropatriarchy and the Three Pillars of White Supremacy: Rethinking Women of Color Organizing" to offer a new frame I call "The Creative Potential of Black Girlhood." Music made from conversations in SOLHOT is used to emphasize how three logics of the creative potential framework, including volume/oppression, swagg/surveillance, and booty/capitalism, amplifies Black girls' critical thought to document the often overlooked creative process of Black girl music making, demonstrate how hip-hop feminist sensibilities inform girls' studies, and, most importantly, move those who do Black girl organizing toward a wider repertoire of actions and conversations that affirm differences among Black girls and differently sounding Black girl knowledge. The creative potential framework shows how Black girlhood organizing is more productive when we listen to what Black girls know, forgo dominant characterizations, and expand on how they share what they know.

I conclude with a series of personal letters that underscore the necessity of envisioning Black girlhood differently than it is described on mainstream television, written about in popular magazines, uncritically interpreted through statistics, and rendered in policies that punish, segregate, and silence. The letters are addressed to people whose love and compassion is a testament to continue this work and who intimately know the necessity of maintaining personal healing while also advocating for the abolition of all forms of Black girl servitude. Moreover, because I am often asked about replication, or ways to bring SOLHOT to wherever you are, I write anticipating this request, even as I maintain that SOLHOT is not meant to be prescriptive and does not offer itself as a successful model of girl programming. Embedded in each letter is a high five and hug, my expressed gratitude to those who get the spirit of the work, even if they call it by a different name, organize with different somebodies, and foreground altogether different issues. The letters represent a kind of personal meditation that on the sly challenges systemic inequalities, appealing to those who inspire and motivate Black girlhood renewal as a space of freedom.

The writing out of how we mean freedom in Saving Our Lives Hear Our Truths is as significant as the dancing out, talking out, and acting out that all goes on in SOLHOT because the word shared extends the vision, improves practice, and widens the cipher. In the pages that follow, I have documented a few moments of how we sensed freedom to mean acting on our desires as Angie, who always keeps it SOLHOT, required—"without worry and consequence." And because there is more work to do with desirous Black girls, there are also, by necessity, more stories to write. This Black girls' song is but one version on an unlimited playlist.

1 Tiara

Endangered Black Girls Instruction 301

"I'm brown,

    five four . . . something like that,

        and I got black hair."

That was the most important thing she wanted me to know.

    Tiara was extremely quiet and often called "shy" by everyone in the after-school program where I met her. When I arrived at her house to interview her about her experiences in the program, her twin sister, the one with the exuberant personality, declared Tiara would go second; I was to interview her first. Her sister told me important details about her experience in the program and then sent Tiara into the living room. Tiara, or, as her sister called her, the "quiet" twin, answered most of my questions nonverbally, shaking her head to indicate yes or no. To indicate uncertainty, which she did quite often, she shrugged her shoulders. My intuition told me that perhaps, before, she used to speak but had long since decided that her twin sister would be, should be, the most audible. At the end of my list of questions, feeling exasperated by a seemingly unproductive interview, I asked her if there was anything, anything at all, I should know about her. She broke her preferred, silent way of being and said rather pointedly but still in a soft voice, "I'm brown, five four . . . something like that, and I got black hair."

I did not follow up with more questions. I thanked Tiara for her time. I left the apartment with her very short response on mindful repeat. I was without a clue about how to analyze one sentence as a unit of data. As a novice researcher, I feared that one sentence would sufficiently fail any rigorous critique made by others. But I knew I had one line from a very important Black girl, whose story I thought should be told. As I struggled to make meaning of her declaration, I realized that I also did not know her well enough to provide a context that could be substantiated by field notes or from commentary by the girls or program staff. Quite frankly, she never caught our attention in a way I documented. Quiet girls are all too often forgotten. But Tiara gave me something that deserved to be respected and handled warmly—her truth.

Tiara's truth was a turning point for me. It was a truth that was singular, small, extremely powerful, and a lesson. I learned that it takes creative means of expression to fully capture the complexities of Black girlhood. Given a single sentence, I used my imagination to create a dramatic context that could give meaning and occasion to what Tiara knew and told me. I drew from a variety of sources, personal, popular, and academic, to create a scene where her declaration could not be escaped or excused. Otherwise, Tiara's experience would be permanently reduced to outlier status and displaced by traditional positivist social science. The fact that she told me nothing else of import about her life left me wondering about other Black girls like her, whose stories may be lost to us, the general public, because we did not have the time, energy, know-how, or desire to hear what they have to say. Overlooking girls who rarely speak, and the passive acceptance of punishing girls who speak out, limits what is known about Black girls and the diverse complexity within Black girlhood. Starting with Tiara's truth, I wrote *Endangered Black Girls (EBG)*, a play based on the lived experiences of Black girls I interviewed, researched, and read about in the news reports of journalists to document a noticeable omission in research and popular literature on Black girlhood: the complexity of Black girls' lived experience and the significance of extraordinary and persuasive Black-girl truths.

ENDANGERED BLACK GIRLS EXCERPT
SCENE SIX: TIARA

> Tiara's identical twin is extremely popular in school; Tiara is not. Tiara sports extension braids pulled into a ponytail decorated with blue and pink beads. Only her "sides" are missing. Teasing for Tiara is normal. She is often teased about her looks; her dress, hair, and skin complexion. Lights up on Tiara at home, watching a television special on "Endangered Black Girls."

NEWS ANCHOR: (*on location*) According to Black girls everywhere: "Popular is you gotta know everybody, and you gotta be half smart, and get the good grades, and you're nice, you're mean sometimes, and you're real together. You're good at all the activities in the school, like cheerleading, basketball, anything else for girls, and most of the teachers like you. You think you gotta be perfect—your face has to look right, you gotta have the right hair, you gotta have nice right clothes, you gotta know everybody."

Experts confirm and report: "Girls have to worry about their hair and how they look and what their weight is and how white their teeth are."

In breaking news: "Intimacy masks Betrayal. Good hair—that's the expression. We all know it, begin to hear it when we are small children. When we are sitting between the legs of mothers and sisters getting our hair combed . . . For each of us getting our hair pressed is an important ritual. It is not a sign of our longing to be white. It is not a sign of our quest to be beautiful. We are girls. It is a sign of our desire to be women. It is a gesture that says we are approaching womanhood—a rite of passage . . . Later, a senior in high school, I want to wear a natural, an Afro. I want never to get my hair pressed again. It is no longer a rite of passage, a chance to be intimate in the world of women." The intimacy masks betrayal, writes scholar, activist, feminist, and spiritualist bell hooks.[1]

In other news, twenty-eight Black girls do not report to extracurricular school activities. Sources report that there has been a consistent no-show because they do not have their hair combed.

1 bell hooks. 1996. *Bone Black: Memories of Girlhood*. New York: Henry Holt.

At a different school, Black girls in gym class rebel. Thirteen Black girls fail gym class. They refused to take the long distance running portion of the state mandatory fitness test due to light rain and high humidity. The girls staged a sit-in wearing Afro wigs, linked arm in arm. They chanted, "Hell no, we don't want no Afro!" One protestor commented, "Black girls have rights, too."

> *TIARA turns the channel. TALK SHOW HOST is on.*

TALK SHOW HOST: Today is the day you have been waiting for, the latest pick for my book-of-the-month club.

> *Applause.*

Now, I have said this before, but THIS BOOK is one of my all-time favorites.

> *Applause.*

The book is . . . *Assata: An Autobiography* by Assata Shakur.

> *Applause. TALK SHOW HOST continues . . .*

Assata: An Autobiography is a thrilling account of one political prisoner's coming-of-age story, detailing her experiences as a Black Panther turned FBI fugitive. This book is going to enlighten us all as Assata Shakur makes a compelling case of the government's role in demobilizing the Black liberation movement. Extremely personal and political, this book should be on everyone's reading list.

> *Applause.*

After the commercial break, Assata Shakur will join us via satellite from Havana, Cuba. Get those mojitos ready. We'll be right back!

NEWS ANCHOR: In breaking news: To meet the demands of so many Black girls who dream of becoming hairdressers and cosmetologists, Wal-Mart opens its first beauty shop. Interested future Wal-Mart employees must be willing to forget the neutralizer on any employee that mentions union. Wal-Mart, everyday low prices, you settle for less!

> *Lights down on television with spotlight on TIARA writing in her journal and talking out loud to herself.*

TIARA: I get—sometimes I get talked a lot about, but I don't get talked about no more. Like, some said that I'll act funny, and I'm afraid to fight, and all the other girls have long hair. My sides, they're kind of, like, messed up, cuz my mom pulled them out when I was little. She didn't take care of it, so now the other girls make fun of me. But there's more girls that are worser than me. But they get teased too, cuz some girls might not look pretty as another girl, and—or she may be ugly, and it's because she hear that people say she ugly, she probably gonna look at herself to say that it was true.

TALK SHOW HOST: Welcome back everyone. I'm sorry to have this happen, but during the commercial break we learned that we can't actually get to Assata Shakur. We tried several times to get through, but the bad connection is our fault. I'm sorry. So right now we will be joined by another activist icon, please join us, activist icon . . .

Applause.

ACTIVIST ICON: Colorism is a result of racism. Racism is pervasive, and it often becomes internalized. That's why people think light skin, long hair is in. Too often when little Black girls are called "Blackie" or "baldy" it is not simply about teasing. The girl that is doing the teasing and the girl that is being teased, if she believes her oppressor, are both participating in the reproduction of a historical continuum of injustice.

ACTIVIST ICON speaks directly to TIARA.

Girls like you, Tiara, are political prisoners. You are being held hostage by your mothers, your friends, your extended family, the media, your teachers, workplaces, colleges with hair codes, blond-wig-wearing pop stars, and consumerism, all constructing the political landscape of Black hair. I speak about this in my book. When I was on the run, I wore a wig, underground. On the subway, I noticed how every other Black woman also wore some kind of hair that wasn't our own. I knew I was in danger, the FBI listed me a fugitive, my picture flashed on every television screen. *I was wanted.* But before riding the number 2 train downtown, I had no idea just how many Black women and girls in Amerikkka also seemed to be underground and on the run. We don't talk about our hair to just anyone because they don't know the Black hair lingo.

TIARA: Can you talk to me about my sides being missing?

ACTIVIST ICON: Do you know what it means to sit between your mama's legs for hours, head being tossed from one side to the other, smelling like grease and burnt hair for days? Have you heard the screams of my sisters running from the comb not made for our head? Have you sat for hours getting extensions added to your hair, missing out on playing outside, missing tutoring sessions, missing your favorite TV show because you gotta keep your head down?

TIARA: I don't have much to say. I whisper when I talk. I don't mind being the bad twin. I fade into the background at school. When you ask my opinion about something, I always say, "I don't know." My mother calls me lazy. My sister says I'm stupid. I am doing what I have been taught. I am doing what she told me to do.

ACTIVIST ICON: Tiara, who are you?

TIARA: I'm brown, five four, something like that, and I got black hair.

ACTIVIST ICON: You are the celebrated obedient Black girl. Too many of our girls are operating on the Black-girl mantra "Keep your head down."

Lights dim.

Lights up on TIARA sitting between MARY's legs, getting a perm. MARY says, "Keep your head down."

H.O.T. GIRLS, RESEARCHER, AND LELA are combing each other's hair, repeating the mantra in the same way their mother used to say to them, "Keep your head down."

TIARA: I'm brown . . .
　　five four, something like that,
　　and I got black hair.

India.Arie's song "I Am Not My Hair" plays while H.O.T. GIRLS get their hair combed.

Lights fade to Black.

WHY PERFORMANCE?

*Many of us should produce plays or poems or songs or other kinds
of performances as ways of engaging with our data and expanding
the interpretive possibilities. (Feldman, 2008)*

I could not address the complexities of Black girlhood using traditional research methods and presentations. Instead, I wrote *Endangered Black Girls.*
Several years later, I was approached to have my play performed by a campus
theater troupe. I was honored and humbled, completely teary-eyed and weak
in the knees. I had no idea if the play would work, if it had wings. I did not
know what it meant to have someone else do "my" show. I could not promise
them they would have an audience. Did anyone care about Black girls' stories?
They wanted me to be involved in the production process. Would I be cast
as the researcher? Would I fight for the integrity of what I wrote? I could still
hear the girls' stories as they were told to me. What if the actors could not
interpret their voices and stories with credibility? In addition, I was a single
new mother, and theater happens at night. Who was going to watch my baby?

To say that the performance of *EBG* was beyond my wildest expectation
in the very best way would be cliché, but it is also true. The director and supporting technicians were brilliant. The initial script was inadequate, but I was
directed on how the smallest moments in the script were detailed enough to
make rewrites and revisions possible and promising. The audience literally
came by the busload, and people were turned away every night. The original cast, six undergraduates and one graduate student, gave new meaning
to the script derived from the girls I knew and wrote about. The girls with
whom I was currently working in the community attended a performance
and thought that I wrote the show based on our very short time together
(although I wrote the script years prior to meeting them), so I knew it was
believable. *EBG* was a success because it resonated and was seen as relevant
to the audience to whom I was most accountable—Black girls.

The first run of *Endangered Black Girls* lasted a week. The outcomes of that
particular production were exponential, with proverbial ripple effects reaching back, moving forward, and multiplying in the current moment. Beyond
increasing awareness of how issues including girl empowerment, identity
politics, homophobia, female friendships, spirituality, responsibility, and
work relate to Black girlhood, the short-lived yet nonetheless local celebrity
enjoyed by all involved, the revisions of the script up until showtime, the

priceless image of me on the steps in the tech booth, nervous to the bone, afraid to look on opening night, and the family and friends that made it possible for me to both mother and work, *EBG* even did more than that. I found myself at the end of Ntozake Shange's metaphorical rainbow, singing a new Black-girl song.

As a student of theater and performance, I have long since known the possibilities of performance. My involvement in *Endangered Black Girls*—from conducting the research; to writing the script; to revisions; to meeting, interacting, and becoming one with the original cast members; to learning from the director of its first production and growing tremendously from her brilliant interpretation of the piece (including the absences and my intentions even when not yet reflected in the script); to witnessing the performances—opened up possibilities for extending the celebration. Researching, writing, revising, performing, and seeing subsequent performances of *Endangered Black Girls* taught me how viable creative methodologies and arts scholarship are for capturing the complexity of Black girls' lives.

Students of performance are familiar with the live energy created during memorable and remarkable productions that have changed the lives of individuals and communities and that have transformed entire political systems. Those who have participated in performance know what the books cannot teach—the ability of performance to serve as an active conduit in the creation of communities of practice committed to new visions. I eagerly await other firsthand accounts in the documentation of why performance is a necessary form of research to benefit those whose performance as research remains in hidden and unsent files, whose story, not for lack of interest, remains on the flat page instead of courageously brought to the public stage.

Why performance? Performance provides opportunities to think, feel, and be with Tiara's truth as it relates to her personal situation, while also illuminating how social inequalities and cultural norms beyond her immediate influence construct her story as plausible. Politically, Tiara and girls like Tiara should be included in conversations about them, even if how they speak is unrecognizable by those in power. Performance enables the affirmation of the particulars of lived experiences. It is our responsibility as researchers and people who love those with whom we work to change systemic barriers to full participation in public life, not to change the people with whom we work. As a radical method, performance challenges disciplinary codes, thereby elevating the more emancipatory elements and affective impulses of social phenomena vital to critical thought, social-justice organizing, and a construction of Black girlhood that embraces Black girls' humanity.

HOW TO DO PERFORMANCE

Imagination is required to challenge academic routines and resist the status quo. Longtime educator and arts enthusiast Maxine Greene (1995) wrote, "It is imagination that draws us on, that enables us to make new connections of the reality we are envisaging" (p. 30). Artist-scholar Mary Weems (2003) related the imaginative capacity of researchers explicitly to knowledge production: "New ideas and reflection incorporate imagination, reason, and the passion that drives us to propose research, to ask questions, and to take risks" (p. 1). Paul Willis (2000) argued that "the *ethnographically imagined* possibility of making connections between art and everyday life is relevant to all of the social sciences, actually to all the ways of making sense of human place" (p. 6). Building on the work of Charles Pierce, authors Locke, Golden-Biddle, and Feldman (2008) wrote that abductive reasoning, or one process by which ideas may be generated, depends on imagination. Moreover, according to Martha Feldman (2008), in research inquiry, applying imagination is one way to expand the data; it is not making up data, but filling in what we know with what we have learned. Feldman's insight clarified that for new ideas to emerge from theorizing, the researcher must be changed and transformed by the work.

As researchers, the choice we make to either explicitly reveal or not reveal the ways we use imagination in the process of making sense of what we claim to know is often related to our identity, our location in the academy, and the methodology chosen to answer our research question. Linda Tuhiwai Smith (1999) made the case as such:

> The notion of research as an objective, value-free and scientific process of observing and making sense of human realities is taken for granted by many social sciences . . . Method is important because it is regarded as the way in which knowledge is acquired or discovered and as a way in which we can "know" what is real. Each academic discipline is attached not just to a set of ideas about knowledge, but also to methodologies. (p. 164)

Imagination is highly subjective. To think through the role of imagination in the research process, then, is to wholly deconstruct objectivity, methodology, and, certainly, what is considered knowledge. The process of knowing with the intentional application of imagination becomes a necessary exercise in interdisciplinarity. Even still, for free imagination, there is no security in such interdisciplinarity.

Questions of identity related to whose imagination may be known as fueling the research process are consequential. Arts-based research by marginalized scholars with marginalized publics, conducted in the academy, is not one of significant but superficial support. Individual scholar-artists of color may flourish in the academy to be the exception; however, on the whole, greater institutional support (at all levels) to do collective and creative work, particularly from the location of the humanities and social sciences, is needed. To do "this" work in an institutional context that promotes engaged scholarship as a marginal enterprise and marginalized scholars as temporary visitors at times, I also colluded with forces that advocated permission-seeking behavior. Questioning the university's categorization of who is worthy of study and engagement in the current political economy of higher education, Aimee Cox (2009) wrote,

> As an African American female anthropologist, I continue to grapple with both the ethics and professional career consequences of attempting truly collaborative research with a group of which I both consider myself a part and also understand myself to be "studying" and, therefore, separate from. I am curious about the implications of practicing public anthropology as a minority scholar under these circumstances. (pp. 52–53)

Cox brings our attention to the ways in which terms like *diversity*, *outreach*, and *equity public* have come to stand in for very specific groups so as to become exclusionary domains. She also articulates that framing engagement or public scholarship as something new or special simultaneously relegates pioneering scholars of color who did this work out of necessity and innovation to the margin and those who follow in their tradition once again to the disciplinary periphery. This is, of course, if their work and legacy are acknowledged at all.

Before, during, and for even a bit after the success of *Endangered Black Girls*, I was not immune to any of the conditions that make an otherwise confident Black feminist question herself, her work, and her artistry. To my dismay, in my attempt to do things that Black women did before me, like write, create art, and profess, I also found myself relating too easily to their historical marginalization in the ivory tower. For example, the more recent celebration of Zora Neale Hurston's spectacular career and revived legacy invites pause.

Cited as one of the premier notables of the Harlem Renaissance, Hurston is typically recognized for her creative fiction, short stories, and anthropological training, and the remarkable story of her dying poor and being buried in an unmarked grave in spite of her accomplished literary career. Zora Neale Hurston, a consummate artist-scholar, wrote, performed, and produced plays before to do so became a university commodity often masquerading as public and engaged scholarship. She not only loved theater and performance, but her application and expertise in staging southern Black folklore, as she knew it and researched, proved that "Zora appreciated us, in any case, *as we fashioned ourselves*. That is something" (Walker, 1979, p. 4, emphasis in the original). Furthermore, the oft-remembered event of Hurston walking into an after-party following an awards dinner in which she won second place, with a colorful scarf around her neck, bellowing the name of her play, "Coloooooor Struuckkkk!" served two purposes at once: she made a remarkable entrance and stopped the party (Boyd, 2003, p. 97–98). I find it plausible that Hurston may very well have also marked her entrance in such a declarative and performative way as playful resistance to those in attendance who held the power to simultaneously celebrate her and deny her artistry. Or as Alice Walker (1979) suggested, it was a performance of defiance, a refusal to be humbled by second place in a contest she did not design.

With too few exceptions, most scholars focus on the content of Hurston's work, with little regard to her innovation in theory and method (Bolles, 2001, p. 39). Black girlhood celebration that attends to complexity as demonstrated in *Endangered Black Girls* also makes it necessary to rethink Zora Neale Hurston's second-place award. About her play, *Color Struck*, a biographer wrote that it was "not a very effective drama . . . really more a sketch than a play, it comes to life only when the folk of north-central Florida engage their wit in friendly verbal competition" (Hemenway, 1977, p. 47). Perhaps, instead of positioning Hurston as second best, the partiality of *Color Struck* was wholly purposeful. That the "folk" were needed to engage the performance could have very well been a part of her intentional performance method, enabling the show to mean something more to the people whose knowledge and culture served as the very premise of the story. Hurston's experimental theatrical practice innovated form and produced new meanings (Goddard, 2007) currently recognized as characteristic of a Black feminist theater aesthetic (Anderson, 2008). Alice Deck (1990) has also rightfully attributed to Hurston the status of progenitor of auto-ethnography, a method of participant observation that includes self-reflexive narrative and relevant autobiographical information about the author to advance the story.

Performance that demands a particular kind of presence and attentiveness from a particular audience, and certainly a whole-hearted commitment from the casts and crew, is exactly the kind of method Hurston innovated. In the case of *Endangered Black Girls*, the performance decidedly depends on what is brought to it by the audience and the performers to make it work. Not just in the way that every show is better when the audience energy is positive, *EBG* is a performance of insider knowledge, whose sense of humor is predicated on a nuanced understanding of Black girlhood culture. *Endangered Black Girls* could very well engender similar criticism as Hurston's *Color Struck* if I did not explicitly articulate how the show's intent is to be accountable to Black girls first. Without the participation of Black girls, perhaps *EBG* is no show at all. Certainly it is not fully legible without Black girls present and accounted for, including girls like Tiara, fully emboldened by their truths. More than a particular genre of theater, Hurston's methodology of performance may not make for first place in theatrical contests, but it does the more important work of facilitating new conversations, creating new audiences, showcasing a different kind of humor, enabling the recognition of a people typically unseen and misunderstood, and moving people around and together, resulting in a kind of profound recognition that is able to transform singular truths into collective actions.

In his articulation of what performance studies ought to be, Dwight Conquergood (2002, pp. 145–46) wrote, "Performance studies struggles to open the space between analysis and action, and to pull the pin on the binary opposition between theory and practice. This embrace of different ways of knowing is radical because it cuts to the root of how knowledge is organized in the academy." One unfortunate result of the radicalness of doing performance work, or creative work as research, particularly from the location of the social sciences and humanities, is that one may encounter the "advice" that creative work is not academic or scholarly because it is not written (in the form of a publishable book manuscript or journal article), and it should therefore be abandoned immediately, until tenure is secured. Radical work like performance is also threatening to many in the academy on a personal level, because they did not successfully navigate the academy doing creative work (even if they were really good, or could have been great), and the most bitter will subtly or outright suggest that you should/will not be either. It is radical work that, even in times when the perfunctory is in vogue, uproots normative assumptions, standards, and expectations.

Performance-based work is different from traditional scientific work—it cannot be evaluated in the same way, it can't be replicated (thereby proving it is or isn't a reliable, successful approach to a problem), and it does not fit into a neat category, all of which makes it a difficult job for bureaucrats to deem effective, efficient, and thus worthy of funding. If "this" kind of work is acknowledged in the academy, it rarely translates to greater systematic access to validation, recognition, and promotion (Scobey, 2002, p. 51). On a structural level, the political climate of contemporary university life, often characterized as neoliberalism, reigns supreme and is culpable in the branding of civic discourse as commercialization, privatization, and deregulation, responsible for producing privatized citizenship and self-interested individuals (Giroux, 2002). Chandra Mohanty (2003) rightfully called out the devastating underpinnings of privatization as it relates to the university:

> Further, it is the racialized, and sexualized, systems of exploitation that underlie and consolidate the everyday material workings of the corporatized university, and the production of consumer citizens. These systems include unequal relations of labor, exclusionary systems of access, Eurocentric canons and curricular structures, sexist and racist campus cultures, and the simultaneous marginalization and cooptation of feminist, race and ethnic, and gay/lesbian/queer studies agendas. (p. 174)

Under a neoliberal regime, the more political aspects of collective and creative work may be destabilized and therefore necessitate further analysis of the conditions of intellectual life as produced by the public university so as to articulate what is intentionally at stake in the doing of performance work and creative work more generally. Research that is creative, public, and grounded in collaboration with marginalized communities, conducted by scholars of color, is always and already suspect.

Endangered Black Girls is an example of performance ethnography. Performance ethnography explores the expressive elements of a culture, focuses on embodiment as a crucial component of analysis and as a tool for representing scholarly engagement, and is often represented as (but not limited to) a staged interpretation of research (Hamera, 2011, p. 318). Although widely utilized and greatly circulated, performance and the doing of performance as research methodology resists tacit understandings about the form, function, and very meaning of Western thought. Those who practice performance as research in the fine arts and theater are typically the first to experience the brunt of the current economic crisis in the university; those outside of fine and applied arts are not regarded as "artists" by their more formally trained colleagues; and those in performance studies represent the interdisciplinary vanguard, meaning that on the daily they simultaneously experience having an institutional home and homelessness. Graduate students in the humanities and social sciences who are interested in performance work are chastised for being amateurs, reinforcing the constant yet worthless endeavor of permission seeking. Never mind that including poems, films, multimedia projects, and other creative texts has almost become standard fare in the syllabi of even the most rigid disciplines—in the business of knowledge production, artistic sensibilities become gentrified by the hard facts. In these very highly positivist times, policies, practices, and norms that result in the disposability of creative artist-scholars of color are typically found on the interdisciplinary margins of the academy.

THE ILLUSION OF PERMISSION

S/he who writes, writes. In uncertainty, in necessity. And does not ask whether s/he is given the permission to do so or not. (Trinh, 1989, p. 8)

She sat there in our very small audience, astute, ready to listen. We were in Denver for the 2010 National Women's Studies Association annual conference, presenting and performing our work about Black girlhood. Tired, nauseous, and diminishing from the merciless early symptoms of pregnancy, I gave a sincere performance of humility and mentorship. Co-presenting with students, I welcomed the opportunity to follow their lead. After our presentation, I listened attentively as they fielded questions from the audience. I delighted in their brilliant responses . . . until she asked a question that awakened my temporarily disabled body.

"Who gave you permission to do this kind of work?" she asked.

During an animated question-and-answer talk-back, she waited patiently to ask—a question she had probably thought about since the start of our conference session, more than likely as a result of her own very important work. To the untrained and inexperienced ear, her question could be answered with a rundown of academic training, study-abroad experiences, artistic mentors, and certificate opportunities. But for those who, because they spend so much time defending their choices, don't really dedicate enough time to developing the art, the craft, and the work, the question required more than a synopsis of coursework. It is a question for those whose energy is so expended by the bureaucratic nightmare of the now corporate university that they just almost cease honest collaboration, or the challenging of boundaries, say, between the community and the university. It is a question for those who find too little solace in interdisciplinarity but settle there because although it is not freedom absolute, it is not as constraining as disciplinary codes. It is a question for Black-women, women-of-color, and queer-identified scholars who think themselves writers, artists, and intellectuals. Considering the lives, deaths, and legacies of women of color in the academy who have paved the way to do "this" kind of work, if one dares to take up their legacy and has been met with a quizzical stare, at best, then the question becomes radical, dangerous even. It is a question often asked silently, to oneself, and deserves greater attention.

"This" is performance work based on research that is in some way collective—by *collective*, I mean some part of the research process could not have happened without collective decision making—and creative, in that it engages the arts; ultimately, the research is sung, acted out, danced, photographed, or otherwise expressively narrated. The "this" is heartfelt, public, and political. The "you" of her question is a bit more personal. I assumed she meant me, a young Black woman who researches and works with Black girls. The "you" could have also been a reference to my appearance as youthful and relatively new in my assistant-professor position. Had she known me, the "you" could have very well implied my status as a first-generation college student, newly pregnant, and a plethora of other identities and situations. Perhaps it was also the tone in which she asked the question that gave rise to all that she was really calling into question. I knew, and she knew, all too well the hauntingly familiar voice that berates a less complicated "you" into seeking permission from someone to do "this," and as such, maybe she fully expected a practical answer.

How do you do *this* work in the academy?

Because I was at times advised that to do the work I was doing, and wanted to do, did in fact require permission, her question resonated. Those who suggested that I could do this work so long as I also did my *real* work made me suspicious, in any case, that permission from whomever I needed it had not yet been granted. As a result, doing collective, creative work, with young people outside and inside of the academy, felt at times like a struggle bigger than it should been. It seemed as if I was doing the impossible, so much so that I often kept quiet about it. I reframed the work, hid my work, denied my work, worked underground, and funded my own research, when I knew I was barely scratching the surface of the kind of scholar I wanted to be.

When questioned by this unassuming audience member about permission to do this kind of work, Black woman to Black woman, I went numb. I heard my immediate response in my head and kept silent. I felt the consequences of her question in my body. The names of people of who encouraged my own intellectual creative journey surfaced on my heart like ticker tape. Looking back at her, I wondered if she had managed to appropriately reframe a question that had at one time been inappropriately asked of her as it had been asked of me: How dare you, as a Black woman, in a corporate university context, do collective and creative work in a place that values individualism over the public good? Or as Hattie Gossett (2002) matter-of-factly worded it, "Who told you anybody wants to hear from you? You ain't nothing but a Black woman!" (p. 194).

My intellectual curiosities beg creative answers. I followed a kind of intellectual trajectory that taught me how to do creative work well, but my training did not grant me the permission. I performed in plays as an actor and wrote performances based on my research, but I did not think of myself as an artist in the academy. Although I have always done this kind of work, I did not always have a name for it. For certain, I could not always justify it. My tradition, really, and the bodies of work whose ideas set me on fire were not always recognized as intellectual or scholarly, so by extension, quite possibly, I concluded neither was I. As with all illusions, there is neither a magic moment nor a wizard in the city that grants permission. However, I can recall three events that specifically made a difference in how I presented myself and thought of my research. I cannot say these events granted me permission, as much as they served as catalysts to unlearn permission-seeking behaviors.

First, I gave birth. As a very pregnant postdoctoral fellow, I was afforded time and space to rethink the limitations of disciplinary norms and commit to a research agenda that would make an academic life worth the investment. The postdoc and pregnancy were a significant coupling, as I was determined to give life to a baby girl and to a work for which I would not mind doing what it takes to make it grow. What would I do that could outweigh the guilt of being away from my daughter? What could I love as much as I was coming to know love to be at that time? I had nine months to birth the baby and nine months to become the kind of scholar I wanted to be. I wrote tons. I sat still. I swung back and forth on my parents' front-porch swing. I was taken care of. I thought hard and positive. I listened to the beating of her heart and mine. Mostly, it was not an intellectual exercise. I had done that part. This work, undoing the discipline as it were, was spiritual. It was less about reading and learning, and more about recovering and rediscovering what I already knew before the training and the degrees. It was reconnecting with who I knew myself to be, and listening to what my aunt said—my aunt who remembers my earliest plays and poetry, who calls me every now and then for a poem, because that's what I do.

Second, I fumbled and I learned from my mistakes. I was invited for an interview at a very prestigious university where a close friend was also enrolled as a graduate student. She knew me well. Well enough to say after my very traditional presentation, "Nikki, what the hell was that?" She was disappointed, and so was I. She read my shadow academic papers and knew of my dreams of doing performance. The traditional scientific stuff is safe. I thought it was what they wanted to hear, but it was not. A senior scholar in the department drove me to the airport to catch my flight home. Wise and still tender enough after all her years in the academy to say to me in a way I could hear, she told me, "Once you get your voice together, say what you really need to say, dress how you really want to dress, you are going to be something." Just like that, she called my bluff. I thought she didn't even really know me. That my scholarship could be mine and that a couple of people were really interested in what I had to say encouraged me. I was on the verge of giving myself permission and making the necessary connections.

Third, I sought academic-artist communities, and I began to make myself known. I observed the way a few women of color in the academy presented themselves as artists, and I took notice. "I am an artist," they would often say by way of introduction, and I began to do the same. It was the utterance that I needed to try out. It would mean I would have to present my work and myself in a different way. Those few words gave me a way to enter into a conversation I wanted to be a part of. A position. A purpose. Those words shifted the conversation in a direction more toward what I was doing, the questions I wanted asked of me, and it required my audience to evaluate my work in a way that was more true to its intention. Saying to myself, sometimes silently, before giving talks of any kind, "I am an artist," worked as an affirmation. Those words, which I still need to say often and sometimes out loud, are an invocation of my wish to do "this" work with authority, confidence, and swagg. My introductory ritual serves the same purpose as Toni Cade Bambara's reminder to Nikky Finney: "Don't let anyone think they can have their 'important' conversations without you, present and accounted for" (Brown, 2008, p. xviii).

Minh-ha Trinh (1989) rightfully declared that permission is an illusory concept and that permission seeking, while comprehensible, is ultimately deceptive. She warned,

> One can no longer let oneself be deceived by concepts that oppose the artist or the intellectual to the masses and deal with them as two incompatible entities. Criticisms arising from or dwelling on such a myth are, indeed, quite commonly leveled against innovators and more often used as tools of intimidation than as reminders of social interdependency. (p. 13)

No one will give you permission to do performance ethnography, specifically, or creative expressions of scholarship generally. The good news is that permission is not necessary. The cumulative work of Barbara Christian has recognized the historical fact that people of color have always used diverse narrative forms as a modality of theorizing, and Black feminism(s) in particular, through its connection to the academy, has been and continues to be incessantly tenuous, is also not without joy and will survive (Christian, 2007). Of greater importance are those in the cast and in the audience who show up and say to you in earnest, "This performance changed my life." A girl will sing for the first time in front of others in rehearsal or in a production that she helped write and own her own voice in desired company. There will be tears. A man well into his earthly years, who walks with a cane and a limp as a result of his former "gang lifestyle," will confess how he felt a part of something he initially thought would be of absolutely no relevance to his life because it was about Black girlhood. Upon your arrival, a light bulb will blow in the dressing room to signal the strength of your power. Somebody's grandmother will pray for you and publicly declare, "This is good." There will be parents that support you. Mentors will emerge from the community, not the university, to create more opportunities for you to grow your work and exercise your talents. Young people will engage with your performances, although they will not buy the book.

TIARA'S LESSON:
ENDANGERED BLACK GIRLS INSTRUCTION 301

When teaching to resist privatization in higher education, creativity is paramount. As a story told creatively and collectively, *Endangered Black Girls* transformed us all. As a performance, *EBG* inspired numerous combinations and creative equations for accessing that spark within us that allows us to live inside of our bodies and be in touch with ourselves. It invokes the energy to create the communities we want to be a part of, if they do not already exist. Particularly, when ideas are collectively and creatively engaged through performance, the bodies, presence, and productions of imaginative thinkers—many of whom are people marked as youthful, Black, feminine, queer—become not disposable and marginalized, but alive, valued as prodigies of the kind of knowledge essential to our collective survival. *EBG* brought people who once thought themselves different from each other closer together, while also inviting those with whom we worked and performed to sense themselves anew.

The original cast of *Endangered Black Girls* demonstrated what I knew intellectually but had not yet experienced through my own art: the possibility of creative work to illumine complexity and simultaneously inspire people to organize themselves. In the case of *EBG*, subsequent productions led to overcoming institutional limits and trends. *EBG* the play and *EBG* as an experience intersected to teach us all something more beautiful about ourselves. It was a quintessential lesson in *Black-women artistry without art* form that we had the privilege to learn together, reading and capturing with song, clay, strings, dance, and ink the joys and pains of Black woman-hood and Black girlhood as a matter of duty—because a person who is sane, secure, and sensitive enough to revere our art is the same person who will emulate our lives (Weems, 2000, p. 94). The *EBG* cast taught me that when the performance is not only relevant to their lives, but also gives life, they are free to create the kind of educational experiences they most desire. When the performance is of service to others, in the way it positively served them then, no obstacle (such as zero funding, transportation, racial differences, or hectic student schedules) is too big to overcome. As Perkins and Uno (1996, p. 4) documented and the cast of *EBG* can attest to, a lack of access to a formal theater space does not stop people of color from making theater. These reflections from a few of the original cast members profess how they created *Endangered Black Girls* as a meaningful experience for themselves.

> *Endangered Black Girls* has not only reunited me with my own inner Black girl but has connected me to others. All of our lived experiences are inter-twined and transcend the lines that separate us.
> —Katherine (Tiara)

> The beauty of *Endangered Black Girls* is that it gives voices to the millions of young women that are silenced. Through this production we are demand-ing that young girls "scream at the highest mountain" to let the rest of the world know that we are here and that everyone needs to take notice. *EBG* is like no other production around and it is beneficial for every young girl, adult woman, and man to see. The stories of these young girls whom we are bringing life to need to be heard worldwide, because I truly believe we can make an international difference. [*EBG*] is one of the best things that God has blessed me with, and I am sure that anyone else that experiences what is [*EBG*] will feel the same exact way.
> —Brittany (Lela/Talk Show Host)

A year ago, I remember reading the script and not really understanding what was really going on, incapable of falling into my characters because I wasn't so fond of them—because I thought they were mean and cold-hearted, or rather—white and bland. I remember the three nights at the theater, how hot it was because the lights were beaming down on us and it was so packed that we had audience sitting on the stage. I remember the standing ovations and the talk backs and Taylor almost getting kicked out of the bar and Doc telling our waitress she was old enough to be our mother. I knew then that I was a part of something great, and tonight, when I looked up at you on the stage and felt the audience move in their seats, I knew that that greatness has only been exemplified.

It's been a long and rough road, but we made it. It was a road that we didn't think existed before, a road none of us have traveled, but I am grateful to say that we all walked, ran, and danced down it together, and have gathered new friends along the way. Perhaps tonight's show wasn't what you expected it to be, perhaps it was more than you expected it to be, but isn't that what *EBG* is all about? Not falling into some category, not labeled, not treated as if it is some entity? Needless to say we have accomplished more than I ever thought we would and in less than a year can have a claim to success.

Yes, there were points of panic and there was the anxiety, the nervousness, the frustration; but you will find that down any road through life. At the end of the night we have to realize that in this endeavor, we are our own masters, and we have created our own journeys, and for now we are on the road less travelled. But as we continue on, we will have more followers, more people to inspire, to touch, to teach, to learn from.

That's what I'm most grateful for—that I learn from each and every one of you, that you inspire me.

In my eyes, and in my heart, tonight was a success. It was a beautiful, beautiful, beautiful, beautiful performance, and I am so proud. I hope that everyone enjoys the rest of their weekend, get lots of rest, get lots of love, give lots of love.

I am not a Black girl. I don't have to be to realize that these stories reflect my own, that I too am "endangered," that I too have been marginalized, stigmatized, and sexualized. [*EBG*] is a celebration, not only of Black girlhood, but all girlhood; and I rejoice that I am able to participate in this celebration by adding my own voice, my own story.
—Catherine (News Anchor)

If the original cast awaited my permission to make *EBG* their own, the South Side of Chicago production[2] might have never happened. The cast showed me that if the university classroom becomes too inadequate, too confining, and too private, they would make educational spaces premised on our interde-

2 *Endangered Black Girls.* Written by Dr. Ruth Nicole Brown. (Re)directed by Catherine Pham. Co-produced by Brittany Baker and Catherine Pham. Original direction from Lisa Fay. Lighting and sound by Dylan Oberling. Music provided by DJ Michael Lee. Original artwork done by Djuana Harvey. TV and all other technology inquiries provided by Nik Njegovan.

pendence. The South Side production made me the student and the cast the teachers. We do not typically recognize undergraduate students as critical to the process of knowledge production; with *EBG*'s South Side production, it happened only because of them. The original cast of *EBG* taught me how (and reminded me again) Black girlhood is a perfectly sensible basis from which to establish a network of relations that make loving and life-sustaining spaces possible. Beyond the cast's and my very own personal transformation, the process of writing, performing, and witnessing *EBG* inspired a space called Saving Our Lives Hear Our Truths (SOLHOT) that makes possible collective transformation. SOLHOT is a small and powerful idea that reimagines Black girlhood. SOLHOT is a radical idea that transpired with abundant support and in a context of excessive warning.

SAVING OUR LIVES HEAR OUR TRUTHS

With insight gained from the process of research and writing *Endangered Black Girls* and the productions that followed, previous experiences of do-ing girl empowerment programming, and rethinking Black girlhood in the context of Black feminism and hip-hop feminism, I dreamed about a space where Black girls would not be an afterthought. Would not exist in comparison. Would not be watched for the purpose of punishment or voyeurism. I thought about a space where we as Black girls would be en-gaged, not bored. Surely, I felt, in this space we would not have to carry the weight of the world in or with us. I did not want us to assemble to become empowered, or to become anything really. I wanted a space for Black girls to be together and have fun. If such a space could exist and Black girlhood could be deployed as an organizing construct, I realized that it would be political and revolutionary. The idea alone countered so much of what cur-rently exists for Black girls. In much the same way, the Combahee River Collective (1995) stated their belief in a politics grounded in "the shared belief that Black women are inherently valuable, that our liberation is a necessity not as an adjunct to somebody else's but because of our need as human persons for autonomy" (p. 234); I believed in such a space for Black girls. I held on to the idea and nurtured it.

The goal/the vision: the celebration of Black girlhood in all of its complex-ity. The means would be collective and creative. The number-one creed of SOLHOT would be the lesson I learned best from Tiara's truth: *When a Black girl tells you something, believe her. When Black girls speak, listen.*

I did not immediately have access to a place to implement the idea. As a newcomer to the community where I was living, it was appropriate for my interests to take a back to seat to current organizing efforts. In the meantime, I went to a local recreation center to volunteer. My intention was to not do anything more than get to know the community I was now a part of through its young people. I introduced myself to Mrs. Regina, a staff person at the center, and she told me they were in need of someone to lead the center's girl group. I thanked her for the opportunity and did the work. Mrs. Regina, I soon learned, was more than her position at the center; she is a thinking woman of faith. She saw, somehow, that I had something more to give. And I did. After a semester of my doing what was asked of me, Mrs. Regina allowed me to do what I wanted to do. What I wanted to do was Saving Our Lives Hear Our Truths. I don't remember exactly how I came up with the name Saving Our Lives Hear Our Truths (SOLHOT), but I did, and it resonated. I knew I could not do it alone, so I sent out a call for others to join me in this work I could not fully describe. People responded. Thankfully, they were and continue to be some of the most powerfully beautiful women and men I have had the pleasure to work with, and together we created a way to do SOLHOT. I organized women who inspired me. Women who I thought were courageous, talented, and from whom I could learn something valuable. Together, I promised those I organized that we could make something really special happen for Black girls in this community and for ourselves. It was risky. We did not really know each other when we started; mostly we only knew of each other. I introduced myself, had one-on-one meetings to get to know people better, shared my experiences, and conveyed my dreams. I really could not offer them much more detail than the time and place we were meeting, once a week for two hours, at the recreation center.

We who came together to organize on behalf of Black girlhood were named homegirls by a homegirl who unconsciously or consciously sought to invoke the brilliance of Barbara Smith and her comrades (1983), as they called themselves homegirls to connote their love for home and reject the homelessness their critics insisted on for them because of their intentional practice of Black feminism. Regardless, SOLHOT continues their Black feminist tradition of honoring certain "home truths," particularly those that address "the challenges we face in each other, to broach the subject of accountability in Black women" (Smith, 1983, p. xl). SOLHOT affirms the challenges of Black feminists before us. Those who do not identify as Black women yet worked with us were called allies. One homegirl later reflected about SOLHOT, "It's a space for us to come together and communicate a sacred revelation that pedagogy, politics, and practice are hard to pull off at the same time but very necessary to our survival as Black girls and women."

We started by working with the girls who already attended the recreation center regularly. Of course, if they wanted to bring friends, they could and did. SOLHOT was open and available to anyone who wanted to drop in. Some did just that and came once. Others girls have been with SOLHOT since it first started. Still others have graduated high school and grown up. About SOLHOT, a few girls offered the following descriptions:

> "It's a place where Black girls can express theirself more and tell about how they get through life and how they feel about being a Black girl."

> "We have so much fun. We take pictures. We talk to each other. We free. We dance."

> "It's fun and—well, you get to do things, and you can meet new people if you've never met 'em before, because it's a whole bunch of different Black girls."

> "It's a program for Black American girls to talk about how they feel about themselves and how they feel about being Black women and stuff like that."

> "It's perfect."

What We Did

We had to have some plan of what we were going to do in SOLHOT. The center required it, and the homegirls expected it. We came up with a loose structure: the content of each session consisted of starting with a Black girl's game (e.g., Little Sally Walker), sharing something of educational value (e.g., hip-hop media literacy), creating something together (e.g., a theatrical scene), and ending with remembering someone who we all wanted each other to know and remember, a libation of sorts, or what we called the incense circle. We created a curriculum that depended on our ability to freestyle. When SOLHOT first begin in 2006, we partnered with the local recreation center. Currently, SOLHOT partners with four local institutions. At each site, on average, twenty girls and five adult women meet once a week for dialogue sessions that typically culminate in a public arts event.

Original Principles

From the very beginning, the most important part of SOLHOT was the way we treated each other while were together. SOLHOT is sacred work. Therefore, it requires homegirls to do the EXTRA work of monitoring our process when we come together, as an act of love. Everyone who attended SOLHOT did not necessarily agree on the following principles, but these served as a close enough description of our experience together to incite productive conversations about what we were doing and what was happening with us because of SOLHOT:

1. Black girls are "TOO LOUD" to be told to quiet down—so do not do it. In SOLHOT we have a rule for the grown folk; you cannot tell the girls to be quiet. This requires us to become comfortable with Black girls' voices—whether they are loud or silent. The reason for this rule is because we love Black-girl voices and we need to get in where we fit in. It is not about Black girls coming to voice. It is all about listening to and loving Black girls' unique articulation of voice and silence.

2. Develop authority—do not discipline. SOLHOT is a "free space." To maintain this idea means that the adults should not "discipline" the girls but rather develop your voice and theirs as a voice of authority. Black girls have been "raised" and they know when they have gone too far; usually another girl will tell them so. Support the girls that are recognized as leaders among their peers. Piggyback on what they said and reinforce what they said and how they said it. This requires listening.

3. It feels kinda like church when SOLHOT is at its best. Not because we are a religion, but rather because we act out of a spirituality. Because many Black girls are "churched" there will be direct references made to Jesus and God. More than that, Black girls who are "churched" often use the language of the church to make and affirm group and individual actions (examples: Amen = I agree, Hallelujah = Praise and Celebration, the devil is a liar = girls' taboo talk). Most importantly, in SOLHOT things happen that defy time, space, place, age, gender, race, etc., so it's a metaphysical experience. Respect the sanctity of Black-girl spaces.

4. Greet each other in truth. Connections are meaningful when Black girls and women are known for who they really are. This means you cannot be afraid to share with the girls the truths about yourself. The girls will probably perceive you as someone who "has made it" (read:

not like them) as a result of your physical appearance. Don't be afraid to tell them how you are making it, your successes and your failures, your dreams and your struggles. It seems that what Black girls really value in an introduction, for example, is knowing who you were raised by and what they taught you that has shaped the person you are today. So go ahead, tell the truth, and get free.

5. You be the change, save yourself! What we do in SOLHOT may be more memorable than what was said. What we do in SOLHOT is up to you. If the girls come up with ideas about doing something (at the center, in the community, change the world) then use your strong Black-woman powers for good and make it happen. Don't leave it up to the oldest person, the most educated, the richest person (or whatever) in SOLHOT. You should not be concerned with saving the girls, but saving yourself and doing what you know needs to be done in SOLHOT. (Many of these principles also appear in Brown, 2009)

Structure

The organizing structure of SOLHOT is organic. Because I initiated the idea of SOLHOT and took responsibility for making it happen, I became referred to as the visionary. In SOLHOT, leadership both rotated and was shared. Sometimes the homegirls would lead, and sometimes the girls would lead. Sometimes we all led together, and at other times, no one led. We took turns creating an agenda and organizing activities. We always deferred to the girls. Participation for all was voluntary. However, during the first year, I was always there. The recreation center and a few organizers purchased the materials that we wanted and needed. We met as SOLHOT for eight weeks. We took a break for a couple weeks and then started the process all over again.

Currently in its fifth year of operation, SOLHOT has changed tremendously. SOLHOT remains without a physical space and has over time collaborated with several local institutions, including the recreation center, the local library, a university campus, and public schools. New leadership has emerged, and each of the four sites now has a different visionary. My position has changed to focus more on encouraging and teaching newer visionaries. While the commitment to celebrating the complexity of Black girlhood has remained a constant in SOLHOT, new practices have emerged. As it turns out, there are multiple ways to celebrate. The new visionaries are documenting the ways SOLHOT is now enacted, and I eagerly await their analyses.

CONCLUSION: PERFORMING SINGULAR TRUTHS, ORGANIZING POSSIBILITIES

"I'm brown,
  five four . . . something like that,
    and I got black hair."

That was the most important thing she wanted me to know.

Tiara taught me sometimes all you get is a sentence, at best. A singular turn of phrase. Something specific. A small work. A question. Tiara's silence and the fractured sentence she offered to me spoke loudly against a backdrop of racism and sexism, making what she managed to say even more valuable than a statement just about herself. Tiara's interview was not a failure. Her quietness was not a problem. That she gave me something I could then put in conversation with other girls' singular truths using imagination led to researching, to writing, and ultimately to subsequent productions of *Endangered Black Girls*. Her truth, dramatized in relation to other Black girls' truths, in and through performance, made possible imagining new ideas, new images, and new spaces of belonging.

Youth programs and the academy have much in common, in that on many occasions what matters most falls outside of curricular concerns, disciplinary norms, institutional standards and rewards. Moreover, the conditions in which creative work specifically and creativity more generally survive in a more privatized university raises significant implications not only for the content of creative work, but also for those among us who are miseducated into believing that permission is necessary to create, to be artists. What is at stake in substantiating the illusion of permission, particularly as it relates to artist-scholars of color, is the paradoxical impossibility of critical thought and creating and sustaining critical communities of engagement in a context where engagement and postracial diversity is all the rage.

The process and subsequent productions of *EBG* inspired me to think of new ways Black women and girls could be present with each other, leading me to suggest and co-organize Saving Our Lives Hear Our Truths (SOLHOT) as transformative collective and creative work. SOLHOT is a space dedicated to the celebration of Black girlhood in all of its complexity. Theorizing the celebration of Black girlhood in all of its complexity as practiced in SOLHOT is absolutely vital to academic and popular literature on Black girlhood and for challenging and changing systemic structures that do not value Black girls' lives. On both fronts, *EBG* and SOLHOT thrive on and value creativity as a necessary resource in collective knowledge production, and they foreground complexity.

Beyond the reality that offices in many academic institutions resemble prison cells, researchers who think outside of the proverbial box, who do research that does not easily lend itself to mainstream disciplinary standards, are often punished and policed. Bodies of intellectual imaginatives, then, are all too often overburdened and dis-eased. Academic appointments displace certain thinkers around and across the university, making them account-able to multiple, sometimes impossible standards and evaluative criteria. The more the military-industrial complex constructs the prison-industrial complex and influences the academic-industrial complex, the more often some of our most creative thinkers are imprisoned, bodies disposed of and explained away as untenurable. The result is not just death of our collective imagination, but also the loss of people with families, who have dedicated their lives to teaching and nurturing generations of scholars. I could name names if I thought this obvious, significant, and admittedly redundant point would not be overlooked in so doing; creative work is foundational to col-lective social-justice efforts and to our individual well-being. It is creative work, collectively engaged, that makes possible a pronouncement of what ought to be, a visioning of how to live, a declaration of knowing who walks with us. This is the stuff of dreams, works of art and practices of science by scholars whose methods and productions are not always legible or tangible but nonetheless serve a concrete function in the world of ideas. This work is necessary and inherently resistant to the production of knowledge as business as usual.

At the end of the day, the most important thing Tiara wanted me to know was,

"I'm brown,
    five four . . . something like that,
       and I got black hair."

2 Black Women Remember Black Girls
A Collective and Creative Memory

"[She] reported that Jhessye's hair had been pulled out and described Jhessye as not looking alive and that she looked like a zombie," the document said. "[She] said that the closet where Jhessye had been looked like a grave and smelled like dead people." ("Search for remains," 2012)

I want you to know and remember Jhessye Shockley.

A 14-year-old girl from Tennessee became a trending topic when a video of her performing oral sex behind a school was posted on Facebook, and instantly went viral. (Miller, 2012)

I want you to know and remember "Amber Cole."

Scott's death clearly underscores the need for more awareness and discussion of depression and mental health issues among Black women and less shame and silence. (Williams, 2012)

I want you to know and remember Jacqueline Scott.

Sakia Gunn, a fifteen-year-old Aggressive-identified African-American from Newark, New Jersey, was fatally stabbed on the morning of May 11th, 2003. Three men were harassing Gunn and two friends while they were waiting at a bus stop, and the three women told the men that they were lesbians in an effort to get the men to leave them alone. (Mazina and Di-Brienza, 2008)

I want you to know and remember Sakia Gunn.

And I got to thinking about the moral meaning of memory, per se. And what it means to forget, what it means to fail to find and preserve the connection with the dead whose lives you, or I, want or need to honor with our own.
—June Jordan (2002, p. 5)

To go from the idea of Saving Our Lives Hear Our Truths (SOLHOT) to the creation of a practice, labor is required. That is, someone must do the work—the organizing work, the academic work, the personal work, the spiritual work, and the community work—not necessarily in this order. Since SOLHOT requires labor, it is worthwhile to think through issues of process, production, capital, death, survival, and recognition. These issues are often discussed among homegirls, with particular urgency given to questions that help us to explicate how we in SOLHOT resist and unconsciously collude with capitalist exploitation premised on the expedient disposal of Black and Brown bodies. Black girls' lives, especially when taken too soon and often as a result of violent action, are not typically remembered. The nonexistent global protests, the absence of national rallies, and the missed calls for structural reform, often coupled with victim-blaming headlines, signify a failed connection with those whose lives, Jordan professes, we should honor with our own. Even still, Black girls living in their bodies know the all-too-familiar expectations of premature and slow death, as they are often the first to be sacrificed, the expected carriers of heavy loads, made to feel invisible and inferior in spite of a historical legacy that suggests anything but defeat.

In SOLHOT, we remember Black girls. We have made up rituals to remember games we no longer play, and we have a way of commemorating conversations that make room for silence and the speaking of taboos. The "incense circle" is a ritual in SOLHOT where we call the names of those we want known and remembered. Jhessye Shockley, "Amber Cole," Jacqueline Scott, Sakia Gunn, and June Jordan, you are known and remembered.

In SOLHOT, we honor ourselves by remembering those we've lost too soon as a way to rehearse what our work is together. SOLHOT requires creating something that has never quite existed, as we've known it, and in order to do this, rituals of remembering are required. For a homegirl to be ready to undertake the labor required to accomplish a task as monumental as celebrating Black girlhood in a way that accounts for complexity, remains critical, instructs humanely, and feels like healing, preparation is a must. Homegirls must remember all the ways they are not alone but connected to others, ancestors, kinfolk, spirits, and communities whose honor it is of theirs to recall, respect, and remember as part of the work of doing SOLHOT. To homegirl is to commit to a very sincere practice of remembering Black girlhood as a way to honor oneself and to practice the selflessness necessary to honor someone else, remembered whole.

In this chapter, I explore how homegirls remember SOLHOT as a sacred experience that makes a liberatory Black girlhood possible. The concept of the homegirl is what sets SOLHOT apart from traditional mentoring programs and youth cultural work. For certain, to *homegirl* is a verb, and because SOLHOT—when it works—does very much seem celebratory, it is often the labor that homegirls attribute to the spiritual and the sacred that best explains what happened in SOLHOT that was so much work, so much fun, and so healing. Memory is the means through which homegirls make sense of the spiritual and the sacred in SOLHOT as connected to their labor. Homegirls consciously and collectively use memory to make SOLHOT more than a program, something bigger than us, a sacred space of teaching, learning, and healing. Homegirls give time, energy, and creative insight to remember Black girlhood as a space of celebration, a playful engagement of being and becoming, as an iterative process whereby the gifts, talents, creativity, and knowledge of Black girls matter. In the doing of all of this, homegirls also remember who they are and how they are or are not up to the task of being present in relation to a very particular community that depends on their presence and being well. As a meaningful experience that has come to stand in as a critical part of their lives, homegirls understand that the doing of SOLHOT is significantly tied to those who were denied a Black girlhood. Their memories of doing SOLHOT locate the urgency of their practice in the awareness that unless they make an earnest attempt to create a space of Black girlhood celebration, Black girlhood may very well not exist at all or be remembered by Black girls as positively remarkable. Based on the interviews of eight SOLHOT homegirls, this chapter features a creative and collective memory titled "Black Women Remember Black Girls" that shows how the creation of a space to celebrate Black girlhood in all of its complexity is to know the dynamic ways in which an intentional Black girlhood directed toward freedom invokes labor and the sacred.

MEMORY AND TIME

When homegirls discussed SOLHOT in interviews, homegirls did not wax nostalgic but named the multiple ways their labor was something more than secular and how their motivations for doing the work reached beyond self-interest. Even for homegirls who moved away from where they once participated in SOLHOT, SOLHOT proved memorable even after several years since their day-to-day active involvement. The cumulative re-memories of making a space revealed a kaleidoscopic framework of diverse and contested subject positions (Shohat, 2006, p. 3) that alluded to SOLHOT as a living archive of Black girlhood possibilities. The homegirl memories of doing SOLHOT honored those before them, affirmed the presence of all involved, called names, recognized differences, and valued complexity—all practices mirrored in their interactions with the girls. An examination of their memories revealed that time—specifically, the way they used, manipulated, and created time—undergirded the spiritual dynamics of the work.

Students of Black feminism, women-of-color feminism, and womanism are familiar with the productive relationship between labor, memory, spirit, and time. bell hooks (2009) wrote,

> We chart our lives by everything we remember from the mundane moment to the majestic. We know ourselves through the art and the act of remembering. Memories offer us a word where there is no death, where we are sustained by rituals of regard and recollection. (p. 50)

In this way, when homegirls remember Black girlhood in SOLHOT, homegirling functions as an urgent process of mastering the multiple, often unsustainable, yet necessary recognitions and rituals of life-affirming recollect and regard. Notably, the interview transcripts and recordings read like extended conversations on a subject that is familiar, beloved, and complicated. Yet even as the homegirls expressed many good feelings about the work, they were also critically aware of the practice—both in a sense of the overall comprehensive work and in their own personal contributions to SOLHOT. Whether the homegirls thought of their last time in SOLHOT as yesterday, last year, or a couple of years past, their memories were animated. Through tone, tears, laughter, silence, extended pauses, trembling, giggles, colloquialisms, and requests to turn off the tape recorder or to have certain things "on record," the homegirls interviewed made clear that a part of what makes the work more than a program is their relation to SOLHOT as a living thing that continues to affect and influence their lives. That memories, in this case of SOLHOT, also allow homegirls to remember themselves, alive, is expertly theorized by M. Jacqui Alexander in her book *Pedagogies of Crossings* (2005). Written in honor of Gloria Anzaldúa and the legacy of *This Bridge Called My Back: Writings by Radical Women of Color* (Anzaldua and Moraga, 2002), Alexander beckoned:

> Can we *intentionally* remember, all the time, as a way of never forgetting, all of us, building an archeology of living memory, which has less to do with living in the past, invoking a past, or excising it, and more to do with our relationship to Time and its purpose? There is a difference between

remembering *when*—the nostalgic yearning for some return—and a living memory that enables us to remember what was contained in *Bridge* and what could not be contained within or by it. (p. 278)

Surface and casual observations of SOLHOT by participants and outsiders alike are usually inattentive to the ways time travels in SOLHOT, ignorant of its purpose. In spite of (or rather because of) popular reference to SOL-HOT as "chaotic" and "unstructured," in depth analysis of the homegirls' interviews revealed that time in SOLHOT functions much the same way as a living memory of *Bridge*, making it possible to examine the more spiritual and sacred inter- and inner dynamics. I suggest that the perceived and felt chaos of SOLHOT is akin to what Alexander (2005) names the *palimpsetic*, a logic of time that structures the "new" through the "old" and a scrambling that "makes visible the ideological traffic between and among formations that are otherwise positioned as dissimilar" (p. 190). Likewise, the supposed unstructured organization of SOLHOT may also be attributed to the likelihood of each moment, conversation, and interaction presenting a surprise. According to Pierre Bourdieu (1980), "to reintroduce uncertainty is to reintroduce time, with its rhythm, its orientation and its irreversibility, substituting the dialectic of strategies for the mechanics of the model, but without falling over into the imaginary anthropology of 'rational actor' theories" (p. 99). In homegirl interviews, certain rituals and routines occurred repeatedly, even if unplanned, just as much as surprise and uncertainty always seemed to undo the formal agenda and curriculum. When time is constructed by homegirl memories, it is not linear or chronological, but rather the making of space to celebrate Black girlhood exists out of time *and* order.

In homegirls' memories, work is doubly referenced as the practices attributed to making a space of Black girlhood through time, as well as the work that memory performs in relationship to the sacred. Homegirls construct their labor as sacred, in much the same way that Black feminist, womanist, and activist organizing traditions that are diasporic and transnationally oriented have named labor as useful. Of the five overarching characteristics of womanism (anti-oppression, vernacular, nonideological, communitarian, and spiritualized), spirituality is named as the open acknowledgment of the spiritual/transcendental realm in which human life, living kind, and the material world are intertwined (Phillips, 2006, p. xxvi). Operating in and operationalizing what Cynthia Dillard and Chinwe Okpalaoka (2011) call an "endarkened feminist epistemology" (p. 149), the relationship between the sacred and spirituality as understood by the homegirls is sufficiently explained:

What we mean by spirituality is to have a consciousness of the realm of the spirit in one's work and to recognize that consciousness as a transformative form in research and teaching . . . However, when we speak of the sacred in endarkened feminist research, we are referring to the way the work is honored and embraced as it is carried out. Said another way, work that is sacred is worthy of being held with reverence as it is done. The idea here is that, as we consider paradigms and epistemology from endarkened or Black Feminist positions, the work embodies and engages spirituality and is carried out in sacred ways. (p. 147–48)

Endarkened, Black feminist, and womanist paradigms are each distinct paradigms yet have in common an understanding of the role of the sacred that may be expressed in work, as work.

Time to give is typically coded as a luxury afforded to those who are privileged with leisure, unconsumed by survival. However, when the work is with Black girls in the name of Black girlhood, giving time is not as important as making time. Making time requires an understanding of labor outside of a secular orientation. Memory and acts of remembering make it possible to unclock time for the purpose of looking at how one travels through time, for example, to access the past as a way to change the future in the present moment. Time accessed as a unique resource allows working and working-class Black women, and those becoming someone else, to know themselves as Black girls precisely through memory and a remembered Black girlhood. Structural inequalities coupled with the material realities of Black girlhood make it necessary for many Black girls to grow up before their time, so much so that bearing responsibility for more than themselves at particularly young ages shapes Black girls' activity around the needs, desires, and well-being of others, instead of themselves. Implications abound and include the possibility of never experiencing a Black girlhood that was "carefree" or innocent. This is, of course, if Black girlhood is actually remembered at all and if they, Black girls, survive the struggle. The labor of making Black girlhood worth remembering, and the sacred work of creating Black girlhood as a space of attempted, even if not fully accomplished, celebration, requires the labor of others (Brown, 2009; King, 2005; Ladner, 1971; Sears, 2010) who often act in a way to honor those who came before them. The act of making the space of Black girlhood exists outside of linear and Eurocentric understandings and practices of time.

Theorizing the sacred in relationship to time is one way to show appreciation for those who most willingly labor on behalf of Black girls. It is no small feat to know how to make Black girlhood, and it is to the credit of the homegirls that SOLHOT does so, so well, consistently. Moreover, when theorized in context of the sacred, homegirls' memories of SOLHOT illumine the labor of making the space, work that is typically and mistakenly masked by sameness (particularly in terms of shared markers of identity). Further, the pedagogical implications of spirituality and the sacred as they relate to Black girlhood inform the ways in which diverse types of knowledge and embodied wisdom are valued and understood as necessary resources in the work of homegirling. As activists, warriors, and gate guardians, homegirls make time for Black girlhood through SOLHOT and create opportunities to recollect themselves whole, as Black girls, or as once Black girls, and as new people, while also and just as significantly making Black girlhood memorable for someone else. Spirit and the sacred are not least among the resources necessary to master an education too rarely taught, invoked, and spoken of in relation to spaces for Black girls and youth more generally.

THE ART OF HOMEGIRLING: A CAVEAT

SOLHOT is sacred work, and, when it is done correctly, it is memorable. However, not all homegirls are skilled in the art of homegirling. Homegirls who do not know how to make Black girlhood will attend SOLHOT and go through the motions disconnected. They do not make time, but rather schedule SOLHOT in their daily activities. Unaware of how the sacred functions, the unknowing homegirls adhere to prefabricated narratives of "volunteering in an after-school program," for example, that at best translates into doing good while they are there. Most of the unknowing homegirls remain in SOLHOT for a single six-week cycle; a few stay longer to enjoy the space as a form of entertainment even as the girls attempt to tell them, in subtle and not so subtle ways, why they are "not SOLHOT." Unaware homegirls are seemingly more focused on everyone else than interrogating their own not-so-correct actions. Those that miss the mark often do not take up SOLHOT as any kind of labor, sacred or otherwise, and remain committed to a "Black girls are the problem, not me" mentality that influences their not-so-deep relationships with other SOLHOT girls and homegirls.

What do the more skilled homegirls know that those who are unaware do not? With an embodied knowledge of how the sacred functions in SOLHOT, skilled homegirls know that before Black girlhood can be celebrated, it must be made. In SOLHOT the homegirls take on the responsibility to make the space and prepare the celebration. This celebratory space is made through time, specifically time that is fluid and transcendent. Transcending and transforming time is a sacred work that they are skilled in because they have practiced it elsewhere, or because they are ready to learn and do the work. They remember Black girls as a matter of practice.

How do homegirls enact what they know? The sacred requires homegirls to bring their full selves and deploy resources they may not even know they possessed until they were told that they did. That they enact what they know means they trust SOLHOT, they trust the process, and they trust themselves. In the presence of others, they love themselves and make time. They also unlearn, depend on each other, and ask questions. At some point in their practice, homegirls begin to think of their own personal well-being as connected to SOLHOT's sustainability. Homegirls responsible for making time believe that Black girlhood encompasses them as well, that the celebration of Black girlhood is also a celebration of Black womanhood, equally complex, and that the celebration of personhood is also a celebration of Black girlhood. Skilled homegirls put into practice the sacred work of making time, understood as a critical means of deregulating normative privileges. They work with time, not against it. Skilled homegirls enact an intimate and artistic wisdom as a way to honor their ancestors and remember Black girls who died violently and too soon while simultaneously changing the lives of future Black girls, by laboring in the present.

THE PROCESS OF CREATING
THE COLLECTIVE MEMORY

"Black Women Remember Black Girls" is a creative and collective memory based on interviews of SOLHOT homegirls. To create the memory, I relied on the transcriptions of eight homegirl interviews who self-selected to participate. The homegirls interviewed ranged between twenty and thirty-six years of age (the majority were twenty-one years old at the time of the interview). All identify as Black women, with several homegirls particularly attentive to their diasporic location as Jamaican, Puerto Rican, Ghanaian, and African American. Importantly, while more than thirty women have worked with SOLHOT as homegirls, the eight interviewed represent those who have most profoundly given of themselves to make SOLHOT happen. The reader should assume that at the time interviewed, each homegirl wholeheartedly believed in the work of SOLHOT, even as they were critical of the practice.

Interviews were conducted once by a homegirl who has been with SOL-HOT since its beginning and worked with me as a research assistant. A professional transcribed all but one interview.[1] One year passed between the transcription of the interviews and my rereadings of them and subsequent analysis. As one homegirl suspected during an interview, "Dr. Brown, I think, has conversations with each and every homegirl," I have had countless in-depth one-on-one conversations about SOLHOT with all involved, especially those who chose to participate in the formal interviews that form the foundation of this chapter. As the original "visionary" of SOLHOT, my participation is unconditional. I bring to the text an intimate knowing of those interviewed, and it matters, as Madison and Hamera (2006, p. 288) noted, because the text lives off the page based on what we bring to it as we read and write. In the writing process, I heard the voices of the homegirls, and I gave attention to the sound of their voices in juxtaposition to each other. I do not identify homegirls or girls by their birth names or traditional pseudonyms. Instead, in the text, I refer to homegirls and girls by a dominant personal characteristic, preferred descriptor, or Yoruba deity. Also, I wanted to show off the uniqueness of each homegirl's personality by not editing language for grammar and word choice.

To construct a collective memory, the process was very much creative. Much like in *Tight Spaces* by Kesho Scott, Cherry Muhanji, and Egyirba High (1999), I relied on a creative force to guide my retelling, a force they name as "She energy." According to Scott, Muhanji, and High (1999, p. 11), "it was from this energy and creative thinking that we gathered the spiritual authority to be critical of ourselves and society by using our many voices from our gender, class, race, and sexuality standpoints." As the single author of the collective memory, guided primarily by the methodological muse of creativity, I also relied on spirit, in much the same way the homegirls advanced remembering as a sacred act, made possible through transgressions of time. My interests in this creative retelling was to resist a simple and coherent narrative structure, to intentionally and thoughtfully place different stories in relation to one another for the purpose of highlighting tension, irony, and contradiction, to include stories that were the most critical of SOLHOT as well as those that were the most endearing, and to create a laborious piece of creative work that mirrors, in some small way, the effort, dedication, and commitment it takes to do SOLHOT. As a reader, I am asking you, just as I ask the homegirls, to be present with the creative memory—staying with

1 One interviewed was transcribed by the homegirl who conducted the interviews.

it even when you think you want to put it down, listening for the nuances, commenting in the margins, all the while interrogating how you desire to enter or foreclose the conversations we've begun. Lastly, even with hauntings of a possible essentialist critique of this creative work, I do not indicate which memories belong to whom, as the written "I" is meant to refer to a collective voice. I chose to write in "first-person plural" (Finney, 2009), which simultaneously honors collectivity and singularity.

Even as I was creative, I was also strategic. M. Jacqui Alexander's *Pedagogies of Crossings* (2005) made it possible for me to demonstrate how homegirls' memories of SOLHOT, structured through time, recall their work as sacred. In the chapter "Pedagogies of the Sacred: Making the Invisible Tangible," Alexander explores the ways spiritual practitioners employ metaphysical systems to explain their sense of self as rooted in their memories of particular experiences as sacred, and how, in turn, those experiences shape their subjectivity (2005, p. 295). Alexander simultaneously intertwined her own personal experience as priest in two African-based communities, Vodoun and Lucumi, with her ethnographic research to ingeniously critique connections between the sacred and feminist theories of the body, to interrogate implied categorizations of "experience," and to question narrow deployments of transnationalism and political praxis that relegate women's leadership and activism solely within the secular. The political implications of Alexander's research addressed hegemonic capitalist formations and the subsequent violence committed as a result. Admittedly, the homegirls' memories of SOLHOT do not contest or critique Alexander's theory, or the scholarship of feminist theorists, endarkened and otherwise, but rather the memory builds on their work by specifically highlighting the function of memory, time, and the sacred as it relates to Black girlhood.

After subsequent re-readings of both the interviews and *Pedagogies*, I mapped Alexander's theory onto the interview transcripts. I first coded the transcripts of the homegirls using generic time codes such as "before SOL-HOT starts" (which was later translated into "The Crossings," and so on). I then creatively edited the memory until there were nine parts. The poem-prayer introduces homegirls' memories as sacred work. Next, "The Crossings" addresses how homegirls thought of themselves and who they were before they actually began SOLHOT. "Initiation" follows and details how each session starts. "Acts of Recognition" portrays the range and the depth of what happens during SOLHOT, especially as it relates to the girls. "The Incense Circle" describes the rituals that mark the session's end. "Sacred Praxis" demonstrates how homegirls process their thoughts and actions, whereby theory emerges from practice and SOLHOT practice informs Black girlhood theory making. While homegirls' naming and unnaming of what it means to make Black girlhood is presented in the section "The Antidote," "Black Girlhood Subjectivity" highlights everything that homegirls attribute to having been made or produced in and because of SOLHOT. The last section of the memory, "Healing and Hindsight," focuses on the promises of making Black girlhood as sacred work. As much as I believe the performed memory speaks for itself, it is worthwhile to tell what their words show: the sacred is directly tied to the affirmation of Black girls' lives and everyone's will to live.

PEDAGOGIES REMAPPED:
BLACK WOMEN REMEMBER BLACK GIRLS

1. The poem-prayer
2. The Crossings . . . foresightings and foresensings
3. Initiation . . . .beginnings
4. Acts of Recognition . . . who walks with us
5. The Incense Circle . . . closings
6. Sacred Praxis . . . afterwords and beginnings
7. The Antidote . . . naming and unnaming
8. Black Girlhood Subjectivity . . . multiple productions
9. Healing & Hindsight . . . interconnections

The Homegirl's Poem Prayer

It's for us, too—
how it impacted me.
. . . I'm passionate about it
and see(ing) the urgency in it.
It's really why I am in . . .
subconsciously.
I tell my mom and my grandmother
it's one of the best places I've ever been . . .
My grandmother's
a theorist,
too.
She's a magician.
She does awesome things.

And so

i

believe(d)

in that.

SOLHOT will always live on in that way.

The Crossings, foresightings and foresensings

The Crossings . . . foresightings and foresensings. In SOLHOT, the individual-
ity of each homegirl matters. As such, the crossroads represents the ways in
which homegirls' personal histories, life experiences, family backgrounds,
and ongoing commitments intersect with SOLHOT. The key concept of
the crossings as articulated by Alexander (2005) is that they "are never undertaken all at once, and never once and for all" (p. 290). In relation to the
making of Black girlhood, the crossings prepare us for the understanding
that SOLHOT as a dynamic space looks and feels different in all time and is
dependent on who is coming together, where they have been before, and the
embodied knowledge and talents they bring with them. The crossings also
allow for dynamism within SOLHOT as the practice of making a space of
Black girlhood celebration undoubtedly reflects different parts of homegirls'
personal histories that they may have never even imagined mattered, until
the time it did matter, in SOLHOT.

I was tired, or I had an assignment to do or something like that.

It's so funny, because I'm like a little kid. I want to be a fireman and
police officer and a unicorn. Actually, my ideal job—I would love to be a
dance therapist—a dance therapist that focuses on working with marginalized communities.

I was born here. I spent the bulk of my time doing on-campus
organizing—like thankless grunt work, unpaid labor for the university.
I'm kind of dull and awkward, but I really do like—despite that, I really
do like kids. I really do like talking to thirteen-year-olds. I think they
have amazing insights on how the world works.

I grew up in public housing where I was called the "rec" girl.

I guess I went into it not because—I didn't go into it thinking I would
have anything in common with them, because I've had a—I've always
been the Black kid that got teased for being white. My parents are like the
Huxtables and you're only allowed to speak proper English. I was very

sheltered. I know I was an awkward teenager/awkward adult, so I know there's gonna be a weird, quiet person that I will probably get along with, just because I know there's not a monolithic Black-girl archetype.

I was most passionate about working with other women of color from the university and working specifically with Black girls.

My mom has an at-home day care. Let me tell you, since '98 . . . what is that—eleven years. I've always had kids in my life and having responsibilities with making bottles, cleaning, all that. At some point, I got discouraged, because they'd be watching *Sesame Street* and I'm like, "We should be doing something. We should be doing something," so then I started taking part in day care and doing afternoon crafts and activities. I think what I had noticed before all the programming thing is that there is a lot of Black girls here being raised by their grandmother or something else because of addiction. And my grandmother has seven kids, and it's just my mom out of the seven that isn't addicted to some type of substance. We've raised my aunt's daughter since she was two. She just started high school today. She was a crack baby. She was on ADHD meds up until three years ago, struggled through every grade—almost failing every grade—finally got off the medicine last year, has improved tremendously, and now, by the grace of God, she's getting ready for college. So, I've seen that, but then I've also been in this academic community where people are talking about this issue but not really living it, and I felt like I could connect with these girls on the most intimate level, because I think that is one of the most intimate relationships—a mother and daughter. I was ready to connect with them on that level.

When I heard about SOLHOT I heard it from one of the other homegirls' mouth. Maybe who I was was SOLHOT already. I don't know. I don't know.

At that particular time I was doing rape crisis work, and so I was really focused on sex ed, rape crisis. I guess I don't really know what the word is but ideas about rape and body image and things like that, relationships—so that was kind of where I was, as far as activities.

I don't consider myself a leader, I consider myself like, I play my role, you tell me the position to play and I play it . . . I'm not—I'm a shy person, if you didn't already know that.

I just like working with people, specifically girls like myself that come from—I come from a working-class family in the South Side of Chicago, so I just like being around my own peers. I didn't even know about this place. My world was the university and the city. I didn't really think of this place as a town, at the time.

Well, I found out about SOLHOT through an internet page, actually. I was doing research, because I was really interested in trying to get involved in some sort of institute that connected the university with the community, 'cause I knew that I was really upset with the way higher ed was trying to change or shape my identity and trying to push people—it seemed like it was trying to push people away from the community, so I was trying to find a place—

I knew that I would be able to do it. I knew that I would enjoy doing it, probably. I knew that it would be a dope experience, but I had absolutely no idea what we were expected to do, at all.

I thought my responsibility would be the same as the Big Sister, Little Sister Program at my high school. It was like, "Okay, you go in. You role model, you do fun activities with the girls, you talk to the girls after school. You kind of just form this relationship," and so that's why immediately it was like, "Oh, okay." It was just like the same thing. It was ironic how, even though the way SOLHOT is ran is so much differently than how it was ran when I was in high school, the outside looks the same.

I was very nervous—very nervous, because I did not know what I was stepping into.

I wanted to work with children. I'm a Black girl. I feel like my—I don't know. I just have a regular life. Actually, I wasn't sure if I could even—if I had any things to offer Black girls in terms of—sometimes I felt like maybe possibly I would have—I initially felt like I was gonna be an outsider in the whole SOLHOT movement, period. I felt like it was so close-knit, and I always tell The One Who Favors Red II this. I'm like, "The One Who Favors Red II," you didn't welcome me. I didn't feel welcomed by you.

I had a traditional upbringing. "Traditional" I guess to me means I went to church, you didn't wear certain things. I probably won't even wear red fingernail polish. To this day I never wore it, because hookers wore that, as my grandma would say.

I kept talking about it, and people are like, "What are you doing?" and I'm like, "I've got to do something. I've just got to get there," so it's anticipation. You're so excited and apprehensive, and then you see one of the girls. When they recognize you, and when they stop what they're doing when they're getting out of school talking to somebody and they stop what they're doing. They know that when they see you it's time to come into the building. Just visually, it's like acceptance almost, and peace—just a comfortable feeling that you don't have to talk about it. I can look at one of the SOLHOT girls and we can know what's about to happen. We understand that this is what's about to go down, because this is what happens every Friday.

I never thought about African American—a Black girl—like political socialization. I never thought about that. I never thought about looking at my girlhood, you know what I'm saying? So, that's what interested me.

I was at first reluctant 'cause I was like, I don't want to do a research project on like Black girls because I know how it can be taken out by administration, like, at-risk Black girls need some fixing, like I didn't need fixing, you know, I just needed to be heard and I was like, and I don't wanna be those people who came to my neighborhood, and it's always about taking, case workers come to your neighborhood and they take, you know, police come to your neighborhood, they take, you know, so everybody always is like what I call data miners, always coming in trying to get information and I was like, I don't wanna be a data miner.

I hated living here. I hated being here.

There I was in this place that was not home—and like the only African American student in my program.

I just wasn't chillin'. So yeah, maybe just coming from class and feeling like I go home for about an hour, and then it's like that hour seems so short and then it's time to go to SOLHOT. It's like, "Man, I didn't really"— I wouldn't say I didn't want to do SOLHOT, 'cause I always look forward to SOLHOT, but sometimes it was like, "Oh, SOLHOT. I really just want to climb into my bed."

So, I mean, you start printing out the emails. So I would always look at that right before. But everybody knew—everybody, and I say everybody, the people that I had to have meetings with, either about the women-of-color reading group . . . so everybody already knew don't call me when I finish before this time like I'm unavailable . . . and I would get—and I think I would be mentally prepared in a myriad of ways because I had to prepare myself for thinking that you know maybe I'm performing, like I am like this down person and I may not be. Am I performing that I know like these girls when they are—they are, you know . . . they are their own people, so am I projecting my own self onto them? You know, so is this just about me? So you know I would go in with those kinds of feelings.

I assumed that because it's not quite a city but still a city there were a lot of issues like boys, sexuality, fights—those sorts of things that would be common. I mean, just given statistics I assumed I would have a similar background, like maybe they didn't have a dad growing up. Or, maybe a lot of them were raised by families of women and a lot of men weren't present in their family structure. I assumed that a lot of them would be into the arts—something, whether it be dance or writing or something like that.

I would normally be getting out of some type of evening class at about 5:00, would run home, get my stuff—'cause I was always lugging some type of luggage to SOLHOT—cameras, equipment, something. And I'd usually—I drove—but my mind frame would even be changing on my way to SOLHOT, because I'd be thinking about, "What do I want to share, as well, with these girls? What can I share today? What's been going on with me?" because they want the check-in.

So, I have to bring them to the space.

I could just tell that it was a place that I needed to be in. I knew that I had a space there and that I needed to be there.

Honestly, I think it was just what it was called, "A space for Black girls." You don't hear that label for you, "This is for Black girls—Black girls, not Black women, not a mixture. This is for Black girls," and that concept of that even being offered to me was just so new. It was like, "What is this about?" And it didn't center around teen pregnancy. Right, the only time Black girls were called together was to talk about boys and teen pregnancy and how to not catch HIV and stuff like that.

And it's kind of refreshing to—it was very refreshing to have that, and that was what I anticipated, like, "I can go in there and use all the improper English I want. I'm not upholding the race."

I didn't walk in assuming that I had anything in common with them. So, I structured my thoughts around the space instead of around the girls. I was really just about ready to quit graduate school, or at least go somewhere else. So, I hadn't applied anywhere else, so I was back in the fall. And I remember seeing a flyer, and I can't even remember what was on the flyer other than something about working with Black girls. I said, "Oh my gosh, this would be fabulous," because I worked for an all-girls camp for five years . . . and that was probably some of the best times of my life, developmentally. I worked there from the time I was eighteen until I was twenty-three when I came here. It was fabulous, that whole working experience and being around women and girls and having that kind of relationship was great.

I don't even remember that being formally said: "These are the things we're gonna do. You do this. You do this." There were no assignments given out. It was just kind of, "You bring whatever you want to bring to SOLHOT," and that was it.

I was telling you before that I went to a predominantly white, wealthy school and so every time I did try, even now and then, it was just completely shot down. People didn't really understand. They didn't believe I was real. They thought it was an exaggeration.

I had a positive situation growing up.

I'd argue that the suburb I'm from is not the definition or the picture painted that everybody thinks of suburbia. It's not, by any chance, perfect, all white families.

So, first on the way, I'm thinking of all the fucked-up shit that has probably happened through the day, that I need to have at the forefront of all my thoughts and emotions so that SOLHOT will do what it will with it. So, it's kind of a prep period where I'll—it's almost like more of a confession. You're trying to figure out all the shit you did, so you've got a working list when you get there. That's kind of how it is coming to SOLHOT. It's like a compilation of everything I want to get rid of.

Initiation, or beginning to practice saving and hearing . . .

Initiation . . . the beginnings. SOLHOT has come to stand in for a set of "terms, symbols, and organizational codes" homegirls use to make a Black girlhood space (Alexander, 2005, p. 293). For example, check-in, the Batty dance,[2] side conversations, and preparations are specific practices remembered by homegirls to initiate SOLHOT. The accomplishment (or not) of each of these practices influences the quality and kind of space that is made. Moreover, that these specific actions and ideas are embodied practices means that homegirls come to know the sacred work of each practice through the body. In other words, homegirls know and have knowledge of how the Batty dance works as a metaphysical resource because they have danced, or not. In Alexander's work, she gives great attention to the relationship between memory, time, and the body, mindful that what can easily appear as secular experience and secular labor (e.g., the Batty dance is only a girls' game or dance) has as much to do with the consequences of cultural relativist paradigms and postmodernity that renders the sacred as only tradition, a lesser-than knowledge that is attributed to a mythic historical past unrelated to the present moment. Alexander wrote, "In this matrix the body thus becomes a site of memory, not a commodity for sale, even as it is simultaneously insinuated within a nexus of power" (2005, p. 29). Homegirls know all too well that they must be well in their bodies in order to make the space of Black girlhood as celebratory as possible. Likewise, how homegirls superficially appear to others

---

2 The Batty dance is a Black girls' game created by one of the homegirls in SOLHOT. A detailed description of the Batty dance is explained in *Black Girlhood Celebration: Toward a Hip-Hop Feminist Pedagogy* (Brown, 2008).

is not enough to conjure the metaphysical resources necessary to make the Batty dance happen, specifically, or to make the space of Black girlhood more generally. In this way, what the homegirls know through the embodied practice of SOLHOT and what clearly comes across in their memories is that their experience and labor as sacred necessarily and by definition resist all-too-easy and superficial designations of SOLHOT as "mentoring" or as a university-sponsored brand of "civic engagement."

You're in there talking and, "What happened?" and then The One Who Favors Red II reminds us that we need to pull it together and get started. And then there—I don't even know how to describe it. When you're there, you're just there.

I'm thinking about all of this stuff. I'm thinking about what's gonna be said in check-in. All of this stuff goes through my mind. It sounds complicated. It's complicated in my head, but I go to bed dreaming about the next Friday, "What's gonna happen?" Also, "What can I contribute to this space to allow these things?"

So, then I get there, and sometimes it's the same as what I thought it was gonna be, and then sometimes it's completely different.

It's like, "Hey, girl." It's just that excitement of, "I'm here. I'm here." It's like every Friday being surprised by your mother's favorite dish that you want.

I come in the space and it's beautiful! And I'm not romanticizing—

And then we do the Batty dance. That always takes forever, because no one wants to do the Batty dance. They'll be there all year, but no one wants to do the Batty dance. There's always four people that does it. So, we have to get people to do the Batty dance. We do check-in. Check-in is the best, because I'm able to talk about how I feel openly and not be judged or not like, "Oh, this is not your time." So, I love check-in. I think everybody likes check-in.

We would be—I was thinking, "Check-in will take twenty"—we would spend an hour doing check in. We were there from 6 p.m. to 8 p.m. By the time we finished check-in it would be 7:10 p.m.

We walk in, we hear the girls say how they don't want to do the Batty dance, "I don't want to do it," but once they get there, everybody seems to have a dance now. Everybody's ready to do the Batty dance. Then, we check in after the Batty dance. Check-in's always fun.

I'm coming in, I'm tired, but I'm excited to see the girls. I'm wondering how their day was. I'm wondering how this activity is gonna go. And I'm thinking, "Okay, what am I gonna talk about at check-in? What am

I gonna say?" 'cause there's so much time, and we don't have time for all of that. So, "What am I gonna say?" I come in, I see the girls, I say hi to them, make little faces at some of them, hug some of them, sit down, figure out what people have to do—

I was usually one of the earlier to arrive, to set up and get the equipment in and just hang out, chop it up with everyone else out there, 'cause they all know who you are.

When we walk into that space there's so much going on and there's so many different people. It's not just the girls. So, it's strange that in a place that I feel like we struggled so much—I would carry that into the room sometimes—we were moved around. We went upstairs, we were downstairs, but all this stuff that we had to do just to get to be at SOL-HOT at the Center—there were moments when I was in the room and I was participating, but I didn't feel as good all the time as I did. I would walk into the Library—I remember the second year—I felt like, "This is ours. This is our space." I felt comfortable, we could talk about anything. At The Center there was a lot of in and out, so the girls would go in and out, the boys would come in and out, people would come in and out. So, we weren't left alone. So, there was always this kind of time in my own mind—my defenses were always up because at any moment there could be some type of disruption.

I would come in, and I usually came in a couple of minutes early. So, I either helped set up or talked with people who were there about what we were gonna do that day. And then girls came in, usually talked about where snack was. There was that complaint about that pizza every week, so that was funny.

It wasn't called check-in, but I remember everybody distinctively coming right out and saying what was going on before we started anything— what happened today at school, what happened today on campus, how they were feeling, all the stuff they had to do afterwards or all the stuff they had to do before—

We always came in with something kind of planned for the day.

Once you come in and step through the threshold, you get your pizza, you get your Sierra Mist, and it's on.

Acts of Recognition, who walks with us

Acts of Recognition. . . . knowing who walks with you is referenced in Alexander's pedagogies as the process by which sacred energies in African-derived spiritual practices "claim one's head" and, in turn, are recognized by practitioners through daily acts such as pouring libations for and greeting specific energies or deities (2005, p. 307). In reference to SOLHOT, it is the informal acts (i.e., greetings) and formal ritual actions (i.e., Batty dance) that occur during SOLHOT that are used to signal the beginning and end of SOLHOT. These particular rituals and the others that are enacted during SOLHOT are dependent on the various personalities and embodied knowledge of each of the homegirls that are often reflected back to them by the girls that participate in SOLHOT. Furthermore, the idea that these acts are dependent on the whole of the group—those eager and those who dissent—to be accomplished is key feature of what it means to homegirl. To homegirl is to never be or feel alone. Even as one is acting out of one's own individual sense of self and spirit, it is the recognition of others so moved in the space that makes SOL-HOT, SOLHOT. Many times what one does to move time in SOLHOT or, stated another way, to keep it flowing, is recognized by someone else, before the person who is responsible is even aware of her positive and necessary contribution. According to Alexander,

> In the realm of the Sacred, however, the invisible constitutes its presence by a provocation of sorts, by provoking our attention. We see its effects, which enable us to know that it must be there. By perceiving what it does, we recognize its being and by what it does we learn what it is. (2005, p. 307)

She contended that this particular type of knowledge demands a serious "rewiring of the senses" (2005, p. 308). In the homegirls' memories, some of them more than others possess the "sense" necessary to recognize with whom we walk in SOLHOT as well as who walks among us. To be fully transparent, in the memory text I identify myself as "The Wind." In my role as visionary, I have become masterfully attuned to knowing how sacred energies claim the homegirls and the girls, and what sacred energy they have to give as a result. As someone extremely comfortable in the disequilibrium of SOLHOT, I am often clear about the various ways "spirit brings knowledge from past, present, and future to a particular moment called now" (Alexander, 2005, p. 307). As a matter of politics and principle, I teach and share what I know, freely.

> You come in, and people are setting up. It's always the OG homegirls greetin', which never changed. Somebody was always happy to see me—always. And that—people don't know that that's good for your soul. You walk in the door and somebody's all, "Hey, girl"—even if they just talked

to you five minutes before, "I'm on my way." You text somebody, you're on your way, and then you still come in and they're like, "Hey, girl." It's always that. It's always the greeting. Usually setting up—there's always something to do—set up the food, chairs, who's up? What are you gonna do? Do we have enough pens? Do we have so and so? If this lady comes in here and asks us what we're doing one more time—" so it was always a little bit crazy at the beginning. Or we might be having a malfunction with the projector. One day I thought you was gonna throw that projector through the wall. You were like, "It is not working, and I am getting stressed out. Oh my God." Then the girls start to come in, and it always would kind of start as little groups. Somebody would be over in the corner, somebody is getting some food, somebody is puttin' their coat up or whatever. But then, it's all these little micro conversations, and then we try to bring it together by doing the Batty dance. But then, sometimes somebody would start this little micro conversation, and then somebody else would piggyback on 'em, and then everybody would kind of get into it. It was usually about either school or boys, "My teacher did so and so today, and I wanted to slap her, because she was actin' so racist." And then we'd be like, "Well, why do you think that?" or "What happened?" and then somebody like The Fine One would be like, "You know what? That's why—da, da, da, da, da," and we would forget, for a minute, what the plan was because we'd be so absorbed into what this issue was or why this person was mistreated. Or maybe they weren't mistreated but they felt they were. Or we'd do Batty dance or Little Sally Walker. And on a good day you'd only have two or three people in the corner. Of course you're gonna have Orisha in the corner. She ain't doin' it. She just sayin', "I ain't doin' it. Y'all better get out of my face. I ain't doin' it." Then you have—people want to get up and show you their new little dance, and homegirls are always trying to learn the latest dances. Then, The One Who Favors Red be snappin' her pictures. She'd run in, shake it real quick, jump out and snap a picture. And then we would gather back around the table, and then our activity would start.

So, the Batty dance. I really pay attention in Batty dance, even when my dance is all messed up, because I think—and I don't know if this is the intention or not—but what's unique to me about Batty dance and what's special about it is that we watch all the ways in which the girls and the rest of the homegirls interpret the dance that you just did. And it's like giving you a little piece of their personality or something. So, I'm always very interested in that. Then, of course, check-in. That's the stuff that really needs to go—definitely comes out at check-in. So, all of the stuff that I've been pre–piling up on the way over—

I think this—it was a mistake that we made, that we gave up on try-ing to do the Batty dance that semester. There was a point at which we'd come—'cause I think that thinking about stuff like theater of the op-pressed and how you could communicate stuff with your body without saying stuff, I think that's something that's cool about the Batty dance. And I think that moving your body and trying to express yourself through your body can sometimes—not punctuate but—yeah, kind of punctu-ate check-in. I think it's a good thing to do before check-in, and I think it gives people the space to actually do things, 'cause they just move their body whereas when we first got there and we'd just sit up and do check-in. I think that's what led to it taking almost an hour and a half. And so I think that getting rid of the Batty dance was a mistake.

Homegirls are excited. The girls are apprehensive and sluggish. Nobody wants to do the Batty dance. I don't want to do the Batty dance, but I'm gonna act like I want to do the Batty dance today, trying to think of a dance, thinking of such a long week, but now it's time to come in and see what's been happening with the girls, trying to draw on those quiet girls.

I'm a sidebar ho is what they call me, so I have a lot of small conversa-tions with the girls.

I know Bright Smile, Quiet Girl was having trouble writing, and I helped her write a poem. And we both enjoyed that. I think that she didn't feel comfortable admitting that she had trouble writing, so I was kind of like the quiet, unassuming, hopefully nice person that was nonthreaten-ing. So, I guess that was sort of my role. When we started doing more group work, I felt like I had more of a space to interact with people indi-vidually. I will rethink loudness, because I can be very loud when I want to be, but in terms of how I deal with people, I usually—when I get excited I get boisterous, but I know there's a couple of times fights broke out and people would be like, "This is not okay," and I'm not—I struggle with straddling the line between being responsible and being an authority fig-ure, and I really don't like to yell at younger people or really raise—I don't like to really yell at anyone, in general, or raise my voice. I guess I was sort of the placid person, but I think that sometimes that translated into— I had to challenge myself to not being present. And it's not that I—I enjoy being there all the time, even during the tense moments. Tension doesn't make me feel uncomfortable.

Then, we go and we sit down, we do check-in—a lot of the girls tell stories. We all tell stories, anyway, with our faces and our hands and stuff. Usually, I'm looking around at everybody's faces. I'm listening to the person that's talking, but usually looking around, watching everybody's faces and gestures and stuff. We do check-in, then we go into some sort of activity. Girls would talk. Usually the conversation would stem something around boys, something about relationships and sex and school being boring, a lot of laughter, a lot of smacking teeth. Somebody would break out into some song—at least a phrase of a song.

So we played music—So I remember one day when we played the . . . song and I was looking at The Wind like, "Really? You are not gonna play this song?" And like, "I refuse to dance to this song." And everything like, "We can't enjoy this! I can't participate in this!" And then the girls started dancing and I'm like, "I don't know if I wanna co-sign, right? To this." So I'm not really even dancing. And then I remember and again this is the same thing I was saying earlier about we need to be able to learn and talk about not just these experiences but method of negotiation. Like it wasn't as much about the music, I mean about the lyrics themselves but the act of camaraderie in terms of Black bodies moving with light bodies and communing with one another in dance.

I remember one night we were supposed to be working on interviews—our journals—and it was just crazy energy that night. Everyone was all over the place and an impromptu dance soul-train line broke out, and we danced for forty minutes. I was sweating at the end, and I'm just like, "Whew, that was nice." That was nice, because we didn't dictate the flow. We just went with it, and I remember that from the first night when we did introductions and stuff. That was one of the nights one of the girls said that—what did she say? I can't remember. I know her face. She was a little tomboy, and she said that she sometimes doesn't feel like a girl. That was the first night. I was just like, "Wow. Okay, it's on."

I feel like even though the places are so different, they're still so similar. Who is that? Her Words Are Fire, she was talking about how she loves thugs, and she loves these men. And I had that same experience. You grow up around all of these boys, and boys get so much attention. Boys get so much attention, like no matter where you are. It's like, "Okay, let's just go and do whatever they're doing. Let's just hang out with them," and I could really relate to that. I didn't think she was crazy for saying she loved thugs. I did, too. I don't think she was crazy at all.

Whenever people were talking over each other and I didn't say anything that day, people were saying, "You weren't being authentic. You weren't being real."

But then there came times where it was like, "No, I have to let people know that there's this other—that there are many Black-girl identities."

And I tried. I tried to at least be—I mean, I was always cordial to her, but she would walk into the room and just—I would stiffen, because I just felt like she didn't have respect for anybody but The Wind. And I kind of felt that way about a couple of the girls as far as, "Okay, if The Wind asks you to do it, you'll do it," but we are all adults. And what is it about The Wind? Is it because she created the program? Is it because she's a college professor? I'm like, it can't be an age thing, because I'm older than The Wind, and I know y'all know I'm one of the oldest chicks in here. And not that it was deference like, "I'm the oldest, you gotta respect me," but I felt like for some of the girls it was like, "Oh, we'll listen to The Wind, 'cause she's in charge. I'm not really trying to hear what you've got to say." For a minute I had dwelled on it to try and figure it out, but then after that I just was like, "Okay, whatever." But Her Words Are Fire—The Wind could ask her to do something, "Her Words Are Fire, could you do social studies?" and she would do it. I felt like anybody else, "I'll do it in a minute." I'd just tell her she had an attitude for no reason, consistently, all the time. I don't remember one day where she just came in and she was just cool. I don't remember one interaction where she was just chillin'. It was always something, "I'll beat that ho's ass. So-and-so—why your hair lookin' like that? You are so ugly. I'll slap you. I'll just—" every day. And I was like, "How could somebody be that unhappy all the time?"

We played outside and we played Double Dutch. And this was before me and Talented Girl got cool—'cause Talented Girl used to be mean to me—and I beat her at Double Dutch, 'cause she told me I was too old to jump, and I was like, "Yeah, all right. When you get beat, don't be mean to me—or don't be something." And I was like, "I don't care if it kills me, I'm gonna jump longer than her. I don't care if it takes me out." And then, after that, we got on this topic of, "How could I be thirty-five years old and be able to jump rope?" and I was like, "What do y'all mean? What do y'all mean?" And they were like, "No, for real, you're thirty-five. Seriously, you're too old to be jumpin'. My mom is thirty-three, and she don't do nothin'," and it was deep. It was deep. And also, those conversations have really affected some of my research as far as what role are you supposed to play when you get to be a certain age? And why could I jump at seventeen or eighteen—or it's really more like fifteen, 'cause once you're eighteen you're really not jumpin' Double Dutch anyway—but why was it okay to jump at those ages and I can't jump at thirty-five? Growing up playing Double Dutch, for me—we played every day when I was younger, but these girls don't do that, and just, "You can't play." I'm like, "It's my rope.

I'm gonna take my rope and go home," and they're like, "How you got a rope?" "'Cause I went to the store and bought one." They were amazed that somebody my age was doin' more than sittin' and whatever—whatever they thought. So, I think I gained some respect from the girls. I'm like, "Ooh, I got a little street credit. I can jump. They think I can jump rope." But then, also, I think it kind of put it in their mind a little bit like, "Oh, you still could be old—" 'cause they were just on that. They're like, "Oh, you're old. The Praise Dancer, you are so old," and I just had to laugh, 'cause I was like—to me, old is seventy-five. And I was like, "Well, I wonder when they get thirty-five, will they think that? Or, will they be like, 'Gee, I'm old'?" 'Cause I have friends who I met at thirty-two who are like, "Oh, I'm so old," and I'm like, "Really? 'Cause we the same age, and I'm not old at all." So, I don't know—

When we were at The Library, and one of the girls kept talking. And I asked her to be quiet, and she kept talking. I asked her to be quiet again, and she just snapped on me. And then I snapped right back at her, and I wanted to leave 'cause I was kind of like, "You know what? This is the girl who can do whatever she wants, can say whatever she wants, can be disrespectful to girls and homegirls alike, and nobody says anything to her." And at that point, I was feeling like, "You know what? I don't know how much longer I can do this, because I'm not gonna come up in here and get disrespected by kids." Then, I thought I had come so far, 'cause I initially felt like that when SOLHOT started two years before, that I had gotten out of that. You know what? It's not so much about, "Act this way. Be this way," but I was really trying to—her and I never clicked—'cause there are certain girls who were closer to certain homegirls, but her and I never clicked. I just thought she had the nastiest attitude, and I thought she was being enabled, and other homegirls probably looked at it like, "We don't want to lose her. She's on the edge," or, "We're just trying to meet her where she is," and I just kind of felt like, "You know what? You come in here callin' everybody bitches and whatever. I'm not gonna be your bitch. I'm not," and she just kind of went off. It was just disrespectful—just blatant disregard.

And I was just like, "We have no boundaries. What do we have?"

I mean a physical altercation ensued 'cause she was like, "Don't touch me," 'cause they were like—they were making some crack about her hair. I don't even remember what was said. It happened really fast. I just remember I saw them approaching each other and then they started fighting and then someone broke them up, and then after that there was a—it was like being in church, and not in a good way. No, I always associate being in church with bad things—as a place of oppression and scariness and bodily management.

I don't remember, I don't remember a bad time. But memory has a way of operating in order like, you know, for survival. And it's been years, it been like four years and I think that for my four years, I just have, I have all good memories, I mean, I have good feelings and maybe that's the way in which, that I want to keep it. . . . I'm like, is it because my memory is playing tricks on me and that, you know, I have to have this, I have to have this construction in order for me to like travel back to when I'm feeling lonely isolated, when I'm feeling by myself, when I'm feeling lonely in a goal to remember that moment? And so I can't have those [. . .] experience, you know I can't have those experiences. Or that it just didn't—I don't recall [. . .] I don't have it.

I have a huge problem with lecturing kids about personal responsibility in a post-responsibility state where if they don't have solidarity with each other, whose failure is that? I have a huge problem telling kids about, "You have to be responsible to each other," because who the fuck is teaching them about—in this fucked-up post-responsibility state to be responsible? Who is setting that example? Absolutely almost no one. There are some people but not many. There are so many promises to them that have been broken in terms of how the education is, how the education system is. Just hearing them talk about things their teachers said to them, broken promises, how big the prison-industrial complex is, how many youth of color are locked up—I can't not think about that. To me, that's always a part of the context, even if it's not there in the moment.

We watched a video first of all the—the video, it was just a simple slide show, and it was sort of to illustrate the dichotomy in the media between the version of the virgin/whore among heterosexual women and the femme/butch among queer women. And they try to include as many women of color in that slide show. And after that, we all kind of talked about the slide show, really briefly, as a big group. We split into groups. You were in my group which we talked about Sakia Gunn's story, and I sort of summarized it for the girls. And we talked about, "Has there been a time you were sexually harassed? Were you scared? Did you think you were going to be killed? If you were Sakia Gunn, would you have said you were gay, or would you just stay quiet and be done?"

At the end, we made "Remember Sakia" buttons and we'll always talk about why we should remember her.

And then, in another group, the girls actually took pictures from the slide show and said which pictures they would like to see more in the media, what kind of person they think they are now. Are they more of a Beyoncé, or are they more of someone else? And that was interesting, because some girls did say that they want to see more Black lesbians in the media which I was really surprised by. No one said that they were that or they wanted to be that, but they wanted to see more, because they hadn't seen any of those photos. They didn't know who these women were. And then, another group talked about the nuts and bolts of sexuality issues and sex issues like how to properly use a condom, what does GLBTQ stand for—things like that. So, they had a really good discussion, I heard.

I remember coming up with the ideas about how to engage the conversation about sex without just providing a bunch of facts or whatever. So many girls are afraid to—some even older women are afraid to name their body or to do these things—so I came up with the idea—the whole "Name your vagina" thing and doing it with the girls. Then, when we started doing it some of the girls were very vocal. Some of the homegirls were very vocal, but then there was another group of girls on the sides of me who was really, really quiet, and I started talking to them, and they were like, "This is disgusting. I don't talk about this stuff in front of people. Miss Movement, do you talk about this stuff?" and I said, "You know, yeah. And actually, the first time I named my vagina was this—" and I tell 'em the story. They're laughing and they're disgusted, but they start doing the activity. And then I was helping them come up with names, and I—I felt like I was more on the sidelines with talking to them or even some of the quiet girls, like Lil' Bit. She's really small, dark-skinned—she would always be so quiet and wasn't able to talk, "Well, I don't have anything to do with it," I was like, "You sure about that?" I'm like, "Okay, tell me," and she'd tell me in my ear, and I'd be like, "That's a great idea," and she'd be like, "Really?" and so she would always look at me, and I would smile at her, and then she might talk. She might not. But I think we were doing cards and saying, "Thank you," to somebody we appreciated. She wrote me a card, and it was just like, "Even though I don't remember your name—" 'cause she always had a hard time remembering my name. She was like, "Even though I don't remember your name, I still know you, and I still love you," and then it was just like, "Love, Lil' Bit."

I guess when the girls talked about sex. I was just like, "Man, what should I really say?" 'cause I know I was like—I don't know. I guess talking about sex, I guess, I was like, "What should I really tell them?" blah, blah, blah, 'cause I wasn't the best little girl growing up, either. And then there was one instance where—I forgot her name. I'm horrible with names—

She talked about being molested.

They'd look at me just to try to size me up, and I would just look at them back and size them—you know what I'm saying? But I don't know.

But it's always been consistent that when I was there I showed up. I was there mentally, physically, emotionally.

I did feel really—I don't know why but I felt silenced. I didn't say anything, even though I was like, "I don't agree with this at all."

I liked being with the older girls. So, the older girls would talk about wanting a job or what they were gonna do when they graduated from high school, going to college—they wanted to talk about sex. They wanted to talk about relationships in general. So, those kinds of conversations could be any given day at SOLHOT.

We were trying to get the girls to talk about something, and they were just being rude. We were talking about abuse, and they were just being rude. I couldn't take it. I kind of just snapped, and I left.

Conversations get difficult. I think one of the girls was like, "That's stupid," and I just lost it.

The last day of SOLHOT, last semester, they decided they were gonna teach us how to dance, and so they taught us how to do the Stanky Leg. It was just so cute, because they were all ready to do it together. They're like, "No, we need to teach these homegirls how to dance. We have to," and they just really enjoyed themselves. It was just so nice seeing them—especially when we were in the cafeteria—so they were in the school setting, and everybody hates school. They are enjoying themselves. There were girls I hadn't seen since the beginning of the semester come in, and they were like, "Yeah, let's do this. Is this SOLHOT today?"

That was my girl. She was just so open and ready for any ounce of knowledge and wisdom and anything that you were ready to put on. She was ready for it. And then Orisha—I could just—every week, you could almost tell which Orisha she was gonna be which week. Was she gonna be hardass? Was she gonna be like she's cute this week because she has little braids in? Is she rebelling? Is she gangster Orisha who just got into it, physically, downstairs and now she's amped up? Or is she sensitive, reflective Orisha this week?

I think we wrote letters one time, and you could mail them or not mail them, and Bright Smile, Quiet Girl gave me hers. And Orisha gave me theirs, and they said, "Just hold on to them." They didn't want me to mail it. They didn't want me to read it. They just wanted me to hold on to it, and I still have those little letters with the stamp on them. They're still sealed. And I hold on to them. It's really a symbol of trust for me. They trusted me, without knowing me. They trusted me, and it's almost like me keeping it closed is a symbol and a testimony to that trust, because I respect it that much. I value it that much.

We do damn good work, regardless of what people say. Money doesn't always—it does help the situation in terms of programmatically it helps, but it doesn't—money can't buy you this kind of self-awareness that you're valuable.

And then the activities, which is the structural part of SOLHOT, is of course the part I hate—not that I hate any part of SOLHOT, but if I had to rate my least favorite to most favorite—only because I can never stick to what's going on.

There was a day that—I can't remember who wanted to fight, but I know Talented Girl was in. She was fighting with somebody—verbally fighting with somebody. I kind of was like, "Look, we're not gonna do that here. If you want to fight, we can fight." And Talented Girl had—even at eleven, had an attitude for days. I felt like I stepped outside of my body and saw myself like, "We gonna fight. Me and you gonna fight." I'm gonna be an eleven-year-old girl and I'm gonna kick your butt—just to stop them from continuing this back and forth, back and forth, back and forth, back and forth. And the way that she looked at me—I was like, "Oh, she's really serious," so it's like, "I'll fight a kid," and they kind of just squashed it after that. They still didn't like each other, which was fine, but I remember her looking at me—and me not being afraid to say that to her like, "If you want to fight somebody, you can fight me."

Yeah, 'cause there's a level of fear these girls don't have. I think it gets beaten out of you as you get older to exist in these spaces that people want you to exist in rather than existing in as much and as far as you possibly can.

I remember when I first met her she came in—I was in there. She came in, she walked up on me with her—she had a Harlem swagger about her, and she walked right up to me, and she was like, "Who is you?" right off the bat. "Who is you? What you got a camera for?" and that was it from then on. I was like, "Well, who are you?" right back at her. And she was like, "I'm Orisha." And we had our connection, because I called right back on her. She thought I was another university volunteer and she was gonna check me real quick, and I came back right at her and we had common ground from then on. But we were doing journals, and it was writing about a painful or something that made you feel like—something you're insecure about. And The Wind was stressing that these journals—while we could share them, if you want to—you don't have to. It was something that you could keep private, but the important thing was for you to get it out so you could see it. Orisha was writing that she lived with her grand-mother, and she was talking about the last time she saw her mother and how they got—I think they got caught by the truant officers, because her and her brothers weren't registered for school and they were home alone. So, when they found that out, that's I think the reason why they got taken. Her mom lost custody, and she had to live with her grandmother. She just bared that, and she didn't want to share it in large group. But then, at the end of the session, she handed me her journal, because we collected them from them at the end of every session. She handed me her journal, specifically, and she had folded the page. And she said, "I want you to read it," and I was like, "Are you sure? You don't have to," and she said, "I want you to read it." And that was like she was trusting me with this—I don't even know what it is—but she was trusting me with it. Out of everyone here, she wanted me to know this about her, not that she wanted me to fix it or she wanted charity or sympathy or pity. She just wanted someone to understand her, for that moment. The next session she was back to herself with her barrier up and hardness, but for that moment she was completely vulnerable and exposing herself. I'm like, "Why? Why me?" And that's what really solidified that we were all collaborators and listeners and sharing together. That really solidified that for me. Shout out to Orisha.

She was talking about an incident that happened with her family. She's from a notorious family in the area—the Johnsons—and they had another altercation. They're very well known for being crazy violent. She was like, "Black people just act so crazy. I just wish I was white." I don't know if I was just so caught up in the celebration of Black girlhood and I had to be checked and brought down to the reality that shit is not all great being— everyone is not as proud as you are. It was like being slapped in the face. I was just stunned. I just didn't know what to think. I didn't know what to say. I didn't know how to respond to her. I felt too many different things. I was angry, and I was hurt. I just didn't know what to do. I was mad at her for saying it. Mad at the way it is that she felt she had to say it. It just angered me. When I went back in—I don't know, because I was pretty angry the rest of the day. All of my responses were out of anger like, "And you need to be proud of your heritage." I was going off on my little tyrant.

This was in 2008—spring 2008. And she told us that she hated being Black. She wishes that she was white so she could be happier. She said white people are so happy, they're so put together, they're so all of these things. But when we asked her how she felt about herself she was like, "I don't have any hard feelings about myself, but Black people are a little different from where I am." That was really hard to hear. That was really hard to even digest just her saying that. And what was even harder about it is that I feel like a lot of people feel that way. I had to think, "Have I ever felt like that? Have I felt like it's so good on the other side—it's so the other side, I guess?" That was just really hard to hear. It was really hard to hear her say that, especially in a room with all Black folks, and she's like, "Y'all ain't shit." there was just so much emotion in her voice when she said it. She was so serious. This wasn't like a, "White people be having fun," you know what I'm saying? This wasn't, "I'm just having a conversation. I'm being silly." She was really serious, like, "I really hate being in the body that I'm in," and that just really took me. That just really got me. I just really—I don't know.

In SOLHOT, we deal with all the things that the girls give us and the ways that they are instead of just shutting them down.

'Cause there's a freedom in being a homegirl. You don't have to live with these girls. You get to go home. These are not your children. But I also know they tell us things that they wouldn't tell their parents. So, what's the balance in that? How would I balance that?

There was another instance, too, where a girl got molested and they talked about it. I think I remember crying. Did I cry? Maybe I didn't cry. Maybe that was just the last day of class and I just left class. But that was pretty intense for me, because whenever I—that was a moment when I didn't really talk about being molested. I never even told my mom I got molested, 'cause that would just freak her out. So, every time I would talk about it, I would be very hesitant. My mouth would get dry and stuff like that, so I think that was a difficult moment for me, 'cause I knew—I think she knew about that, and she wanted me to talk to her about that or say something in class or in the space, and I did or whatever, but that was difficult.

It felt good. It felt good to say something.

We clearly had our conversation about sexuality—talk about the night everybody cried, right? You remember that conversation?

I remember, "I just don't like gay people."

"Why?" "'Cause my mother told me that I shouldn't like gay people."

The Incense Circle, closings

The Incense Circle . . . re-crossings and closings. Alexander wrote, "The dead do not like to be forgotten, especially those whose lives had come to a violent end" (2005, p. 289). In SOLHOT, we have a ritual for remembering those who have passed on called the Incense Circle. As the ritual goes, we stand in a circle, hand everyone an incense stick, and someone will stand in the middle with a lit candle and invite each person to light their incense as they tell us about someone they want us to know and remember. In SOLHOT the incense circle is the ritual that most affirms and confirms our practice of making space for Black girlhood as a spiritual work that is sacred. In the incense circle, our will, both individually and collectively, to remember ourselves, our loved ones, and unknown affiliates with whom we desire to connect is the practice where the most intangible elements of the work come the closest to being immediately seen, felt, and sensed.

And then there would be some sort of closing. The One Who Favors Red II usually would say some closing words. I felt like it was like the last words in church or something like that. It would just be like, "All right, y'all. Make sure y'all do this," or whatever. And then it would be over. Some of the girls would hurry up and leave. Some of the girls would stick around and ask a couple of questions, and then we'd walk out, make sure everybody had rides, say bye to the girls at the door.

And then the Incense Circle, and then more laughter, and then on my way to drop Hoop Earrings off on the other side of town—but that's SOLHOT.

And then a few people always have to leave early—be it a homegirl or a participant—and then we'd have either the candle ceremony or the lightin' of the incense or the—why can I not say this?—homage to the ancestors— one of those moments where we're trying to bring it together, when we're trying to be serious but somebody's always saying something—"This is for the negroes in the street. This is for the pimps," and you're like, "Do I feel like fighting that off? Do I feel like arguing?" "Nope, it's fine. Say what you're gonna say," and then somebody will really say something like, "I want you to remember my aunt who died of breast cancer two weeks ago." "I want you to remember my cousin who—" whatever. It'll sober you. I'll be irritated with somebody 'cause they bein' loud over in the corner, and then somebody else would say something, and it'd just be sobering like, "Damn, that's what they're dealing with."

Then, libations—I never feel like I have enough to bring to libations. Sometimes I can really feel other people release their shit and really heavy stuff. I can feel the weight of it, so I just never feel like I have enough what- ever you want to call it. I just never feel like it's deep enough—some of the weight. And I don't know if that's me not digging enough inside me to pour out a heavy libation of my own, but libation's always deep. Sometimes we forget to, and I can even remember thinking some days, "Whew, I'm glad we did not do libations today." Some days I just wouldn't be able to take it.

And then we'd do—what was the thing we did at the end? I know it, too. We'd do some type of call and response to reaffirm and strengthen our bond that we made that day, because it was always breakthroughs, or someone has conflict with this homegirl this week and, "The One Who Favors Red told me to sit down," or something like that. We'd reaffirm and strengthen those bonds before the next session.

And then we'd come back together to close in the Incense Circle. I feel like the only two constants were us coming in and checking in, the Batty dance and then closing together. But in between that time, anything could happen. Anything was possible.

And by the end of SOLHOT we are loud and open and laughing or crying and completely raw. I like to use that word—completely raw by the end of SOLHOT every Friday, no matter what the topic of conversation is. But I think it is a process that happens, from beginning to end. Then, when we leave, the girls linger. They don't want to go home, but it's also the weekend for them, so they're excited about going home and enjoying their weekend. But they linger and we linger, just because it's hard to stop that. It's hard to put a cork in something that's just flowing.

Sacred Praxis, afterwords and beginnings

Sacred Praxis . . . afterwords and beginnings. Sacred praxis in SOLHOT is represented in the time homegirls dedicate to theorizing from our practice, practicing consistently, and practicing the theories subsequently created. This reiterative process is how we come to know something more about Black girlhood than when we first began. It is the time dedicated to rethinking what was heard and said in SOLHOT in conversation with others that improves future practice. Sacred praxis requires us to rethink what we previously believed to be true, against our actions and reactions to the girls' thoughts, talk, and theories about how the world works. Alexander wrote, "practitioners have to be present and participate in a community; they must show up, in other words, for this appointment, to the ceremonies that rehearse over and over again the meaning of Sacred accompaniment" (2005, p. 310). Homegirls who practice SOLHOT come to understand something more about Black girlhood based on their practice that is greater than those theories created about Black girls but not with them. Furthermore, sacred praxis is the ground from which coalitional work is made possible in SOLHOT, even if not always engaged.

SOLHOT is just not from 3:00 p.m. to 6:00 p.m. or 3:00 p.m. to 5:00 p.m. SOLHOT is every day. As long as we're Black girls, it's SOLHOT.

I'm thinking about the girls. I'm thinking about, "What happened in SOLHOT? How can we make SOLHOT better? What can we talk about next week?" I'm thinking of things like that.

I know we're all gonna die one day, but I just hope it never stops, or goes in the opposite direction that it's going.

I want to be in the space, because I don't want to miss anything. I just want to be a part of it. I don't want to be outside of the inside joke or the event that happened. I don't want anybody to have to tell me—I'm not sure if I've missed a SOLHOT. I think I may have missed one, but for the most part, if I can help it I always try to avoid missing SOLHOT.

I'm constantly thinking about her. I'm thinking about a question that a homegirl asked me that I didn't know the answer to, and I told them I didn't know the answer to, but they still look at me with puppy-dog eyes like, "Why don't you know the answer?" And it's like, "But I really don't know the answer, because even though I'm older than you I still don't know."

Then I'd go get in my car and I'd be like, "Whew, I made it." And then I would get in my car and put on some kind of music and think.

I'm usually doing a recap of all the things that the girls said, just trying to pull it together and figure out what that means and, "How should I address that?" if I feel like it's something deeper or if I feel like, "That's something I need to address. How should I do that when I see her the next time? What does that mean? Do I feel like that, too?"—that type of thing.

We were walking to the cars to talk about what that day was like. And then, additionally, we would go home and write sometimes.

First of all, I usually never leave SOLHOT alone, and I think that's something really special. I either have some girls with me to take them home, or one of the other homegirls, we're gonna go hang out or study or whatever. But I never leave SOLHOT alone. That very, very, very rarely happens. So, I think that's significant. I just can't figure out what the significance is yet. But I think I definitely know it's significant, because I can't really get past what happens after SOLHOT.

We don't just leave like, "All right, The One Who Favors Red, you be good." I like that I can send an email at 2:00 in the morning, and somebody will be like, "I read it. Give me a second to get back to you." I really appreciate that. I like that at the SOLHOT exhibit, when you were talking I was like, "Hell yeah, The One Who Favors Red." That's really deep and I just met you.

"I feel special." I felt so special, like they noticed, even though I may not have said too much or I may not have been the loudest or I may not have said as many cuss words or I may not have like—maybe I just wasn't the loudest one in the bunch, but they noticed. And they notice when you're missing. And just leaving SOLHOT in anticipation of doing it all again that next Friday.

I just always remember them hanging back to walk out of the Center with us, because it meant something to be walking out together in a whole little crew. And you could see—I saw changes every week—confidence, them being more articulate in what they're feeling—but that was the SOL-HOT day. I normally didn't go back home right after. I would go to a café and write. I wrote a lot during it, just reflecting and thinking about, "Okay, what can we do next week?" And that was good. I love SOLHOT. I do.

I thought about a lot of the girls were complaining about how their teachers would just say really messed-up stuff to them. A lot of us would leave SOLHOT pissed like, "Who are these people?" and so I was like, "Maybe we should have organized a trip to a school board meeting to say something—"

Literally I walked away and I remember calling my mom . . .

I mean, I often go home talking about SOLHOT, but that was a day I was just like, "I don't know what to say. I don't even know what to say." That was a difficult conversation or a difficult thing to keep replaying. That was very difficult. I think everybody went home like, "Yeah, that—" there was no way to come back from that.

I think some girls played jump rope afterwards, and I couldn't even bring myself to—I was just like, "I'm about to go home." I wanted to go to sleep after that, but then, too, that's on your mind. I felt like that was really, really heavy on me that whole week.

"She's practicing SOLHOT, so I don't have to worry about her." Sometimes it's not. Sometimes I feel like there are girls that might not be feeling SOLHOT at the moment, or whatever the case may be. And I worry about them, but not about what happens to 'em. I just think about 'em more.

And coming from our SOLHOT space, that was the legacy that was in me like, "Find another Black girl. Find as many other Black girls as you can and put them on. Let them know they can do it. Education is not a privilege. Let them know they can do it."

I think there are many times in which I felt—coming away felt like I wasn't included in the group because I wasn't adhering to this one, collective identity that was sort of being built in SOLHOT.

I would always walk out of there with a new perspective—like that my issues were so small—so small compared to—whatever, my baby daddy ain't doing this, or I don't have any money, or I'm in this PhD program but I really don't know what I'm doing. I just always walk out and be like, "For real? Your problems? For real, they're not—they're okay. You're okay." So, yeah—

And so I went home a lot feeling like people thought that I hated the girls or I hated the other women and that I wasn't being—celebrating this Black-girl identity we had created as a whole in SOLHOT. So, I think those were the days where it was hard, but I never knew really how to fix it because I was so quiet. I would want to interject, add a pause, but those pauses never really came up.

I started to do that more, and my friends and my girlfriends are like, "Where is this coming from?" and I'm like, "I don't know. I just feel more like I need to assert myself." So, in very small ways—or I found more instances where I was like, "You know, it's not okay that I'm quiet. And I should try harder to be more outspoken in these situations," so little steps.

And then I think at the end—later—me and Orisha—'cause I saw her later. She had her baby, and I saw her at an event at another school, and she was so happy to see somebody from SOLHOT. And then it was so emotional, 'cause I was like, "Why you don't come around?" and I was like, "If you tell me you haven't been comin' around 'cause you had a baby, I'm gonna get you. Why would you think we wouldn't want to—you know we love you, and we gonna love your baby," and she wanted to cry, but you know she's hard. And she was so excited that I was so excited. She was showin' me pictures on her phone, and I was like, "Oh, he is so cute," and she was so proud. But she didn't really know what to feel, 'cause I think she kind of faded to the background like, "I got this baby, so now I'm supposed to be an adult or whatever," and I'm like, "What does that got to do with you coming around to SOLHOT? You can bring the baby." I was like, "You gotta come back. We want to see you. We care about you. We miss you," and she just couldn't stop huggin' me. She was just, "I know, right? Girl—" after a while I had to walk away from her, 'cause I was about to break down, 'cause she was just so—like she needed to hear that—not necessarily from me, but—and then it was so sweet 'cause her little boyfriend—her baby's father was just so there for her, and I was just like, "Oh, that is just like a—" and they're super young, but she was like, "Yeah, he watches the baby all the time, and when I have to go to school he doesn't do his after-school stuff, because he—" and I was like, "A brother's doing that, and he only about seventeen." It was just real—and they were still together, and they were still—I guess her mom was watching the baby, and they wound up coming—it was like a carnival. So, they just playin' carnival games, just bein' together, just doing teenager stuff. And you never really would have thought they had a kid at home or whatever. They were just laughing and joking with each other. It was really sweet. It was. It was just like—I was like, "Wow, just hold on to that for as long as y'all can." It was sweet.

I actually went out to—I guess you could say dinner. I took them to Buffalo Wild Wings right at the end of school, so that was interesting to see what their take on SOLHOT was. Who did they like in their space? Who did they not like in their space?

And I'm like, "I can't commit to once-a-week or twice-a-week sessions and still be moving toward doing my other stuff." Yeah, and then also, I think the last—yeah, the last time we were at the Center, The Wind was out of town quite a bit, and it was Oshun, The Fine One, and two other girls, and me. And the Center was kind of giving us a hard time, the girls would keep coming in and out. Nobody was really committed. The girls really—it seemed like the majority of them were not interested. It was just different. When we were upstairs or in that other room it seemed like that space was ours for that time. In that back room people were coming in and out, in and out, and even though The Fine One and Oshun have strong personalities, I needed another OG home girl to kind of help set the pace, 'cause it was just different, 'cause we were trying to do a video—a documentary—and the other two girls were just super nice, but they really did not understand the concept of SOLHOT.

It forced us to look at one another in a different way—it forced us to like forgive ourselves . . .

The Antidote, unnaming and naming

The Antidote . . . naming and unnaming. For Alexander, healing work is the "antidote to oppression" existing in various forms; it is the crux of spiritual labor (2005, p. 312). In the process of healing, she argued there must be a cause which mobilizes everyone. In SOLHOT the cause, as previously mentioned, is the creation of a Black girlhood that homegirls recognize as within their power to manifest and, depending on their practice, may or may not come to exist. The cause is personal as much as it is political, as homegirls are intimately acquainted with the various outcomes of not experiencing anything like a girlhood. SOLHOT comes to matter as both the cause and the solution of making Black girlhood and then honoring the complexity that is involved in its attendant celebration. That healing is an outcome of SOLHOT is evident throughout the memory text. When homegirls remember the more healing aspects of the work, they become more strident about what SOLHOT is and what it is not.

I just feel like I'm SOLHOT on the inside. I am SOLHOT.

It's not an organization. It doesn't operate that way.

I think that calling it a political project and also I think calling it a cipher really speaks to how—the relational nature of how information is passed and how people relate to each other and what the importance and purpose is of it. And so I think that—it is hard to describe, and sometimes I'm like, "You would have to go."

I always tell people that SOLHOT is a space where everyone contributes to creating a safe environment for people to express themselves. And that's how I describe it. I say we're not the traditional mentor program. And I always tell people, "We don't mentor. It's not, 'I'm telling you what to do, and you need to act like this.' We get away from those notions of the politics about respectability. It's more about embracing the Black body." That's something I tell people. People don't always understand what I'm saying.

First of all it's a grassroots organization, and again I know you all object to the idea of it being called an organization, but it is.

It's the movement to get what you want, so that's what SOLHOT is. It's a movement of girls who are trying to get what they want to be free.

I don't like that a lot of the homegirls come into the space, again—to judge. I don't like that they don't want to be vulnerable. They don't want to say what's on their mind, or they don't want to speak up—whether it's to the group or whether it's to somebody—one of the other homegirls in the space. I don't like that they don't want to be challenged. They feel like, "Oh, everybody else is wrong, because I feel bad about something." I don't like that. I feel like the only way for the other homegirls—and even for the girls who know how you truly feel inside, or that you really want to say something—is to come out and say it. And I don't like that people feel like they can come to the space and don't want be vulnerable but still want to judge and still want to critique. I don't like that.

It's about coming into this environment, as a Black girl, to say how you feel and get how you feel so that you can feel better about yourself and be able to cope with the environment around you. It's like a support system.

If you're not willing to be vulnerable and you're just angry, you're not gonna get it.

I am being challenged to question my beliefs. I'm learning all the time. Again, I get to have a good time. I get to just act a fool, if I want to. It's just fun. Everybody is with me, so I enjoy that. I like that it's a learning space, and it's a fun space, and it's just a good space. It's like whenever you had a really good feeling in your life, I think that's what SOLHOT is.

What SOLHOT did is to start where they are. Don't talk to them where you want them to be, like what are you interested in and that's how you talk about those issues.

I think we did a good job of being like, "We're here because we value your knowledge," and I think that that is political to tell someone that their knowledge is valuable, but I think an explicit statement about it like, "And the broader scope of this is that we think Black girls can change the world. We think that you guys have the capacity to do that"—I don't think that was communicated often enough.

SOLHOT is just being who you are at the moment, because it's needed. And that's how I explain it. It's like a structured—it's like an organized, unstructured kind of setting. It's organized in the sense that the homegirls create this environment for the girls to come in and be unstructured and all over the place—if that makes sense. It's like a circle. It's like if you draw this straight circle, but then you draw zigzags all in the middle of it. It becomes abstract.

Some days I feel like SOLHOT is the, "You know what? And this is what the fuck happens. You see all that fucked-up shit that y'all put up in place up there up top." I feel like it's where we sit back and say, "Look at this mess that they've created." And in that sense, I feel like that's where the most change comes from—from those spaces of, "What is this?" That's where revolutions and movements come from.

SOLHOT is about breaking down those barriers that we've been brought up to believe, or even informing us that there may be another way to look at stuff. So, feeling comfortable about being a woman, about being a girl—it's okay to be a Black girl or a Black woman.

Yeah, having that freedom is political—and just a space that is very political.

SOLHOT is unexpected. You never know what's gonna happen when you go into SOLHOT. You think you had an agenda, but you really didn't. You got to about two points on that agenda, and then Anetha says, "I want to talk about something else today," so it's definitely unexpected. The first day at the School when they asked us, "What is an orgasm?" It took me back a little bit. I wasn't prepared. I wasn't prepared for that. It's unexpected. It's unexpected. It's dope. You learn so much.

I'm tired of defending it. I'm tired of explaining myself to folks. I'm tired of explaining issues, but I guess this is what SOLHOT is all about—

having those difficult conversations with other people who don't even come to SOLHOT and stuff like that.

And I don't even think this is done purposely, but SOLHOT was kind of pitched to some people as being the space for everybody to be themselves, but who can really be themselves at SOLHOT? And so I was asking The One Who Favors Red II, "We don't want to become this space where the ghetto Black girls come to SOLHOT," so I'm like, "Can SOLHOT work in a suburban space, the way that we want it to run? Can it run in a suburban space?" So, in that sense I'm like, "Can SOLHOT be full of people who are different? Can SOLHOT work outside of spaces that we've created or that we are in, ourselves?" I'm sure SOLHOT is something totally different than what The Wind envisioned it to be from the get-go. And how will we accept it if SOLHOT is something different than we thought it would be after we're no longer at the university or something, or we're no longer living here? Will we come back like, "What is this? This isn't SOLHOT. This isn't how we used to do it back in the day." I really, really, really think about how can SOLHOT operate outside—and how can it speak to girls who are not, I guess, the stereotypical—not to say that this is what SOLHOT has become or this is what the space of SOLHOT pertains to. Can it be for girls who are not low-SES? Do queer girls come into SOLHOT? Do Asian girls come to SOLHOT? Do they stay into SOLHOT? I don't know.

I say that it's a homeplace and I feel affirmed. This is not like just poetic. This is like for real . . . I mean I feel called to have been in that moment at that time however brief, it's been life affirming. It's taught me a way to even see, like, see the little girl—[crying].

To just sit there and be like, "Oh yeah, I really enjoyed that conversation that those girls had," that's just not cool, "I really enjoyed that." This isn't a TV show. It's not just for you to sit back and enjoy. So, that's how I feel about that.

It's funny, because I guess sometimes more people get it than I really give credit for—like my granddad gets it.

But when we are in SOLHOT—or in all the different ways that SOLHOT exists—it's like the denial or affirmation of all those things that were—all these theories and all these ideas that people thought they knew or people think that they know. And so I think that's why it's political, because it's that space. It's the place to say, "No, that's not true." We always say, "I'm here." That's really deep to say, "I'm here. You can't take that away from me. This is what we created. This is what it is."

It was like the secret society—the Underground Railroad–type thing.

I dislike that everyone in SOLHOT doesn't necessarily practice it. 'Cause it pisses me off. That's one less person that I could share this with, or that I might want to. And it pisses me off that sometimes people see this as a way to—sometimes I feel like people want to commercialize us, from outside to within—commercialize us as a clique—

I like that there were no black-and-white rules and no hierarchy of power within the space. Even though The Wind initiated, developed, and was running the entire project, she was always so open to discussing, "What should we do?" and developing with us and being so collaborative, because a lot of times when people bring you on these projects—and I've had experience before. They want you for this specific purpose, to fulfill this, to get X, to get Y, so they can finish their project. And I think she didn't have any set expectations, but only to complete the six-to-eight-week period that we were doing, just to make sure we met when we said we would. But what we did in those meetings was completely organic. I felt like that. I don't know behind the scenes if it was, but I felt like that. And we did have structure. We had structure, but it just wasn't stifled by control—control, control, control, control. I just love the energy too. I love the energy. I love the space. Even the air seemed different. You know what I mean? I just felt empowered. If I had to make it all into one word, I felt empowered every night.

SOLHOT is something you really have to want to do. And you have to want to do SOLHOT outside of three to five on Fridays, 'cause SOLHOT definitely—you carry SOLHOT in your purse, basically.

I remember that first meeting when The Wind was distinguishing that we were not mentors because we were also gaining the same things that the girls were gaining. It wasn't this unequal platform, but that it was a learning space. It was a space of love and nurturing and openness and that we were basically there just to facilitate that. And I remember her saying, "Girls this age have so much energy. You can't stop them from being themselves. Trying to contain them is only gonna silence them. If they need to get up and be active and shake it, let them do it. There's no control. There's respect, but there's not authority in this space." And that's what really struck me like, "Okay," 'cause before it was clearly like we were the authority and we were doing—

We were all collaborators.

SOLHOT is just a way for a Black girl to be—it's a way for you to be however you want to bring yourself. That's where we're gonna meet you. If you come in and all you want to do is sit and write in a journal and not say too much, that's fine. If you want to come in and talk about that boy, that's cool, too. If you want to dance, or if you've got attitude—if you come in cussin'—as problematic as that is for me, it's good. I mean, I don't really think there's been anyone who's come in and been themselves and it was rejected or wasn't—it's just like SOLHOT is a way to be. It's a way for you to be exactly who you are from three to five, or four to six, however long it is. And we get into, "It's this little space where Black girls can come, and we can celebrate," and that's a wonderful definition for folks who can't even conceptualize that we need our own space. But I think—for us, for the homegirls—I'm like, "We're just being in all our glorious, dysfunctional, happy, great, problematic ways. We can just be."

Even though SOLHOT is a space for Black-girl celebration and we're working with Black girls in the community—reading The Wind's book and everything it's like, "It's not about you." That statement always stays with me, but at the same time, it is so much about us. What we see as what it means to celebrate or who we're celebrating or what experiences we're celebrating—

I also say it's a place that's just as much about the girls as it is about us, and sometimes maybe even more about us in the sense of—I just think about how long we've gone through school, how long we've been conditioned and how long we've gone through the whole socialization process. And they've had less years than us, so at the same time we're trying to create a space for them to be celebrated, but we've gone so long of not being celebrated. So, what does that mean in terms of trying to create the space for them? I tell my mom and my grandmother it's one of the best places I've ever been in. I feel both challenged and supported. I feel like loved and not liked. I feel like a family—like a typical family. Sometimes, "I really don't like you right now, but I'll always love you" kind of thing. I also feel like—I haven't really talked to my mom about this, because I'm still processing it, but I feel like it's a painful place in the sense of so many women are coming with all of our stuff, and we don't necessarily lay that out. So, it becomes both a recovery place but also a painful place, and both a community place but then also an individualistic place in the sense of—I felt real alone last year. I was like, "What the fuck?" People think I'm not involved. People think I'm not present. I'm sitting here and saying I'm present. Okay, I'm going through this stuff, but then at the same time I feel—I still feel obliged to be there, but then I still have people saying, "Well, maybe it's just not for you. Or maybe you don't want to be here. Or maybe you aren't—" and I'm just like, "How many times do I gotta keep telling you? I keep coming back," but in the midst of all this pain and frustration it was still—I still felt enough of a connection. And I don't know if it's a sense of inner responsibility that I feel to other Black females, but I still couldn't let go of it, where I know some people—if I would have told 'em about it they'd have been like, "What are you doing, Movement? Let it go. If people feel this way, go," but I couldn't go. It'd be like turning your back on family. So, I think overall it's a beautiful place for that reason.

But when we were in New York and we all went out to dinner, that's SOLHOT. That's a SOLHOT moment. Whenever we see each other—me and The Kinda Shy Homegirl saw each other when I was at home in LA. That's SOLHOT. Those are the moments that still feel like I'm participating in SOLHOT whether I'm physically with the girls—we become Black girls when we're all together, so it hasn't—not physically being there with the girls—and I still hang out with you, so there's still opportunities for me to hang out and participate in SOLHOT, just not in a particular way—I remember The Writer posted this Facebook story in her Facebook tag where she was at the grocery store and this little girl saying that she wants to be a Black girl—not Superwoman, not Batgirl. She wants to be Black girl. And I'm like, "Oh my gosh, me, too." That's my first response back to her, so I felt like we're having SOLHOT via cyberspace—virtual SOLHOT. So, I think I've expanded what SOLHOT is. It's not just a program that takes place. I think we've all expanded the definition. It's not just what happens at the Center or the library or wherever we are with the girls. It's whatever happens when anybody that's ever participated in SOLHOT gets together ever again. That is what it is.

There are no boundaries.

Black Girlhood Subjectivity, multiple productions

SOLHOT produces much. Tangible productions in the form of articles, books, T-shirts, and theatrical productions are most valued by secular audiences and outside observers. However, in SOLHOT the production of meaningful relationships has been and continues to be the production, what those who do SOLHOT value most. The memory text also makes visible other intangible and worthwhile productions, including Black girlhood subjectivity. In SOLHOT, we learn what it means to have a self, and whether the selves we have built are strong enough to be in the company of the greatness of our peers. This is how SOLHOT works for everyone, not in a selfish way, but very much as a process of interrogating ourselves, with love, and in community. For many, it offers the opportunity to rethink the goal of making a space for Black girls that does not operate out of reaction to white supremacy and identity politics, but out of love for being a full participant in the creation of a space that depends on one's expressed gifts and talents and ability to show up, fully present. After SOLHOT, homegirls think of themselves as Black girls and are interested in affirming the lives of other Black girls, in and out of SOLHOT.

I will go to spoken-word stuff, and I will try to share things that I wrote with people. I started a band with my friends. I'm the lead guitarist and the singer. I would never sing in front of people, and I do that now—just things that I would never, ever, ever do. Definitely, the first semester after we did SOLHOT, I was super pumped and I ended up actually starting a spoken-word workshop at the detention center with the girls there, which was so cool. I enjoyed that a lot, and because—and I know that's why I was like—I knew I needed to challenge myself to—just in the group dynamic of Sister Circle, something needs to happen where we're recognizing each other's talents.

We left no—outside of the girls and their word of mouth or that type of thing, we left nothing for the School to say, "SOLHOT is that shit," or, "SOLHOT was there," but they know SOLHOT works. But they don't know SOLHOT was there. I think the best thing that we did was the conference. That was the highlight for me—the panel—yeah, the panel. I'm like, "This is what I want to see—Black girls telling their own stories and for them to just get up there and say it how they want to say it and everybody can understand and everybody is listening and attentive." So, I think SOLHOT needs to try to do stuff like that more often for the Black girls—in the community, on campus—but you're right. What did SOL-HOT produce? We produced graduates, I guess. And we produced girls who came in one way and have a whole 'nother meaning of Black girlhood at the end.

I'm really into this whole Black-girl studies thing, especially the homo-sexuality angle. I think about them all the time when I write and do my research. I think about their stories when I'm reading a theory and the stuff in books—always comparing their stories to the literature. So, that's in my work. I think that also another way that I've been inspired by the program, it's made me really think about what it would mean to be in-volved in Black women organizing and Black feminist organizing. I think a lot of the issues I'm finding in SOLHOT were written about in the 1970s and the 1980s among Black lesbian feminists that I was like, "Oh, that was a thing of the past," but it still holds true today. It's really hard. You would think that Black women is such a—I don't know what the best word for this, but sort of a specific or narrow identity that we could so naturally and easily come together to support each other and to do things as a group. Then, you realize there's so many other identities within that group. It just makes it so real for me. And so it makes me really think about feminist theory and also Black feminist organizing and women organizing that if I do anything up here, I'll definitely take away the lessons I've learned from doing SOLHOT. I think those are the two major ways.

I think SOLHOT has helped me to deal—not deal with—but family issues and the education I'm getting from SOLHOT. And the education I'm getting from the university has helped me to help my family. So, SOLHOT is something—everybody who knows me knows SOLHOT. So, maybe everybody is a part of SOLHOT, because I let them be. I share my stories with them, and I share my experiences. SOLHOT has helped me find out who I am.

After I did SOLHOT in the spring, me and two of my friends ran a summer camp in the community. I wouldn't have done that. Not only did we run a summer camp, we ran a community kitchen to run the summer camp. We had a restaurant—definitely wouldn't have been able to do that without SOLHOT—just engaging with people and thinking through what it means to be present and trying to talk to people and put yourself out there even though they might not always accept it, but knowing that it takes coming back multiple times to create a relationship or connection with anyone is something that I learned through doing SOLHOT—just so many things. I wouldn't think that my grandma's a theorist. Definitely, I have a much better relationship with the women in my family. Now, I'll just call my mom and be like, "Tell me about yourself." And I think that that wouldn't have happened if I wouldn't have done SOLHOT.

SOLHOT changed the way I thought about collaboration, the way I thought about sharing information and empowerment. I always thought, previously, if you shared something that it was ultimately taking something away from you. That you were losing something, because you were giving something. But SOLHOT changed that. It made me feel like I was gaining by giving. And though I didn't necessarily know what it was I was gaining, at that moment, it felt better to give away the experience and the knowledge. It felt so much better to share that than it did to hold on to it and keep it for myself. We're in an academic environment. It is competitive, and you do have to achieve to distinguish yourself, but I've never been around—especially other Black, educated women—so willing to share and nurture and advise and bring you into their circle. I always felt like a colleague, not like a production assistant running around on the set of The Wind's production. I mean I felt like I was at the table with all of you. I'm an undergrad thinking, "Can I do this? Am I qualified to share my opinion?" I felt so empowered like, "Yeah, I am. I can. They care what I think. For real, they care what I think," and that's changed my entire attitude.

How you were able to be so free and give the audience so much of yourself in that performance. Whatever that freeness you feel in the Center— you finally decided it was okay to share that with the audience, and that's because of SOLHOT, in part.

And I met some fantabulous women in the process—people who—everybody a great respect as activists and scholars and just smart people—but then also people who I would kick it with. I would come to y'all couch and be like, "I just need to lay here. Could y'all feed my kid? I brought him a can of pork and beans. I just need to be near y'all." Or I remember when we went for The Wind's birthday, and we were in the foyer. And you was like, "You know what? For real, you being ghost on us, it's not gonna work. You need to come back. Whatever you're going through, we can work with you. For real." Right? That right there, you can't buy that. You know what I'm saying? You were like, "For real, whatever reason you've been gone—" and a lot of it—most of it the personal stuff that I just couldn't open my mouth to say or be embarrassed, mad, whatever—just not wanting to—and then I'm gonna tell you this. I told Yemaya—I was kinda tellin' her, and I'm like, "I want to talk to them, but I'm so ashamed," and she was like, "Why?" and I was like, "I don't know." I said, "'Cause I always want to be happy around y'all, 'cause y'all make me happy." You know what I'm saying?

Just how learning from each other's experiences and everyday lives. You know, being in a Black feminist or womanist environment where lived experience and wisdom is just as important as what you learn in the academy. I mean, we can learn—I was learning something every SOLHOT session from these girls—putting a CD in the toilet and flushing it. I was like, "Come on, now," but it worked—and just little stuff like when they go to a dance they don't let a boy get on them right away unless it's a certain—and you're like, whether that was similar to what you did when you grew up or whether it's something completely different—just the exchange of information.

It also just—didn't remind me, but it reaffirmed to me how much Black women mean to me and how committed I am—no matter what people say or how people try to push me out—not to say that people push me out, but I've always felt an affinity toward Black women, even ones that hate me, literally. It's something that is a part of me that I'll always be pushing for, even if those people aren't pushing for me. So, it kind of reaffirmed that. It reminded me that work with Black girls is hard—not that I didn't know that—but that it's hard—but how important it is. And on a personal note, I think that the struggles that I saw some of the girls going through with guys reminded me of the crap that I was going through and kind of pushed me like, "Well, I gotta be doing better than this. I can't go back to ninth grade and high school and all of this stuff. I gotta believe what I believe in and just keep thinking forward." Yeah, and it reaffirmed to me that everybody is doing a lot of the similar work much differently and that I have to be firm about what I'm doing and that if I know what I'm doing, whatever everybody else says doesn't matter—not that it doesn't matter literally, but if I know what I'm doing then when people call it into question, I'm not really concerned about it because I know a little bit of what I'm doing. And I say a little bit, because I don't think we can ever truly measure the impact that we had.

It has shown me that there is so many ways—how do I put this?—how you can combine what you love to do and what you have to do, like your research. We're doing research. We're also connecting with ourselves, connecting with these girls who are a reflection of ourselves, 'cause we are girls, or used to be girls, or are a little further along the evolutionary stage of girlhood—but also performing research, also connecting with the community, also finding out more about ourselves.

So, it was nice to finally be in a space where I'm like, "You experience the same exact thing. Thank you." It was finally being validated rather than being written off.

And then getting SOLHOT recognition on campus from The Wind. In terms of it being an actual community-based research project that I don't think that any department that she's affiliated with really understands the impact in—nobody else is doing that kind of work in the community. And I think it's interesting that we have all these initiatives and these PR statements that we say about the university embracing the community, but really there's no—when somebody's actively doing that in the way that The Wind has—and basically starting SOLHOT from the ground up—there's not money, there's not resources applied to it, and kind of getting that recognition where there are other programs that don't set foot in the community, or they handpick the people that they want to do stuff in the community. They get all this kind of funding and this recognition.

The fight that goes along with telling people that it's—the validation of trying to constantly validate SOLHOT to other people, and even sometimes the people that actually participate in SOLHOT. I think that kind of work gets exhausting. It's necessary, but it's exhausting, and it takes a lot out of you. So, it kind of hinders the progress that can be made sometimes. It gets hard to tell people. How do you tell somebody that you are valuable and you should be here? It's like validating your own existence. It gets tiring, especially if people are unwilling to listen.

The people that have been a part of SOLHOT and continue to be part of SOLHOT definitely need to know that they are valuable in this kind of work, whether or not SOLHOT goes away or continues to grow.

Regardless of whether it exists in this physical space or not, SOLHOT will always live on in that way. There will always be SOLHOT if we're always pushing towards making Black girls' voices heard.

I think it's definitely given me a new way to look at all the dope shit that Black girls and Black women do that kind of gets—and there's a good and a bad to being stepped on. Nobody ever sees you coming when you're stepped on, which is a powerful thing to have. It's changed me in that.

It's makin' me aware that I'm a Black woman, and I have obligations to my community, and accountability. That's what I'm saying I think SOLHOT has done, definitely.

That it's not just about me.

I'm gonna cry.

It's not about myself, at all.

I think it's not just the girls, but also you guys—you, The Wind—just being in that setting where I don't have to explain myself.

Healing & Hindsight, interconnections

Healing & Hindsight. . . . interconnections. At its very best, practicing SOLHOT shows us how we are all interconnected. The beauty of organizing under a Black girlhood construct is the immensity of who enters when Black girls are invited and made to feel welcomed. Within Black girlhood as made in SOLHOT, we know and acknowledge that we are making spaces for us all. Alexander wrote,

> Since colonization has produced fragmentation and dismemberment at both the material and psychic levels, the work of decolonization has to make room for the deep yearning for wholeness, often expressed as a yearning to belong, a yearning that is both material and existential, both psychic and physical, and which, when satisfied, can subvert and ultimately displace the pain of dismemberment. (2005, p. 281)

To be and belong in SOLHOT is to express a desire for healing, a space to acknowledge the mundane and the majesty of a Black girlhood that cannot be taken for granted. To say, "I am SOLHOT," is an open acknowledgement that homegirls make space through time to intentionally remember Black girlhood. It is a statement that speaks against fragmentation and dismemberment that would suggest volunteering after school for a couple of hours is sufficient for doing work so big and so sacred as to require metaphysical skills. To do SOLHOT requires mastering several kinds of knowledge—of the body, interior and personal, and of the body collective, extending beyond one's self. The kinds of interconnections sponsored when SOLHOT is accomplished as sacred is the stuff that requires enacting love, trust, honor, loyalty, duty, and humility, on the regular. Doing SOLHOT is a grand setup to practice love, and to value life and living, insisting on the well-being of us all.

Homegirl means I can relate to you. You know where I'm at, I know where you are. We know each other's stories. You're my homegirl. You're my best friend. There's a lot of words you can interchange with that. I feel like if you're my homegirl, we're supposed to keep in touch no matter what life experiences or stages we're going through.

I thought it would be more of a me as the older person in a leadership role, not so much—because there was a lot of emphasis in meetings about not looking down on the girls because of their age or not creating this sort of "I'm in a position of power, and you're not" relationship—so something that was not so domineering. But I definitely thought of it as me, as the adult, I would be in charge of keeping SOLHOT together.

But I do think it's important for everyone to really try to think through the full landscape of what being present looks like. I know for me I definitely felt convicted in terms of not bringing myself to SOLHOT, not because I didn't want to but I thought it was—"I don't need to be in the spotlight. I'll just listen and engage and support other people doing things," but I don't think that's productive, because I think there's so many different skills and talents, just between the homegirls that there should be an opportunity for everyone—'cause that's gonna hit different—connect with different girls.

So, I think that it could have been structured in such a way that there could have been something physical produced from each session, that then we can go back, "This was the year we did the yearbook. This was the year we did the film-festival short. This is the year we did the picture gallery." And I think it's starting to shape into that, but the first session I felt like that's what was missing, because the girls didn't really know— they need material motivation like, "What are we working toward? Are we just talking every week? Are we just meeting every week? Is this a club, or is this like—is this a group, or is this an organization that I belong? Is this something I belong to? What is my role and my account-ability in this?"

I mean the only thing that I had reservations with was when it became a research project.

We had Yung Sister, with that beautiful voice. The Master Storyteller is clearly an actress—all of these great talents, all of these great—Queen, she writes some beautiful poetry—all of these things. And if those were put together—if those were like, "This is what we have. This is what we've come up with," and all of the ideas are still there. They're just in a different form. I think that's a good way of showing what is really going on. I don't know if— you can answer this for me—but some type of article or response, or some-thing like that. I don't know if we could do that. I don't really know how all of that works, but some type of thing that says, "This is what happens here." Yeah, something like that—something concrete that says, "This is what it is."

I don't know that I found my exact place. I know I want to be a better writer, a better wordsmith, verbal artist to keep up with—or if I could have that ease with speaking and writing that I do with moving, but that's also part of my research in researching movement. The way you move or the way you feel or how you can make an audience feel you through space—how you do that with words on paper. I've been reading a woman in my department who's done movement research. That's a big part of her research. So, maybe continuing to be a part of SOLHOT can help me kind of get there, and if not, I'll just keep dancing.

If you know what it is here then you know what it is there—so what-ever. But the knowing of not being able to be there—the knowing that it is there and that you're here, you know in whatever kind of you know mar-ginalization [. . .] that's a whole other kind of yearning, it's a whole other kind of longing, it's a whole other kind of like wanting to belong because you know what it felt like to be belonged—

I was really afraid. I think that a lot of queer people get afraid about working with young people, especially in a Black community. I didn't know how their parents would react. And I also, again, was so concerned about keeping SOLHOT, as a group, together that I didn't want any of the girls to stop coming to SOLHOT. That was my big fear—or for the girls to sort of separate themselves from SOLHOT and sort of divide over who was like, "Who cares?" and those who were really against me. So, I felt like I had to hide that for the sake of the group.

I feel like now the accountability is there, but there is an undermining as to the work that it takes to trust somebody in this type of space, because I think it's just assumed, "You're gonna come in. You're gonna be yourself." Okay, well, some of us haven't been ourselves for a while. Some of us have been hiding our self, and that self only comes out after ten o'clock at night when all the work is done. "Okay, so now you want me to come in front of you. Okay, you have all these relationships with other people already. I'm coming into this space, you want me to be myself, whatever that is," but not taking heed of the fact that for so long many of us couldn't be ourselves, or at what cost could we be ourselves? Now, yeah, come into this space for this Black-girlhood celebration. There's an assumed trust that isn't necessarily there, but it's like we're supposed to operate in that way, I think.

So, I think that—when it first started, I felt like there was a lot of emphasis on many different ways to speak, but that fell to the wayside when a lot of the girls said that they didn't like to write, they didn't like to draw, so then it just became about talking morally. And that was the unfortunate thing.

I felt like that could have been a space where we could have started to turn things around. But that would have been a really difficult balance, because we would have had to teach girls to read and write, and was that a space for that? We didn't have that much time.

We hadn't had a serious, meaningful conversation about queer issues before that.

And then it's also hard to put it in such black-and-white terms like that, because it wasn't so much homophobic as it was heteronormative and that there were definitely queer girls on both sides, both homegirls and young girls. But I think we all felt like for some bizarre reason, we all felt like for the group we all had to be heteronormative, and I don't know why—just to keep everyone sort of happy and together.

'Cause it was a story personal to me, talking about generations of—I was going to talk about generations of abuse in my family, and for them to not really see the importance of that—and I get it, they're young. But in that moment I felt like I was really emotionally vulnerable, so I don't think they kind of—hindsight, I know that they don't understand, necessarily, always the importance of hearing people through when they are emotionally vulnerable. So, for them to kind of cut me off and then to hear, "That's stupid," it was hard to rationalize with them. I'm like, "This is a child saying something that they don't really get." So, my immediate response was to close down and protect myself, but it was hard 'cause I was so angry 'cause I don't think they understand how important it is and how truthful it is when somebody's telling them something from an emotionally vulnerable place that they not—even if they don't like it, even if they don't—it's a two-way street, so me being emotionally vulnerable lends to you listening. You have to be able to listen, and it's a trust factor. So, for me to be vulnerable means that I have to trust you, and for them to shun that, I felt like I couldn't trust them. But I had to think about how old they are, too, and where they're at and all the stuff they had been through.

I have to go back to because I am important—and that my story is not my story alone but it's connected to other people's stories again, something that already happens in practice in SOLHOT—I mean you see how this is like—but yeah again you could keep on doing things that everybody else is suggesting that you could do or you could do the things that matter—

So, I felt like sometimes it wasn't productive—the yelling, the fighting—it just wasn't—and the attitude that came sometimes just stank and so I think the girls saw at the Center how much—and they may not have, but maybe they felt how much we struggled to be there, so there was probably a decrease—and this is my assumption—that there was a decrease in the level of attitude and maybe a decrease in our own attitudes, whereas at the Library, we just walked into the space and we'd come in here and yell and scream. There was no struggle to be there. There was no active work to be there by everybody, so maybe that's why there was this level of—just a lot of screaming and yelling. I think we took things for granted that we didn't take for granted before, being at the Center—the work that went into being in that space.

If we have to walk to the schools to do it, we ain't got no gas money, keep doing it.

"At the end of the day, we still all are Black girls."
—Says the homegirl to whom I promised I'd include how Fine
    she is somewhere/how in the text

3 When Black Girls Look at You

An Anti-Narrative Photo-Poem

Field note
Incident occurred December 2007.
I wrote this February 9, 2008.

I was there when it happened. Running a program after school in which the local school is generous enough to provide the children with "supper"—school lunch food (yuck). After gazing at the portions and figuring out what it is—a chicken patty, extra dry, stuck between a bun—the girls decided they would rather get back to SOLHOT and work on their photography project. We leave the lunchroom. The girls walked slow, taking in everyone who passes by and everything he-said, she-said. They were laughing, giggling, and pushing in jest. I reached the room, where we were working, first.

The girls came in. They sat in a circle and we begin to talk about what's next with our project. Interrupting our conversation, a white middle-aged woman comes in and demands our attention. With hand on her hip, she chides the girls with much attitude and overwhelming power. She says something to the effect of "You can't play and push each other in the hallway!"

"Why were you being so loud?"

"Don't you know how to act like ladies?"

She goes on and on, and I hear it much like the girls, "blah blah blah." I'm listening to her and think, "Who is this woman? Why is she raising her voice at the girls, at us?"

The woman proceeds to remain out of control and out of order and demands that the girls tell her what they were up to. She demands an apology. I am appalled. I think she actually wanted them to respond with some kind of confessional statement like, "I'm bad. Please forgive me."

I pay greater attention to what each girl decides to do in that minute than I think about intervening. Dead silence. The silence does not last for

long because, this time, the desired silence is read by the woman as making more trouble. Now she demands they speak! They can't win for losing.

A response. One girl (who loves to talk) says, "Sorry." But she smacks
her lips at the end of the apology, prompting a few smiles and giggles.
I laugh too, out loud, but for only a second. The rest of the girls said
nothing. Silence. The woman continued to chide them, and I would say
verbally harass the girls, until finally she stopped. I don't know why. I don't
remember. Maybe it was because I was giving her a serious "look" by that
time. Or maybe because another school official, the girls' counselor (another white woman), was also present the entire time and agrees to handle
it (though with a decidedly progressive approach). The woman leaves.

What is absent in the above field note is the everydayness of the event. I
did not describe how the cold, already sterile school environment iced each
word of the interrupting woman's speech to make time stand still. Although
I documented that the woman did not retreat after seeing me, my surprise
to her obliviousness is understated.

Not overly preoccupied with the usual ethnographer's dilemma, to intervene or not, I was focused on the girls' responses. SOLHOT exists for the
value of the girls; my research is decidedly focused on what happens when
Black girls get together. I was not, am not there to document the experiences
of those who work at the school. But this moment represented an intimate
crossing: when we do SOLHOT in school, we work hard to create our own
thing, but we can never operate completely outside of the context in which
we are located—often, a context the girls have much more experience in
navigating.

Looking in the eyes of each one of the girls present, and reading their
body language, I learned that their response to this kind of situation was
also routine. In response to her attempt to manage them, the girls also knew
how to manage her. Their ritualized response signaled to me that while she
was inappropriate, there was nothing particularly new or shocking about
her behavior. But I was beside myself. I was outside of my body looking at
her looking at them while watching how they looked to each other. The girls
interrupted the public shaming with defiant glances that were directed toward
the woman. To remain calm, they checked in with each other, as a reminder
to keep their heads up, necks extended toward the ceiling if they had to.

However, I could not understand how these kinds of events are normalized
into anyone's schoolday. I could not understand her admonishment of the
girls being too loud and too quiet, and how they could effectively be doubly

punished for their noncompliance. After this scene unfolded, we carried on with what we were doing, and though the event stayed on my mind, and was debriefed with the other adults present, the girls never mentioned it to me again. It seemed to be no big deal.

The more I work with Black girls, the more unsure I am about how to explain with any kind of absolute certainty what produces a Black girlhood so devastatingly devalued that, more often than not, invisibility becomes boring, a nonissue. Yet, in this moment of pervasive nonrecognition, without sound, word, or physical contact, the girls and I were in kinesthetic communication. I learned that they had been there before. I saw them practicing what they have been taught—"If you don't have nothing nice to say, then say nothing at all"—in response to the woman's demand that they speak. Terribly irritated by her disruption, the girls' seemingly passive compliance suggested that they were much more interested in doing what was planned in SOLHOT than in extending the moment with this woman any longer than necessary. These intersubjective insights—what happens when we Black girls see each other in context of being "othered" and effectively rendered unseen and dehumanized—guides the analytical foundation of this chapter. I do not focus so much on what that woman did not see, but rather on what we saw, how we recognized each other, our shared understanding, and our knowledge that was taken for granted. In this re-viewing, my goal is to also make visible the responsibility of the viewer to hold a productive uncertainty about what is being seen and to prompt discussions about challenging institutional norms and interpersonal actions that do not recognize the humanity of Black girls.

SOLHOT, after-school programs, and youth activist groups operate and are located in institutions, like schools, that too easily collude with systemic marginalization. For example, educational scholars have documented the ways in which high-stakes-test scoring, the school-to-prison pipeline, No Child Left Behind, and other systemic issues disproportionately penalize youth of color. Also, on an interpersonal level, students may experience racism, sexism, classism, and homophobia as the result of school staff and teachers simply doing their job (Cohen, 1999). Therefore, it is important to examine the ways in which we relate to each other and maintain self-reflection about the spaces in which we work in order to remain aware of the multiple ways the institutions constrain and enable the greatest visions of ourselves.

To articulate how Black girls are seen and by whom, the following questions guide this analysis: When Black girls and women create their own images, how do they negotiate the politics of representation, and what new knowledge is produced? What do humanizing representations of Black girl-hood look like, and how are they (re)produced and embodied? When I look at those in SOLHOT and they look back, what story emerges? How do Black girls and women see each other? What are the limits of sight-centric identi-fication and knowing?

My answer to these questions is decidedly performative. Based on photog-raphy created in SOLHOT, I offer an anti-narrative photo-poem. I define an anti-narrative photo-poem as an active and creative text that critically engages dominant images and stereotypes through the manipulation of language for the purpose of producing a mutually dependent relationship between image and word, producer and consumer, injustice and action. The anti-narrative photo-poem allows me to create a performance text that intentionally invites discontinuity—a kind of discontinuity that invites the reader to think again about what they saw, and to act as if how Black girls are seen, by whom, and with what response, matters. It is an opportunity to practice what D. Soyini Madison (2010) calls performative-witnessing, a body-to-body commitment and engagement based on a politics of the body in action with Others (p. 25).

The anti-narrative photo-poem suggests that the school official's behavior is all too familiar, so common, in fact, SOLHOT girls know the script and enact a well-worn performance of Black girlhood docility, the precursor to performing respectable Black womanhood Yet, because of my consistent work with Black girls, I understood the silence as communication. Creatively assembling twelve of the photographs taken in SOLHOT, I use embodied knowledge, my adult authority, and educational privilege to make explicit what needs to be said. I am not attempting to speak for the girls. I am speak-ing for myself based on what I know as a result of sharing the same time and space, and mutual love for each other, as Black girls. To make explicit what was shared between us, I created the anti-narrative photo-poem to speak back to the particular ethnographic moment described at the beginning of this chapter.

Beyond the use of photographs taken in SOLHOT, I relied on the writ-ing practices and methodological innovations of June Jordan (1969) and M. Nourbese Philip (2008) to create the anti-narrative photo-poem. Both Jordan's and Philip's work make possible a retelling of events that foreground the kind of use and manipulation of images and words that does the seem-ingly impossible: it blurs the boundaries between knowing and unknowing while requiring an embodied response. John Berger (1977) asserted, "If the new language of images were used differently, it would, through its use, confer a new kind of power" (p. 33). Jordan's and Philip's respective contributions have conferred new configurations of power that Black feminists and others have acknowledged and applied on a larger scale, and this micro-intervention builds on the legacy of Black feminist creative scholarship. This particular anti-narrative photo-poem demonstrates how the use and teaching of knowledge and talents that were previously unseen, buried, and/or colonized are reclaimed, given space to emerge, and put to use in the service of SOLHOT; it offers the viewer an opportunity to redirect and resist a gaze of inferiority all too often directed to Black girls. Black girls and women in SOLHOT see those who render us invisible, and this particular kind of recognition makes possible the intersubjective knowledge that is of great use in creating new pathways for understanding the actions and behaviors of Black girls differently.

The anti-narrative photo-poem invokes a new way of relating to both the subject and author, while also arguing for diverse re-readings of a person or social phenomenon previously assumed to be known. This contribution works in the direction encouraged by feminist scholars who insist on dismantling the singular, oppressive white supremacist gaze as the defining eye and, with it, its colonial objectifying and classificatory power. Scholars of decolonization and critical pedagogy have long called for new ways of belonging that are not anchored in white supremacy and archaic notions of racial difference and hierarchy. My objective is to critically engage the direct and necessary interrelatedness of representation and lived experience, through the ethnographic archive and performative repertoire that is SOLHOT, for the purpose of articulating new and different paths of justice that are accountable to Black girls in particular.

Before the anti-narrative photo-poem is presented in this chapter, I discuss in detail the dominant image of Black girls in the United States. Then, I address how photography came to be in SOLHOT. Next, disciplinary considerations regarding the use of images are briefly considered. Given that images have at times stood in as the dominant signifier of an objectifying gaze, I suggest that woman-of-color feminist innovations that have put photography in service to communities offer a more just method for the use and analysis of images. Foregrounding the contributions of Jordan and Philip in context of creative feminist scholarship, I highlight their innovations as methodologists, though typically they are not recognized as such. Lastly, this chapter ends with what I present as the evidence, the anti-narrative photo-poem.

THE DOMINANT IMAGE

As a woman of the Black Diaspora in the midst of saturated Black women and girls images it's important to pause to pose urgent questions to ourselves about our histories, institutional structures, and disciplines.
—*Nelson,* Representing the Black Female Subject in Western Art, *10*

In the United States, images of Black girls are hypervisible and persistent as sexualized property (Nelson, 2010), hip-hop accessories (Peoples, 2007; Pough, 2004; Pough et al., 2007; Sharpley-Whiting, 2007), and prototypes of resilience (Evans-Winters, 2005; Stevens, 2002). Historical stereotypes of Black women and girls as Mammy and Jezebel, confounded with contemporary representations of Black girlhood as strong Black women (Beaubeouf-Lafontant, 2009), video vixens (Stokes, 2007), and thugs, divas, and wannabes (Cox, 2009) make for an even narrower range of available narratives that speak to the complexity of Black girlhood. Moreover, punitive social policies ensue, seeking to punish Black girls for their contested behavior that, although typically nonviolent, is perceived as threatening and problematic. Likewise, in gender-specific spaces concerned with "girls," Black girls are always and already constructed as needy, typically included to be the implicit and explicit objects of reform and etiquette training (Brown, 2008). More often than not, the assumed logic for "working with Black girls in the community" is to reform their waywardness and to provide adult supervision so that they will not become sexually active. The familiarity of this logic, in response to my identification and co-organization of SOLHOT, speaks directly to the ways Black girls are constructed by the intersection of heteronormative, patriarchal, racist, and sexist oppressive conditions as already, and in all ways, seen as a problem to solved.

As an example of the hegemonic discourses that govern Black girls' lives in schools, Edward Morris (2007) found in his study on African American girls, "'Ladies' or 'Loudies'?: Perceptions and Experiences of Black Girls in Classrooms," that while they performed well academically, they also faced unique obstacles as a result of how teachers deployed race, gender, and class in relation to understanding Black girls' behavior. Employing an intersectional approach, Morris found that school processes aimed to reform Black girls into a particular model of womanhood reproduced inequity and marginalized Black female students. The disciplinary gaze focused on the bodies of Black girls (and youth of color, more generally) meant that educators' attention is

geared toward controlling their mobility in a way that reinforces racist, clas-
sist, and sexist notions about how young girls are supposed to act, particularly
in urban public spaces. Morris's explanation also offers a plausible explanation
of the woman's behavior in the field note that opened this chapter. Her concern with the girls' volume (on a continuum of loud and quiet) was directly
correlated to her admonishment that they were not performing docile Black
girlhood femininity, the precursor to respectable Black womanhood, as she
preferred and expected.

In SOLHOT, we gather together to create and deconstruct the institutional
narratives and visual images that do us in as Black girls and women day after
day. We read and critique mainstream music videos, we question why Internet
searches of "Black girls" result primarily in pornographic images of Black
women, and we relay to each other in drama and in jest the myriad ways we
cope with the all-too-common racist teacher and street harasser. We question
why we remain disproportionately locked up, raped, and victims of violence.
We collectively gather to have these discussions primarily because the injurious material realities of contemporary Black girlhood continue to create a
desire to come together, to be heard and to be seen as who we "really are," as
language goes in SOLHOT. Spaces like SOLHOT make sense to those who
attend because they present an opportunity to be seen on our terms. However,
even in spaces like SOLHOT that are dedicated to the celebration of Black
girlhood in all of its complexity, we sometimes do not recognize ourselves.

One compelling explanation for such misrecognition among one another
in SOLHOT is that we, as those who identify as Black girls and women, are
not immune from consuming and ingesting stereotypical images. According
to Nelson (2010, p. 5),

> The visual arts in the West form an oppressive repository of stereotypical
> representations of Black female subjects that the subjects themselves were
> forced to consume daily as they saw themselves imaged and imagined
> through white eyes and white social perceptions, in public and private
> spaces through elite and populist practices alike. Vision itself then must
> be questioned and questionable.

Nelson makes clear the necessity of calling into question sight-centric appeals for recognition. In the West we look and we see something that we
attempt to differentiate because we believe we know it via seeing it. However,
this privileging of the visual, essentialized as "worldview," results in a faulty
correlation between knowing and sight (Oyewùmí, 2005). Therefore, the
oft-cited syllogism "seeing is believing" is emblematic of Western logic and

breaks down when considering how sense is made outside of the West and by those in the West who deploy diverse cultural meaning-making strategies that privilege more than the visual. We know because we hear, feel, act, and experience. We also do not know.

In "Sense and Subjectivity," Ngô (2011) addressed the relationship between visibility and power in context of disability theory and war studies. Complicating representations of blindness, Ngô demonstrates how blindness is typically represented as negation, and sight is privileged over all the other senses as a technology of knowledge production and power, producing uneven constructions of subjectivity. Refusing Enlightenment logics that assume "visibility as the foundation for being recognized as having personhood," Ngô urges a more complex stance posing the necessary question: "But what does it mean to recognize evidence of being a person, a citizen, with legitimacy in late capitalism, under a neoliberal state, in an era of empire?" (p. 119). Conceding the tenuous realization that conferring personhood based on visibility is "uneven and often unavailable" (*ibid.*), particularly for people of color and women, this makes it possible for visibility, at times, to result in increased surveillance and, at other times, death. These tensions are compelling and particularly instructive for demonstrating the limits of Black girls' visibility. Many times, youth of color are punished because of what someone, typically with more power, has seen and surmised as truth.

In SOLHOT, though the woman at the school saw us, we were punished for it. Ngô's insight encourages a critical examination of how Black girl bodies are required to unjustly negotiate binaries of voice and silence, invisibility and visibility, and control and being. I attempt to handle the tensions with care, arguing that the anti-narrative photo-poem is generative of a kind of resistance that undermines visibility as an inherently positive value and invisibility as a strictly powerless domain. At the intersection of photography, which emphasizes the visual, and poetry, which relies on the manipulation of words, the anti-narrative photo-poem renders a more just representation of Black girlhood that, when performed, the poem, as an advanced representation of Black girlhood, provides an antidote to the kinds of interactions that construct Black girls' subjectivity as passive and problematic. Contrary to popular and common sense-making strategies, the anti-narrative photo-poem makes it possible for Black girls to be seen and our lives affirmed.

It is the images created in and because of SOLHOT, coupled with the words/story that emerged in relationship to my extended practice of participant observation, that allowed me a particular, unique, completely subjective, and beloved position from which I sat with the photographs, our conversations, and collective experiences. Just as much as I looked at the photographs and "saw" the girls, the poem that emerged from that experience extends beyond what was seen, includes uncertainty, and makes possible a new image. The evidence for my argument, in the form of an anti-narrative photo-poem, is the result of tending to the complex ways my own resistant subjectivity informed what I wanted to make known. Nevertheless, the anti-narrative photo-poem engages a kind of recognition premised on being in prolonged engagement with and for the well-being of Black girls.

HOW PHOTOGRAPHY CAME TO BE IN SOLHOT

The more we know about how the photography came into existence, the more we can judge its validity.
—Harper, "On the Authority of the Image," 403

The way photographs came to be in SOLHOT resembles the inherited legacy of African American photographers, from Roy DeCarava to Gordon Parks, who documented the everyday humanism of Black life. Moreover, technological access to devices, including popular (or low) photographic images taken with digital cameras and cell phones, is ubiquitous. Girls and homegirls often come to SOLHOT with cell phones, smart phones, and/or digital cameras in hand.

Since SOLHOT's beginning, a staple in its curriculum was an exercise in documenting beauty; disposable cameras were introduced as a tool of documentation and artistic production. We often placed the photographs taken by girls in SOLHOT in relationship to images and objects of beauty found in mainstream media. We used our images to create posters and collages. We looked over pictures and enjoyed what we saw in our everyday lives as beautiful.

Simultaneously, Candy, a SOLHOT homegirl, graduate student, and research assistant, especially enjoyed taking pictures to document our process. She became known among the girls and the homegirls as the one "with the camera glued to her hand." After a SOLHOT session, Candy would often send a couple of pictures via email to the homegirls. Her photographs quickly became a welcomed way of documenting our work, affirming our presence, and reflecting on what we learned while outside of the moment of practice. The pictures were powerful. When I viewed them, I was at once reminded of how I felt and who was there, and I relished the opportunity to see things that I did not know were going on because I was either preoccupied or busy elsewhere. It was very exciting, particularly during the first year of SOLHOT, to know that something that started as a suggestion was indeed magical. In SOLHOT we created a kind of Black girl/woman way of being that allowed us to practice love. What we did and how was often hard to explain in words. Candy's photographs became like additional pieces to the puzzle that was the magic of SOLHOT. They allowed me to pair a visual image with our practice, which I fully understood but also could not fully explain with words. Also, I liked that I could forward, via email, pictures to others who were not there and that the photos could prompt a response that was very similar to what was experienced by me, without much writing on my part.

As SOLHOT continued, I came to expect the documentation. On a couple of occasions when Candy wasn't there, I took pictures. They were bad, unfocused and poorly executed. In my pictures I saw half a face, the reflection of fluorescent lights, or waves of light because I was moving as I took the pictures. The very best of my pictures were average. In Candy's absences, I noticed that my pictures were just pictures, but hers seemed more like art. They conveyed more than just who attended SOLHOT for a particular session.

"You're an artist, and your gift of photography is so valuable," I told her. She objected. Again I said out loud and wrote in an email to her something like, "I don't know how you do it, but you do it well." Again, she objected. "You are an artist with a very special gift that I hope you will share with us and the girls in SOLHOT because that is SOLHOT," I proclaimed. "How do you know so much about taking pictures?" I asked, repeatedly. She claimed (and pretended) to not know. To me, her photography seemed trained in a very impressive and specific way. The more I insisted, the more she resisted, until she finally shared this truth: "My father is a professional photographer"—casually qualifying her statement with another truth—"but I was raised by and grew up with my grandmother." That was enough of a confirmation for me.

In the telling of how photographs came to be in SOLHOT, it's important to share this homegirl's story. I do not think photographs would have come to take up so much space in how we worked together, as it did, if she had not been a part of SOLHOT, if the girls were the ONLY participants, if we assumed that we as the adults already knew all of our gifts, and if we did not constantly change the curriculum to account for how things were actually used and valued in SOLHOT.

Candy has her own telling of this story that is equally valid. She recalled the story as such:

> In SOLHOT, when the girls dance I dance too—well, sometimes. I was afraid to dance. I didn't want to. But I kept coming back because I wanted to be there, right there being free with girls. So, I began taking photos of us dancing. The girls came to know me as Candy—the girl with the camera. It was just that simple. I am not a professionally trained photographer. The only history I know about photography is that my father has lived his life taking pictures and that's how he met my mom. On my own, I never considered my photos to be that complex or evidence of some gift or piece of art. It was only when I began to see the girls taking photos themselves that I came to believe in the power of photography and how incredible a talent the girls have when the camera is in their hands! . . . They taught me a language through which to connect not only with them but to also reconnect with my father.
>
> Only in our work with the girls have I come to understand how important it is to own this gift of photography, trust in it and share it freely. Since this recognition, I find my photography of and with Black girls to be about finding freedom and to serve as a way to let the world know we are here. When asked about the choices I make when I take photographs in SOLHOT, my answer is always very simple and short—I take photos of Black girls and women as my way of saying, "I see you and I believe in your beauty, your brilliance and your right to be here."

As long as Candy was in SOLHOT, the photographs were about art. Because she had a gift and was willing to share, we too could and did learn how to take artistic photographs. Her camera was cool, and her passion for taking pictures was irresistible. Moreover, even if she did not think she was a skilled photographer, as in formally trained, other girls who too perhaps had a more skillful eye and hand by way of some previously unacknowledged experience were recognizing themselves as good with the camera. In SOLHOT we were creating art and artists that emerged from our lived experiences.

The pictures in the anti-narrative photo-poem are the result and product of a collective SOLHOT experience. A SOLHOT site emerged particularly around photography, and it is these photos, taken by the girls and myself by way of learning from Candy, that form the basis of the anti-narrative photo-poem presented at the end of this chapter. As art, our pictures allowed us to see each other in ways that at least appeared to be more under our control. Our collective dialogue about our photographs and our lives allowed us to engage in new conversations, such as the surprise of someone proclaiming she was ugly when we all knew otherwise (and told her so). We held multiple photo exhibits for the public. We negotiated with enthusiasm how we would pose and if the space we presented our photos in was worthy of seeing us. We wrote poetry next to our photographs to tell an important story. Rarely did we literally write about what was in the picture, but we delighted in creating composites, in developing multiple nonlinear storylines that excited us and all somehow formed a cohesive statement. The taking of photographs quickly came to be identified as an expected SOLHOT practice. Furthermore, we were developing a methodology, as there became a SOLHOT way to take, display, and circulate photographs.

Photography became a beloved practice of re-searching who we are and who we were together. Even still, photography did not feel legit to Candy. But this wasn't just about Candy. This is how many of the graduate students started to feel about SOLHOT. "Are we doing what we were supposed to be doing?" they wanted to know. "Are we getting the data?" "Do we have a method?" "Are we doing it right?" "Why do you, Dr. Brown, insist on calling what we do art; won't it take away from our credibility as scholars?" These questions emerged from practice and became an entrance from which to theorize and offer a studied response to what we were and are doing in SOLHOT.

The visual representations we created in SOLHOT enabled us to learn about ourselves; they helped us to communicate with others; we resisted what was said, thought, and seen about ourselves and about other Black girls. As the founder and co-organizer of SOLHOT, I wanted to keep do-ing the work and get on to what I thought were more pressing issues and questions, but, as "the professor," I also felt a responsibility to respond to the growing concerns about methodology. My response was strategic and brief: "We are doing photovoice—go look it up." Although photovoice is a contested method, the term was academy-sponsored and would be therefore seen as "legitimate" to graduate students. It worked. We continued to take our pictures and write our stories; all the while, I knew that the way we were using photography, as a research method, was innovative and not yet named in anything I had read or in which I had been specifically trained.

DISCIPLINARY CONCERNS WITH IMAGE

In the discipline of anthropology, the camera is a common signifier of ethnographic fieldwork. Given that the method of ethnography has now taken on transdisciplinary identification, so too have discussions about ethnographic practice, as various disciplinary norms have both transformed and set up new standards about what constitutes and troubles participant observation. As a result, although taking pictures while conducting fieldwork is typically assumed as a common practice, consensus over what to do with the photographs once collected does not exist.

There are several approaches that have made the use of the photograph central to ethnography. Photovoice, visual sociology, and/or new media ethnography are just a few methods that have well documented and theorized the significance of images in the process of knowledge production. Visual sociology is primarily a subfield of qualitative sociology and related to visual ethnography as developed in anthropology through the recording, analysis, and communication of social life in photographs, film, and video (Harper, 1994). Photovoice, developed by Caroline Wang and Mary Ann Burris (1997), emerged out of their research on public health in which she relied on action-research methods that put cameras in the hands of those directly experiencing a social problem for the purpose of using those photographs to give voice to the issues of a particular community, with the goal of creating change at the level of policy. In Wang's approach, the photographs give voice to issues that were previously ignored or unjustly relegated as marginal. New-media ethnographic approaches are diverse and use still and/or moving images in the process and/or presentation of research. As technological ubiquity and accessibility have changed the landscape of communication, it should be of no surprise that researchers in the academy have also capitalized on and complicated the use of the camera as research.

Although images, primarily photographs, are typically standard in ethnographic studies, the use of the camera, and subsequent representations of who was there, is wrought with controversy. For example, although methodological advances in ethnography are widely practiced, visual forms of documentation and analysis are rarely taught and encouraged in graduate programs. As the graduate students who worked with SOLHOT suggested, taking photographs was fun but highly questionable as a methodological contribution. In early ethnographic studies, images were thought to represent the truth—the modern version of what was there (again, seeing is believing)—and as a result became a recognizable technology of imperial colonialism. Photographs were not used to provide deeper meaning but rather presented in place of description and analysis, as if the photograph could speak for itself (Berger, 1977, p. 7). In the research process, once information has been coded as data or thought of as evidence, the researcher has begun an interpretive process.

To date, researchers have taken a more reflective and critical stance on the uses of photography in knowledge production. The provocative question for Shohat (2006) is, "What happens when we reverse the conventional point of view to examine the gaze of the scientist, making it the object of critical analysis?" (p. xiii) Presumably, when the gaze of the photographer is critically acknowledged, a more complex narrative emerges that accounts for what is seen and by whom. Such a narrative provides greater possibilities for imagining multiple explanations and considerations for how that picture/image came to be. Likewise, the still image itself, the photograph, also has a narrative story. The narrative structure of photography differs from the written word, yet when the story is made explicit with words coupled with the images, the redundancy or contradiction, or all the possibilities in between, expand the range of meanings and explanations. When skillfully practiced, photographs, in company with critical analysis of their reason for being and of their creator, make it possible for the viewer to hold multiple ideas, times, spaces, and dreams in their mind's eye at the same time. As a final product, the form of what is created, even with its intellectual and academic content, may seem more like art than the traditional positivist science project. But this too is largely dependent on the gaze of the researcher.

The graduate students with whom I worked zeroed in on a long-standing debate within discussions of visual methodology. Since photography was first introduced in the field of ethnography, there has been a split between those who saw photography as description ("documentary" photography) and those who saw it as art (Harper, 1994, p. 405). Arguably, contemporary meditations on photography in the research process are no less finalized. In her photo-journal book, Ruth Behar (2007) concedes, "But looking to the discipline of Anthropology didn't give me much inspiration or guidance for how to use photographs artistically in ethnography. In fact, I learned that most anthropologists frowned up one the idea of being artistic in their use of photographs" (p. 259).

Working in tandem with professional photographer Humberto Mayol, Ruth Behar's *Island Called Home: Returning to Jewish Cuba* (2007) is innovative in its documentation of Jewish revitalization in Cuba through photography and essay. As Behar instructs, when the researcher aspires more to the arts than the sciences, it seems as if the questions about the research and the researcher's credibility multiply exponentially. According to Berger (1977), "when an image is presented as a work of art, the way people look at it is affected by a whole series of learnt assumptions about art" (p. 11). Embedded in this tension is the question, to whom does the meaning of the art properly belong—to those who can apply it to their own lives, or to a cultural hierarchy of relic specialists? (Berger, 1977). In SOLHOT, our photographs were and continue to be for us first—taken, used, and circulated by a very traceable collective of nonspecialists. I insisted they were art.

As an ethnographer of SOLHOT and scholar who, like Behar, aspires to the arts, I believe in the creation and use of images as a practice of decolonizing methodology. The camera, when used for the benefit and in service of the communities in which the images were created, can open the door for greater imaginative possibilities that extend beyond static truth claims and identity politics. Artistic applications of traditional ethnographic methods make possible the unthinkable: a strong consideration of the validity of both the tangible and intangible measures of social phenomena. In the research process, rarely is everything seen and therefore recognizable by the researcher. There are methods that account for the absences, outliers, and unknowns, and an art-based method such as the anti-narrative photo-poem is one method among many. Furthermore, the SOLHOT way of using photography made clear another obvious yet rarely acknowledged insight: Doing research can be fun and pleasurable.

ANTI-NARRATIVE PHOTO-POEM: A CREATIVE METHOD

> *We do not see those we do not know. And, in a nation suffering fierce hatred the question, race to race, man to man, and child to child, is WHO LOOK AT ME.* We answer with our lives. *Let the human eye begin unlimited embrace of human life.*
> —*Jordan,* Who Look at Me, *back book cover*

> . . .
> rse us in
> —*Philip*, Zong!, *167*

> *es the cur   se s they cu*
>   their own words

To write an anti-narrative photo-poem, I needed a guide. I sat with the photographs created in SOLHOT, and I stared at them intensely, referred to my field notes, replayed familiar voices, and acknowledged the complexity of what I had experienced. I needed a method and writing practice that would allow me to make sense of the photographs while also foregrounding much of the nonsense that went into producing photographs of Black girls in schools. I needed a strategy wherein I could present back to the girls of SOLHOT a story that was accountable to what I heard in our conversations and silences. I wanted this analysis to do double work—to speak to the girls of their beauty, and to talk back to the authorizing voices that refused to see them. I very much wanted to acknowledge my own voice as the author of the final story presented in this chapter while recognizing the varied and significant collaborations and contributions of those in SOLHOT, without which this story could not have been produced. It seemed to me that the story I yearned to tell had to work well on paper but could also be easily translated into a visual performance piece, so much so that readers could imagine themselves as active audience participants. As discussed earlier in the chapter, the work and methodological contributions of June Jordan and M. Nourbese Philip provided primary references. Their respective books, *Who Look at Me* (Jordan, 1969) and *Zong!* (Philip, 2008), served both as an analytical and methodological template from which I could set out to do what I envisioned and also challenged me to own my artistry.

Norman Denzin (1994) noted that women-of-color poststructural interpretive styles call into question much of what now passes for truth in methodological discourse (p. 510). Denzin's observation is confirmed when we consider Jordan and Philip as women-of-color methodologists who, to the detriment of ideas, are not often recognized as such. In particular, Jordan's text makes possible a systematic learning of how to cross-write (in my case, to recognize the fluidity between Black girlhood and womanhood, my voice, and the girls in SOLHOT), build a mutually constructive relationship between image and words, and remain honest (a signature of Jordan's writing style). When skillfully read and applied, Jordan's *Who Look at Me*, as well as the vast numbers of short stories, essays, and poems she has written over the years, proves instructive for how to write in a way that moves the reader to participate, to act. Astute readers of Jordan's work must not only engage their senses to grasp the full meaning of the text, but they must also be moved to action. Her work, as with the anti-narrative photo-poem presented in the next section, asks of reader-witnesses to answer with their lives.

Beyond methods, accounting for Black girls' and women's lived experience also transforms. Carole Boyce Davies (1994, p. 3) wrote that once Black women's experience is accounted for, assumptions about identity, community, and theory have to be reconsidered. Davies (1994, p. 36) offered the concept of "migratory subjectivity" to define how the subject positions of Black women writers are not just constituted but, in being constituted, have multiple identities that do not always make for harmony. She wrote, "In the same way as diaspora assumes expansiveness and elsewhereness, so too do migrations of the Black female subjectivity" (Davies, 1994, p. 37). Then and at once, we may understand what it means to exist within multiple realms simultaneously, challenging space and time as fixed notions. The knowledge created from an examination of how we belong, or not, to many communities in various ways is important to how people make sense of their lives while making space for senselessness to also hold a place of significance. Philip's work becomes a prime exemplar from which to interrogate how Black women writers are able to transcend and transmit the kind of subjectivity that is beholden to multiple times, spaces, ideas, and audiences. In *Zong!* (2008), Philip does not include the images used as research transcribed in her poetic telling; instead, what she does exceedingly well is intentionally tell a story that does not make sense. Her work is instructive in that it resists the call to sense making that is so dominant in academic inquiry. Some things are uncertain, and preserving the uncertainty in the retelling of events is not only admirable—it is also a skill that can be learned and taught. It was Philip's work that allowed the "anti-narrative" of my own analysis to emerge and have a valued place in the story that has been ultimately created.

In analyzing the methodology of Jordan's and Philip's work together, concepts such as cross-writing with images and spatial interventions on the page may be used as a foundation on the path to understanding how interpretive writing may be applied to create new avenues of knowing and unknowing, transforming static and binary renderings of authorial power. The altered form of Jordan's *Who Look at Me*—paintings (painted by notable and not-so-known artists) and Jordan's continuum of a poem or disjointed poetic fragments, depending on how you look at it—demonstrated her early commitment to truth-telling plain Black speech with a Black girl/woman touch. Jordan acknowledges that the idea of writing to the specific paintings published in the book belonged to historian and children's author Milton Meltzer. Yet the way she executed "cross-writing" resulted in an aesthetic that Jordan would come to embrace (and perfect) throughout her writing career. Richard Flynn (2002) noted that a "cross-writer" writes for both adults and children, conveys adult and child concerns dialogically, and theorizes childhood in relation to historical and material concerns. He rightfully contended:

> Jordan's writing, for children, for adults, and across what are ultimately artificial adult–child boundaries recognizes the limits of the confessional and rejects the "bleached speech" of a therapeutic culture in favor of living language. By crossing genres, by recognizing the relationships between history and politics and the personal, and by promoting discovery rather than foreclosure, Jordan delineates a poetics that combats the regressive tropes of childhood embedded deep within the culture and proposes new tropes that may well be revolutionary. (Flynn, 2002, p. 138)

Jordan's ability to use Black-girl language and convey Black-woman wisdom is especially revolutionary and also revelatory. Many scholars of Black-girlhood studies and Black feminism contend that there exists a specific kind of fluidity between markers of Black girlhood and Black womanhood, as a result of a political economy that forces the young to assume great responsibility in terms of working outside of the home and fighting to maintain a sense of self in a context that diminishes Blackness and femininity. In response, many older Black women seek to reclaim a girlhood that was denied and/or stolen, sometimes through a singular speech act of referring to each other in moments of tenderness as "gurl."

Who Look at Me transforms any sentimental impulse typically attached to childhood memoir into a complex, rhythmic text that impels the proper action—of looking and responding with love. It encourages an honest love that simultaneously enables those who would paint a people Black or white, along with those whom the world forgot could say yes and no, to always live. Simultaneously, June Jordan intervenes in the visual technology of the West to categorically reject the passivity (and therefore dehumanizing) of the one being seen. Intervening in the West's sight-centrism, she reminds the reader that knowingness comes by the kind of practice that requires "answering with our lives," a wholehearted and embodied engagement of multiple senses that promotes an embrace of humanity and living.

In Philip's *Zong!* (2008), based on the legal decision *Gregson v. Gilbert* (1783), Philip offers a senseless and meaningful representation of 150 murdered Africans who were thrown overboard a ship named *Zong* so that the owners could collect insurance monies. The legal document of the court case is the only known existing documentation of the tragic incident, yet Philip courageously relies on memory and water to recall how navigational errors of *Zong*, carrying 470 enslaved Africans en route to Jamaica, made possible the insurance claim that enabled the insurers to receive payment (to "recover their loss") for the "destroyed cargo" (Philip, 2008, pp. 189, 116). Philip, a trained lawyer, sat with the legal documents in Vermont to fashion a novel about *Zong* but became convinced that poetry was more suitable because it allowed for "the mystery of evil" of the event to persist (p. 190). She wrote, "A novel requires too much telling . . . and this story must be told by not telling" (p. 190)—convincing the reader that we too bear a certain responsibility to answer and to witness the unfathomable.

Philip's anti-narrative in poetic form intentionally documents the contradiction and complexity of that fateful and destined event through a particular writing style that offers praises to "water of want" to initiate remembrance of "the disorder, illogic and irrationality of the Zong!" (p. 4). She utilizes the power of poetry formatted on the page to intervene as the story came to her, warning that "poems can no more tell the story than the legal report of Gregson vs. Gilbert masquerading as order, logic, and rationality" (p. 197). The form and content of Philip's excerpted poem that opens this section demonstrates just how well she succeeded to "break and enter the text to release its antimeaning (p. 200), noting particularly the use of space, silence, separation, and movement to convey meaning and less meaning. Philip's spatial intervention with the written word on the flat page is brilliant and also characteristic of other exiled women who relay their experience with multiple displacements in their writing (Morrell, 1994).

At the end of the book's poetic journey, Philip leaves the reader with an anchor, a reflection on the particular methodology used to share such a powerful story. She wrote,

> When I start spacing out the words, there is something happening in the eye tracking the words across the page, working to pull the page and the larger "meaning" together—the eye trying to order what cannot be ordered, trying to "make sense" of something. (p. 192)

Complete with rigorous methodological reflection and glossary of "words and phrases heard on Board the Zong" (p. 183), Philip's text is valid in its refusal of meaning making. It should not be an easy read, and it is not. To engage Philip's text respectfully, the reader must do the work or risk collusion with those who profited. Taken together, the works of Jordan and Philip provide a rich and complex foundation for using poetry and image to tell a story, even those stories that can't be told.

Furthermore, both Jordan and Philip are of Caribbean descent, with strong familial ties to Jamaica and Trinidad. Specificities of Caribbean culture are significantly tied to their parents' homeland, as well as to North America. In their study of second-generation Caribbean-Canadian spoken-word artists, Flynn and Marrast (2008) argue that in the process of making and producing art, diasporic border crossings result in the important naming of experiences, claiming space, and negotiating and redefining their identity in ways that are contested, contradictory, transgressive, and counterhegemonic. Focusing on spoken-word artists/performers while also acknowledging the generation of artists and poets that preceded them, including Philip, they argued:

> These artists engage in the process of border crossing, borrowing from other Black artistic forms to create and produce a syncretic and hybridized mix revealing certain affiliations and continuities in terms of broader diasporic concerns. Simultaneously, through their work and performances, these artists produce new cultural forms that acknowledge the specificity of their unique subject position as Black Canadians. (Flynn and Marrast, 2008, p. 4)

Language becomes a critical signifier of migratory subjectivities. How one is known as a thinking person is inherently tied to communication, written and oral. A proponent of Black English, Jordan has notoriously written and acted on behalf of interrogating the cultural imperatives of diverse literacies. In her essay "Problems of Language in a Democratic State," Jordan (1985) argued that because Standard English remains the enforced standard in not only the state and business world, but also in education, it encourages a lack of accountability and perpetuates an epistemology of ignorance. So what kinds of language insist on accountability? Philip turns to poetry, a form perfected by Jordan as well. For Philip, by subverting the very purpose of language— comprehension—poetry as a form makes it possible to speak in one's own tongue, thereby pushing against the boundaries of language (Philip, 2008, p. 197). How Jordan and Philip came to know what they know and articulate is demonstrative of the very best methodological practices.

At the end of the day, I used poetry to create a textual conversation with SOLHOT photos to invent a new story of Black girlhood. Because I was there with the girls when that woman came in and attempted to deny them a sense of self, I felt the senselessness of the event. However, at the time, I did not have the words to explain why that moment was both familiar and spectacular. At that moment I just wanted to be there with the girls, as this is the primary investment of SOLHOT—to remind Black girls that we are right here with you.

The moment stayed with me, haunted me even. Philip taught me that it was necessary to remember the event and to keep company with it, as a means of resistance. Jordan inspired me to write a text that would also be a call to action. I wrote what happened, voiced what we as Black girls and women knew about what occurred, and allowed the senselessness of it all to remain present. It is an unsatisfying poem at best, but one that I hope moves the audience to action and further conversation.

The anti-narrative photo-poem presents a new way of seeing Black girls, produced by being with the girls in SOLHOT week after week, making photography and building relationships. I wrote this poem while sorting through the literal thousands of images made in SOLHOT. I wrote alone, in meditation, and I had to become skillful in the balancing of voices, theirs and my own. I performed the poem out loud, when invited to speak, and I read it differently every time. After each performance of the poem, silence ensues. Bodies uncomfortably shift in seats; people stop playing/working on their smart phones, sleepy heads awake, and eyebrows transform shapes, all indications that the poem works. The silence mimics the silence of the girls' response to the woman at the school, and the audience becomes implicated, as witnesses. The rethinking of Black girlhood begins with thoughtful questions and sincere concern.

THE ANTI-NARRATIVE PHOTO-POEM

When Black

girls

look at you.

when Black girls look at

you.

you called my name

                                                    I answered.

DON'T GET MAD!
                              you asked.
                                                    I answered.
                              you called.
                                                    I looked.
          and now.
                                        you

                                                                just

                                        don't
                                        know
what

                                                                              to
                                                                              do.
Do you?

                                   Reeeeelaaaxxxx.

                                                                              Dang!
(what is your problem?)
left unsaid
                        but
                                        I continue

                                        to see you.

          I'm smiling …..

                                                                knowin' what
                                                        you
                                        don't see

          She said genius?

          Dead silence.

          Yup Genius!
                        in me.

really, I don't know why or how you got this position.

but I ain't gon' let it
stop

my shine . . .

or my girls, either. cuz we just too cute.

heheheh

Intelligent.

hehehehe

Loved.

And cared

for ....
....
...so we survive

Cold metal lockers
And uhhhhh what is dis?? (disgusted)

most of the day.

Till we fall into
Hugs and homework.
Tired mamas
And working daddies.

And bein' everyone's everything and doin' this and that for my grandma
CUZ
That's what you supposed to do for someone
you love.
Don't   you   know   that?   ?   ?   ?

well trust me

then why you

yellin'

Dang!

You be trippin'

And I ain't gonna speak …. cuz you not worth my swagg.

can't you

you can't
See me.
See me.
See me.
Dang!

If I had to shoot me
         to show you
what I have to live for

                      I would do it.
                      With RAISED
              FIST!

PROUD.
hand on hip.

              You know what that mean . . .

uh huuuhhh yeh watch me do dis and juke it like dat and hahha
hhaaahhaa hahh haaaa

grl . . .

                    she don't knw
                'bout dat. Hahhh ahha
              stop.

      Stop!

            Stop playin' .....

10

dang!

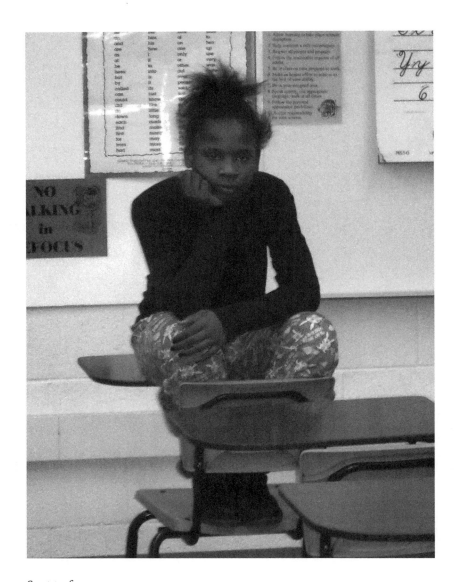

Sent to focus

again. Focus on YOU. To see
more clearly . . . maybe. What you
want me to do.

Not laugh.
Not love.
Not be.
Me.
Black.
    Why   you   gotta
move me.
Black girl.

                Why   you

    gotta send me D
        O
           W

              N

                                here.
Away.

                        I'm 13 years old.

    Why you
gotta s   e
    p   a
        r
                 a   t
    e   me from everybody else?
Knowing something

                        Why you tryna

make me be quiet.
                  I am not

    Why you takin' me out?

dumb.

                   I will take this

camera
And SHOOT!

               I already know how to

use
it
    duh.

and I know

you won't like dis.

Let me see.

Yup.

I want you to see me here.

Focusing again.

on the price my mama gotta pay for milk.
    on the price I gotta pay for you to look at me.
        on the price i gotta pay to be loved in school.

It ain't

free.

but it's fun.

Sometimes.

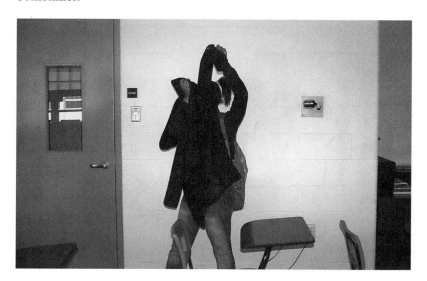

Waitttttt!

Wait. Wait. Wait. Wait. Wait. Wait. Wait. Wait. Wait. Wait. Wait.

WAIIIITTTTTT!

WAAAAAAA ITTTTTT!

I saidDDDDDDDDDDDDD
                    Hold Up!

I got

        Gotta

             I just gotta
Wait a min ...

        A min ...

                            Can you hold on please?

        Dang!

                            I said I'm almost ready I just
Got to
        Gotta

                            Got to do

        Do

    My

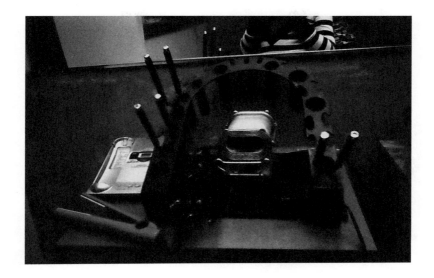

hair.

And if you don't know this, then you don't know nothin'.

so waddd up?

w   hooooo you lookin' for?

                                           Who?

you wanna see?

                       Oh   YOU
                             tryna see
Her?

                                           Why?

(no answer.)

                                                        Dang.

did you see that?

           Yeah, i heard about it.

I wanna see her too.

                           She my cousin!

No. for real.

Ha hahaha.

Yeah she pretty!   Yup.

      She wassssn't no scary chick.

           I was kinda

Scared of her.

Shhhhhhhhhhhhhhhhhhh!

I thought she was an excellent listener.

               She was MAD!

ANGRY at you about that!

      shiddddddd. she was pissed the fuck off about that!

         You

made

her mad.

      And you ain't her mama.

          And you ain't even say sorry.

            I think she

   um....

Well.. I don't know.

       (looks around) wondering who gon'

say sumthin' first.

      Um, dang! YOU GO.

NO. YOU GO!

          OK. Wait.

Aiiiiiiiiiiiiiiiigggggggghhhhhhhhhhhhhhhhhhhhhhhhhhhhhttttttttttttt

      T!

          dang.

                        She
    gone.
                                                    Expelled.
        She
                        gone.
                                                    A fight.
        She   gone.
                                                    Moved.
    Again.
        She

                        gone.
                                                    Used her other
    mother address so she can go to a new school.
        She

            gone.
                                                    Alternative

        School: called GO!   Get. Ready. Set.
        She   gone.
                                                    Don't nobody
    know.
        She
            gone.
                                                    This was
    wack.
        She
        gone.
                                                    Needed to take
        care of herself.
        She gone.
                                                    Said it was too
    much drama.
        She gone.
                                                    You kicked
    her out.

She gone.

                                        Disappeared.

She gone.

                                        Couldn't

come, had to take care of the kids.
She gone.

                                        At the Juve.

She gone.

                                        At the Club.

She gone.

so you can't see her.

oh now you wanna feel a certain way?
                    whateva.

                                        i created this.

4 Bad Days
"If You Hit Me, I'm Gonna Hit You Back"

Black girlhood should not be a fight.

Stories about fighting, violence, and punishment frequently emerged in the interview transcripts of SOLHOT girls.[1] When I asked them to tell me about their good and bad days, all of their bad-day stories were about fighting and punishment. Mostly they talked about fights between girls and acts of violence that resulted in some kind of disciplinary action. The reports and dramatic reenactments of fights along with the subsequent regret, pride, and remorse were retold as an everyday occurrence. Their detailed accounts about fighting were especially prominent because the girls responded so briefly to all other questions.

Before going over the transcripts, I had not for a moment desired to write about fighting and Black girlhood. I did not want to talk about Black girls and fighting because it seems so, well, predictable. Fighting, typically framed in the research (and therefore also in educational policy) as a "behavioral problem," is nonproductive. Also, I did not want to invoke mythologies of personal responsibility or stereotypes of inner-city violent Black girls. Fighting Black girls are commonly sensed to be in deficit, lacking in character and home training, and quite honestly I just did not want to go there.

1 The interviews were conducted during their sixth and seventh grades. The girls ranged in age between eleven and thirteen. Eight girls were interviewed the first year. Out of these eight, five of the same girls were interviewed the next year. Twelve interviews were conducted in total. Of the two girls who were not interviewed, one moved out of town and the other was absent on the day the interviews were conducted. All of the girls identify as African American. A transcriptionist transcribed all of the interviews. The second year, a graduate student conducted the interviews, and they were all transcribed by a research assistant (a different graduate student). In the transcripts presented in this chapter, I (Ruth Nicole Brown) am identified by I2, and the homegirl is identified by I.

Researchers currently writing about girls and fighting share a similar concern with the lackluster ways Black girls, girls of color, and inner-city youth
were previously framed in academic accounts. In *Why Girls Fight: Female
Youth Violence in the Inner City*, Cindy Ness (2010) persuasively documents
fighting as a necessity survival mechanism for those who grow up in low-
income urban neighborhoods and gives attention to how mother-daughter
relationships influence girls' behavior. Careful to not blame mothers, Ness
(*ibid.*, p. 91) identifies a "double-generation dynamic" at play when mothers
and grandmothers who grew up with the need to defend themselves in the
public sphere encourage their daughters to do the same. Beyond sociological
influences, Lyn Brown (2003) argues that misogynist and patriarchal messages
embedded in popular media normalize fights between girls at the expense of
showcasing solidarity and the power of sisterhood that are also a vital part
of same-gender relationships among girls of all races and backgrounds. Both
Ness and Brown speak back to disciplinary conventions while maintaining that
fighting is a completely responsible outcome in a completely less-than-ideal
social and cultural context that marginalizes girls and women.

The literature on positive youth development cites violence-prevention
programs, mentoring, caring relationships with adults, and recreational programs as practical solutions to the problem of youth violence, each promising various amounts of success (Jones et al., 2009; Rhodes, Bogat, Roffman,
Edelman, & Gallasso, 2002). In regard to African American girls, Jody Miller
(2008) suggested that relationships with caring adults is critical to addressing violence against girls in disadvantaged communities because they are so
routinely blamed for their victimization; strong individuals who are genuinely concerned can facilitate disclosure, challenge the insidious message
that they are at fault, and guide them to available resources and programs
for assistance (p. 213). Programming is the typical recommendation to stop
fighting, acknowledged as common adolescent behavior (Cotton et al., 1994,
Talbott et al., 2002). In Saving Our Lives Hear Our Truths, there is no pro-
grammatic response to fighting. Furthermore, situated in a small urban city
surrounded by agriculture and farmland, girls in SOLHOT live in a place
often constructed as the opposite of (and therefore better than) the inner city
because of its imagined relative lack of violence. However, for the girls and
homegirls in SOLHOT who frequently travel between urban and non-urban
spaces, violence and fighting are unavoidable, endemic to living under white
supremacy, capitalism, and patriarchy. In lieu of radical systemic transformation, programs and services offered as practical solutions to curbing violence
provide short-term refuge, with the quality and kind of relief provided almost

always dependent on people with the creative capacity to build relationships in spite of dwindling social-service provisions, and with a political consciousness that resists victimizing those they serve.

During SOLHOT, we talk about fights, and we do not talk about fights. The girls bring their stories about fights of all kinds. They talk about who fought over the weekend and whom they are going to fight next. They talk about who got beat up and their experiences of being jumped. Sometimes, we hear about fights that happened at home, among family. Those that like to fight pride themselves on their abilities. The nonfighters remain observant. On a few occasions, the girls have come to SOLHOT with activities they devised, organized, and led to address fighting. While there have not been any physical altercations in SOLHOT, we have witnessed many an exchange of violent words. Rather than peer mediation, or being sent to an administrator's office, some girls use SOLHOT as a means to resolve their issues with other "females." SOLHOT does not have a party line.

Reading through pages and pages of interview transcripts, it was the stories about fighting that elicited the most emotion and instigated extended voluntary narration. Fighting takes up and demands a tremendous amount of the girls' energy. Their stories suggest negativity and criminalization are commonplace. As Black girls, they must give a lot of attention to fighting, as they are seemingly always on guard. The tacit wisdom regularly shared in SOLHOT that it is never the one who started the fight but the one who acts in self-defense that is caught and subsequently punished is also casually mentioned after the interview's end. In the presence of these very same girls, I delight in their genius; their brilliance is tough. Everything about fighting is the polar opposite of how I know them to be in SOLHOT. The juxtaposition jars.

The girls' bad days remind me that we are all complicit, and so, we write.

Our responses to the girls' stories, lived experiences, and fantastic tales about fighting are emotional and take a poetic form. Poetry makes it possible to speak uncensored, challenge misperceptions about young people of color, and extend necessary conversations that remain in the heart of those who listened, well after the last verse was spoken (Jocson, 2008). We write poetry in the privacy of our own sanctuary because we love the girls, because we are the kind of people who journal, and because we find comfort in words written about uncomfortable situations. We write because, like most laborers, the work stays with us. It stains our hands and changes our physicality, mentality, and heart. When we are feeling courageous, we share our poems publically and perform. More than documenting the sad, tragic, uncertain, and unexplainable, through performance, we testify. Performance creates a space for us, the girls, our families, our friends, and the larger public to come, gather, and know that someone is listening, is right there with them, is still struggling over the very same issues as they are. When we perform, we want the girls to know that we've heard them. We write to try out another perspective. We perform to show ourselves another way. It is the performance of poetry that comes out of our nonpoet selves that make possible counterintuitive thoughts, so necessary to the practice of freedom. The bad-day stories do not sit well, and poetry does not behave, so I try—actually, in SOLHOT we all try—to reclaim them with love.

ONE

INTERVIEWER: So, tell us about a day where you had a really good time at school.

NICKIE:[2] Let me see. I don't recall one.

I: What about a time you had a really bad time at school?

NICKIE: Okay, when I was about to get jumped.

I: What happened?

NICKIE: I don't know. They just don't like me, but now they do.

I: How do you know they were going to jump you?

NICKIE: Because girls in this group told me they were part of it.

I: They tricked you?

NICKIE: That day, I had told Mama, before I was knowing they were gonna fight me, because they were planning for a long time. So, I told my mama that people wanted to jump me, and my mom—she didn't come up to the school right away, because she was working and going to school and stuff. So, when she asked the day that they were gonna really, really jump me, I didn't know—my mama just showed up, though, and it was at the end of the day. They were all standing right there, waiting for me to come outside. I was walking outside, and my mama snatched me. She didn't snatch me, but she grabbed me, 'cause I didn't see her. She brung me to the main office, and then she talked to the dean. And then the girls said something like, "I don't even know why she want her mama to come out here, 'cause her mama could get it, too." These girls—

I: These girls went to—they go here?

NICKIE: Yeah.

2 All girls' names used in this chapter are pseudonyms.

I: The girls that fought Mariah?
NICKIE: Mm-hmm.
I: Why do you think they singled you out?
NICKIE: I don't know.
I: So, are y'all friends now?
NICKIE: No.

TWO

TINA: This girl kept trying to fight me, and we almost fought one day, and I almost got suspended. It's all over now, but—
I: You knew her?
TINA: Yeah.
I: Why was she trying to fight you?
TINA: Over some instigating stuff. I was like, "Well, if you want to fight, let's fight."
I: Oh, so y'all did start fighting?
TINA: We almost. She was in my face, and I was in her face. So, we almost did.
I: Do y'all get along now, or—
TINA: Yes.

THREE

TIANA: When my friend said—well, I'm not gonna say her name—but she went back and told all these people that I said stuff about them, and I said—I might have said it. I didn't say nothing bad about them, but I spoke their name up, and it was stuff bad that they did, but I never said nothing about them. She went back and told them. That was a day that—one of the associates didn't like me, but he might have still talked to me. That's all that matters, because I say if you don't want to get people telling 'em stuff, then you need to confront it with the person who they said it, instead of just getting an attitude right then.
I: Right and going off of what people say.
TIANA: So, I didn't care. I was still smiling.
I: After they tried talking to you and stuff?
TIANA: Mm-hmm.
I: So, you didn't get in trouble or anything?

TIANA: I was bored. I was upset, because I feel like they'll talk to me the next day and y'all was just trying to gang up on me, talking about me, talking about I said something about you. Then, the next day they're talking to me. I think that's kind of fake.

FOUR

ALEIA: Me and Tanay got to arguing, and I had to go to detention 'cause I just wanted to hit her.

1: What was y'all arguing about?

ALEIA: 'Cause . . . she just got to looking at me, and she was talking about me. She told somebody not to talk to me. I asked her, and she said—then the person that she told me that she did. And then we got to arguing and stuff. Then, after that I hit her.

1: Did you mean it?

ALEIA: Yes.

1: You landed—I didn't know.

ALEIA: And then she go tell me to hit her. I was gonna hit her, and the teacher got in the way and so then I had to go to detention.

12: Just for the day?

1: Did detention help?

ALEIA: Mm-mm . . . in the morning we was gonna fight, 'cause I was like, "If you hit me, I'm gonna hit you back, we're just gonna get going at it." And then she brought it to me, and then I put my hands to her and then she gonna just sit there and get all up in my face. It just got ugly.

1: So, what happened? Are y'all friends now? So, what happened?

ALEIA: We both talked it out after all that stuff happened, and that was it. And then we made up.

This is when the fighting began
I was not yet two years old.
June Jordan (2001, p. 14)

In her memoir, *Soldier: A Poet's Childhood*, June Jordan described fighting as the definitive activity of her Black girlhood. For many Black girls, including Jordan, soldier is a choice metaphor. Soldiering implies many things, most obviously war. To battle, soldiers often have to leave home, home assumed to be a place of safety and comfort, for the battlefield, the supposed unknown. Fatigue, posttraumatic stress disorder, and death describe the more injurious possibilities of soldiering. Soldiers, enlisted to do the work of the state, also signify duty, honor, patriotism, and nationalism. Fighting is what soldiers do.

Fighting was the definitive activity around which Jordan's selfhood and community space were built. Jordan fought everyone, physically and with her words. In the intimate space of home, fighting was prominent and implicated abuse. Fighting was also invoked as a way to negotiate space outside of her home. Fighting occupied her school memories and community interactions. It was above all else how she came to self-identify and how others identified her, as a fighter.

According to Jordan, her father taught her how to fight beginning at two years of age. He provided her with daily training. Jordan's father taught her how to fight because he wanted a boy. Jordan (2001, p. 41–42) wrote,

> I had to practice a complicated litany of manly virtues and combat skills.
> You never took your eyes off your opponent.
> You never showed any weakness or admitted to any pain
> You watched for every opening to strike or to defend yourself . . .
> The point was to stay on the alert.
> The point was not to be beaten . . .

Jordan makes the case that fighting as a girl was a way to resist all that it meant to be socialized as feminine. Granville, Jordan's father, had hoped that as a Black girl fighter, his daughter could more easily access the illusory promises of white male privilege. This is consistent with the research of Nikki Jones, who found that by the time a girl is known as a fighter, she has embraced an identity that directly contradicts expectations of normative femininity, but it also makes her more vulnerable to retaliation (Jones, 2010). As a fighting Black girl, Jordan wrote that her father's intentions were well-meaning though misguided. Fighting did not actually translate into transcending Blackness and femininity so much as it provided a short-term outlet for her frustrations over restrictive and unjust identity politics. Jordan loved her father, and he loved her. Nevertheless, Jordan penned this causal and casual explanation of her father's tenacity in raising a soldier: "Probably it seemed easier to change me than to change the meaning and complexion of power" (2000, p. 18). How can we change the meaning and complexion of power to absolve Black girls of fighting and violence?

If power were transformed on a structural level, fighting would not take up as much space as it currently does in the personal lives of Black girls. If power were the target of change, rather than individual Black girls, they would not have to service their body as the site of change on which everyone else inscribes their own version of justice and survival. So much of Black girlhood, even if one did not grow up a soldier or fought in the same ways as Jordan, is about the fight. As Valerie Kinloch (2006, p. 9) acknowledged, "Jordan fought, literally, for her life in her parents' Bedford-Stuyvesant house as well as out in the racist world that she sought to change—and sought to change her." In SOLHOT, the stories girls share about fighting encourage us to do as Jordan preferred—to transform power.

SOLHOT wants you to know and remember June Jordan.

S.U.R.V.I.V.O.R.[3]

> *All characters enter dark stage*
>
> *V1, V2, and V3 enter and deliver lines at will*

V1, V2, V3: Imma survivor I'm not gon' give up. I'm not go' stop, I'm go' work harder. Imma survivor I'm gonna make it. I will survive and keep on surviving. Imma survivor I'm not gon' give up. I'm not gon' stop, I'm gon' work harder. Imma survivor I'm gonna make it. I will survive and keep on surviving.

> *Spotlight on V1*

V1: I am a survivor, yes Survivor

> *Spotlight on V2*

V2: I am a survivor, yes a Survivor

> *Spotlight on V3*

V3: I am a survivor, yes a Survivor

> *Lights up*

ALL V'S: We are survivors, YES Survivors

V1: Look at me! See my war scars! I have been to Iraq yet I have not left this country. I wake up, get dressed, get my siblings dressed, and I'm out the door. Out into to the war zone. Ready to fight because fighting is what I have to do. Ready to fight because . . .

3 Written by Porshe Garner.

V2 AND V3: Fighting is not a choice.

V1: Not a choice when I have to go to school, do homework, and study for tests with virtually no help. Because no one at home understands this work.

V2: Get a good look at my war scars! I'm angry and confused, but of course everyone thinks it's just my Black girl attitude. Not once have you stopped to ask me about me! A harmless Black girl. So this is my war stance and look. I have to protect myself and be ready to fight because . . .

V1 and V3: Fighting is not a choice.

V2: Fighting is not a choice when I am dealing with things you didn't have to deal with when you were a student. I'm just trying to make it to school and back safely! Who knows what student will come to school today upset and decide to take it out on us all. Or what police officer will mistake me for a burglar and kill me dead.

V3: Get a good look at my war scars! Don't I make this look great! I make an entrance into any place with my head held high because of who and whose I am. Do you? I am brilliant, beautiful, brave, and of course a fighter. This is my war stance. I have to protect myself and be ready to fight because . . .

V1 AND V2: Fighting is not a choice.

V3: Fighting is not a choice because Some people do not want me here. And guess what? That heightens my motivation. I am a fighter. I don't give up. I won't quit. I can't quit. Because winning is what we do!! Winning is probably what some of you don't wanna see me do.

V1, V2, V3: Winning is what we do! King Kong ain't got nothing on

V2: ME

V3: Her

V1: She

V1, V2, V3: US

All characters exit stage.

Destiny Child's 1995 hit single "Survivor" and the girls' stories of fighting inspired this homegirl's poem. For many Black girls in SOLHOT, soldier is not only their choice metaphor of Black girlhood, but fighting to survive is understood as the definitive organizing system of Black girlhood. Fighting is the discourse middle-school girls use to discuss issues as old as they are apocryphal. Power. Self-definition. Personhood. Self-defense. Survival.

Self-determination. As indicated in the choreopoem, Black girls cannot take girlhood for granted and by extension cannot assume a structural response of protection, as it has never been available. Given the oppressive conditions of Black girlhood and womanhood, survival, as many Black feminists have articulated, is a daily struggle (Collins, 1991; Lorde, 1995).

State negligence in assuring the protection and survival of Black youth is explicitly recognized in "S.U.R.V.I.V.O.R." as a culprit. Referencing local and national events of school and community violence—"Who knows what student will come to school today upset and decide to take it out on us all. Or what police officer will mistake me for a burglar and kill me dead"—the choreopoem identifies that travel to and from school, an otherwise mundane event, exists for Black youth as a life-or-death event. That death could come at the hands of a police officer is a reality SOLHOT girls know well. On Friday afternoon, October 9, 2009, police fatally shot an unarmed fifteen-year-old African American young man named Kiwane Carrington (Dolinar, 2009). Carrington was a friend to many of the girls who participated in SOLHOT, and his fate was understood as linked to their own.[4] Nikki Jones offers the concept of "Ghetto survivors" to describe adolescent inner-city girls who develop innovative and effective strategies to ensure the basic need of survival that many of their middle-class counterparts take for granted (Chesney-Lind and Jones, 2010, p. 215). Fighting is one such strategy.

"S.U.R.V.I.V.O.R." represents how transnationalism and diaspora matter to Black girls who live in a small urban city in the middle of the United States and more frequently, due to constraints of capital, age, race, class, and gender, experience confinement than mobility. "I have been to Iraq yet I have not left this country" offers Black girlhood as a specific, local, and urgent site of struggle. Home, school, and abroad are noted governmentalities whose indifference toward Black girlhood refuses any sense of safety. Incite! Women of Color Against Violence (2006, p. 2) named the challenge women of color face in combating personal *and* state violence and the development of strategies for ending violence that *do* assure safety for survivors of sexual/domestic violence and *do not* strengthen our oppressive criminal-justice apparatus. The complexity overwhelms us all, but SOLHOT's utilization of performance offers possibility.

---

4 For more on linked-fate theory (originally used to explain Black voting behavior and preferences), see Michael Dawson (1994).

Jordan (1995, p. 8) instructed,

> If you dream and scheme about the self-evident, as well as the potential, reasons why public performance, publication, and media appearances are natural and necessary steps to the acquirement of power through language.
>
> Then: You will probably find yourself launched in an unpredictable nerve-racking and marvelous adventure in democracy and education.

Performed as a part of "A Black Girls' Song," a theatrical performance written and performed by SOLHOT girls and homegirls, this piece "S.U.R.V.I.V.O.R." in particular was written by a homegirl and co-performed with two girls. There are very few people in SOLHOT who think themselves poets and performers. Yet performance gives the homegirls the time needed to make sense of what is heard in SOLHOT and to offer a response that, regardless of impact or effect, is honest. Victim, aggressor, and perpetrator are all present and accounted for as audience and performers. Homegirls put their bodies on the line to honor what girls share in SOLHOT, especially when it is about fighting. Performance gives us the space to say to the girls and the audiences they bring with them: This is what we heard, this is what I believe, and let's keep the conversation going. Performing poetry is courageous and powerful.

Homegirls perform poetry by themselves and/or with the girls because—in our fifty-five minutes of fame—we can author our stories, name our problems, and propose solutions with a sophisticated intentionality of how we make it public. When we respond to girls' stories of fighting in a publically poetic form, homegirls want them to know that we love them and believe that Black girls deserve protection and care that is not patronizing nor patriarchal. Even if we don't know what the solution looks like exactly, poetry gets us closer. In Maisha T. Winn's (2011) study of the Girl Time theater program for incarcerated and formerly incarcerated girls, she interviewed Julisa, a teaching artist who performed with the girls and concluded, "when she gave her all, the girls gave theirs" (p. 65). Effective as a method of solidarity, homegirls' poetic responses relate to the girls, connect the state and the personal, and address the usual problem and a differently proposed solution.

"S.U.R.V.I.V.O.R." suggests that freedom does exist; even amidst constraining circumstances of "no choice" and even still, we Black girls make it look good. In this poem, as in life, it is possible for Black girls to win in a game of no choice. The relationship between homegirls and girls as revealed in the choreopoem allows us all to go "beyond mere survival to speculate about liberation" (James, 1996, p. 22). How beautiful is that?

FIVE

> 1: Why do most Black kids get in fights?
>
> ALEIA: Because they don't like each other.

SIX

> KEISHA: I like school but, some things and some things and some
> people in the school, I don't like. And I just try to find a way of run-
> nin', but I don't think that works.
>
> 12: So, what are some of the things and people you don't like?
>
> KEISHA: Some people is like some of the teachers and some of the
> teachers like, I'm not gon' say names and stuff because of some of the
> teachers . . .
>
> 1: It's okay.
>
> KEISHA: But, some of the teachers they just don't understand me. Like
> I always say to the dean or the counselor that they don't understand
> me or I don't understand them and we don't understand each other
> and I get sent to detention or they call the dean to talk to me and I get
> angry with what she say and I either go to detention or have to spend
> my lunch in detention or have to go home.
>
> 12: What don't they understand about you?
>
> KEISHA: About like, when I like, when something goes wrong, I try to
> tell them or I take it into my own hands and I get caught and I try to
> them and I try to explain what happened, they don't they, they don't
> listen and they just, okay I'mma go to detention right out and then
> write me a referral cuz I get mad and upset and I tell, not ahh not ahh
> and I get angry and I be disrespectful to them because they don't lis-
> ten to me and they just send me to detention without even listening.
> And I had to go to detention. And that makes me mad when they say,
> "detention, detention, detention." I'm tired of going to detention and
> tryna be and tryin' my best not to go to detention.

SEVEN

> TINA: 'Cause most teachers—if you go up to her and be like, "Hey,
> I've got a problem," and they be like, "Well, you need to go to a peer
> leader," and don't nobody always want to go to that.

~◇~

"She was afraid to look at herself just yet" is the breathtaking opening line in
Toni Cade Bambara's (1982) "A Girl's Story." In this story, the reader is introduced to the main character, a Black girl named Rachel Ann (called Rae Ann
in most of the story). At the beginning of the story, Rae Ann is entrapped
in a bathroom attempting to make sense of her very first menstrual period.
Rae Ann is afraid. To overcome her fear, she invokes her relationship with
Dada Bibi, the woman who tutors kids at "the Center." As a writer, Bambara
knew how to represent those resources Black girls often create and rely on
to produce a specific generational currency, a kind of Black girl capital, and
arguably a community good. Rae Ann's relationship with Dada Bibi is one
such example.

Dada Bibi is cited as an uncommon teacher. For example, she helped Rae
Ann make a map of Africa, which "she swung her feet away from" so as not
to destroy it, because "the bright colors of Mozambique distracted her for a
moment," allowing her to "picture herself in Africa talking another language
in that rich way Dada Bibi and the brother who tutored the little kids did.
Peaceful, friendly, sharing" (Bambara, 1982, p. 152). Dada Bibi was an artist
and storyteller. She maintained that it was important to give attention to
the female characters' point of view, in spite of the kid's typical and general
unwillingness to do so. Dada Bibi was on purpose. Dada Bibi, according to
Rae Ann,

> didn't even fuss where you been little sister and why ain't you been coming
> around, don't you want to know about your heritage, ain't you got no pride?
> Dada Bibi never said none of them things ever. She jus hugged you and
> helped you do whatever it was you thought you came to do at the Center.
> (Bambara, 1982, pp. 153–154)

Dada Bibi was imagined as a fashionable bridge between Rae Ann's girlhood
and impending womanhood.

In Bambara's stories, women in the community, women like Dada Bibi, are
absolutely essential to liberatory visions of freedom. To heal from the systemic
oppression and deeply rooted inequalities that construct Black girlhood in
the United States as "lesser than," Black girls cannot and should not be left
on their own, alone. Avery Gordon (2008, p. 268) suggested that Bambara
clearly instructs that one cannot mend the broken pieces on one's own, given
that resistance to healing is so fiercely rooted in a self-protectiveness that feels

absolutely essential. Leading by example, Bambara never leaves her Black girl characters alone, without help. In the quality and kind of relationships Black girls have with Black women in her stories, Bambara articulates a collective and transformational power that heals.

Ruth Wilson Gilmore (2007) offered a definition of *power* that is inclusive of people's ability to make power and, by extension, transform it in relationship:

> Power is not a thing but rather a capacity composed of active and changing relationships enabling a person, group, or institution to compel others to do things they would not do on their own (such as be happy, or pay taxes, or go to war) . . . People can and do make power. (pp. 247–248)

Dada Bibi could have very well been a homegirl in SOLHOT. Certainly, homegirls too are uncommon teachers, artists, storytellers, and, at their best, on purpose. Dada Bibi is the woman who could have taught little June Jordan how to do a power analysis that would teach her to question the system, more than she was taught to question her self.

Dada Bibi and Rae Ann, the homegirls and the girls in SOLHOT, and the kind of relationship I wished Jordan could have also recounted, all exemplify a relational and transformational kind of power. It's the kind of power that could undo the seemingly natural correlation between Jordan's and the SOLHOT girls' theorization of Black girlhood as soldiering, between the necessity of fighting and the dream of living freely, between falling to pieces and a whole-some healing. The relationship affords a power of possibility that enables us "to shake the ground and make movement happen" (Gilmore, 2007, pp. 247–248). In SOLHOT when we are really full in our relationships with the girls, we do indeed use movement rhetoric, organizing logic, and activism from which to build a new kind of Black girlhood not predicated on violence.

Bambara's Black girl characters are especially memorable and seem to be the writer's choicest personae from which to examine the human condition. They are complex, thinking people, and it is their relationship with Black women through which they offer insightful commentary about life, living, and freedom. Writing of Toni Cade Bambara's collective works, Avery Gordon (2008) acknowledged, "For Bambara, healing is the process by which you hold that counter-intuitive thought and overcome the resistance to a truth that doesn't so much set you free, as set you up to practice a freedom that improves upon use" (p. 268). Without the courage of the girls in SOLHOT to share their stories of fighting and violence, without the vulnerability of the homegirls to respond in poetry form, without the performance and the being in relationship together, we would not know healing in SOLHOT. It is exactly through our relationships, in our speaking to each other by name, and in our resistance to the status quo that we hold those counterintuitive thoughts that allow us to improve upon use and practice Black girlhood as a practice of freedom.

SOLHOT wants you to know and remember Toni Cade Bambara.

EIGHT

1: But they're waiting for you to act right or something?

SHA'RHONDA: Yeah, all of us, so they can be able to trust us, because some of the people be leaving the classes, and we on our little no passes and stuff—lockdown. People be fighting and stuff.

1: Is that what they call it this week—lockdown?

SHA'RHONDA: Lockdown, because these two boys was fighting outside. It was horrible.

1: So, let me get this straight, though, because I keep hearing stories. So, there's no passes this week because of something that happened before? So, the whole school got punished?

SHA'RHONDA: So, the whole school—nobody could go out without somebody escorting them.

1: And where are the two boys? What happened to them?

SHA'RHONDA: They up in class now. They were all up in classes like two weeks ago.

1: And they got the whole school—

SHA'RHONDA: Locked down.

NINE

MINA: Umm, well when I got in trouble with the principal.

12: What happen?

MINA: Umm, Somethin' 'bout fightin'. Somebody said that I said that I wanted to fight her, but I didn't.

1: Uh-huh.

MINA: Yea.

12: Then what happened? How did the principal find out?

MINA: The girl went back and told that somebody said that I was gon' fight her, but I don't even know her.

1: Uh-huh.

12: So then what happened? Both of you all both got called out?

MINA: I mean yeah both of us did, but we didn't get in trouble.

1: Oh, ok.

MINA: Yeah:

1: But you both got . . .

MINA: That was the first time I was in the principal's office.

1: What do you think you have to deal with, as a Black girl, that other students don't have to deal with?

MINA: Uhh, [*long pause*] like people thinking we're bad.

TEN

KEISHA: Because he had push me and ran up the stairs and so I had pushed him into the wall and then he got hurt. Like one of these walls, and he got hurt and I went to tell the teachers, and they told me to go to detention and fill out a statement. I went in there and filled out a statement. The dean told me I had a week, because he could've died. They said he was this close from dyin' because I had hit him, I had pushed him down real hard and he was losin' a lot of blood so I had got a like a week of in-school and out-of-school suspension. So, I had start crying cuz I was upset because I didn't want the boy to get hurt and I wasn't meanin' for him to get hurt. I was just tryna get him like don't hit me because I warned him more than one time. Cuz he has walked past my house and he hit me, call me B's and stuff like that. So, I guess he wanted to take it to school. So, when I did that and got sent to detention, I started cryin' cuz I didn't mean to hurt him and I also didn't wanna go to detention. So, I went and talk to my counselor and she calmed me down and now she put me in SOLHOT. When I talk with my counselor, it helps me calm down and some things I don't do no more that I used to do.

12: Like what?

KEISHA: Like get angry. I take it out on myself or I'll do bad things that'll hurt me. Then it just wouldn't be right.

ELEVEN

1: If something really bad happened to you in school, who would you go talk to?

TIANA: I would call my mom, because everybody in this school, they try to make it seem like they want it to be a safe environment, but then the teachers kind of—when you tell other people, "Somebody's trying to fight me," or something, the teachers just—they'll never be like, "Well, you're safe here. They can't fight you here," 'cause all they do is call the police. And all they do is say, "Okay, sit here."

I: They call the police for fights in school?

TIANA: There was a fight outside with these girls. It was in front of two boys. It was a white girl and a Black girl. The Black girl got sent to jail, I think because she lost—the white girl lost.

I: The fight?

TIANA: Mm-hmm. They say it's not self-defense, 'cause the white girl here are friends. They say it's not self-defense if somebody hits you and then you end up beating 'em up. That's not self-defense. That's what happened to me last year.

I: You got into a fight like that last year?

TIANA: On the bus with this girl, because she hit me first. She pushed me.

I: They didn't send you to jail, though. We would have known.

TIANA: They suspended me for two weeks.

A BLACK GIRL'S TRUTH[5]

For each time that we gathered with the girls, we would share some snacks. More often than not, the snacks consisted of lemonade and Flamin' Hots. This was time when we would catch up with each other. You know, check in about our respective days. Doing this always grounded us and connected us to each other before we would venture out and start taking photographs.

On this particular day, during our check-in time the conversation centered on a fight that happened in the park over the weekend. The fight involved several Black girls from the neighborhood and one of those girls being someone in our circle. In the academic sense, it was a moment of "participant observation."

For me, her initial describing of the event led to an outpouring of her thoughts about her ways of being in the world. Ultimately, our conversation forced us all to think about what and who we are really living for.

We were trying to dispel the myth about the police
We were trying to dispel the myth about having a baby JUST to have something to live for

5 Written by Claudine Taaffe.

We were trying to dispel the myth that you Black girls do not have
   anything to live for

She moved me
She moved me so deeply
That I did not know what side of the research question I stood on

So I decided not to take sides
And listen
Listen as though my entire existence depended upon her willingness to
   trust me

She spoke of ideas and declarations, of misgivings and bad judgment

She shared all of herself with the exception of her eyes which took
   snapshots of only the carpet
She snapped her collar
From right to left
And back again
Perhaps an act of resisting
Any outpouring of questions and concerns
Coming her way
She flowed
She flowed
As though
This day
Was like any other day
She moved and grooved in her seat like a break dancer challenging the
   competition

The park
Following the call of a play cousin
Black girls against Black girls
Black girls and Black girls
BLACKGIRLS

Loyalty
Love
Challenge
Family
Honor

My conditioned mind envisioned
An unnecessary beat-down
Where everyone was the loser

The fear swelled up inside of me
And a desire to turn back the clock
Laid on my heart

Still
She declared
A victory
A necessary act of ritual
The fact that they won the fight
Overshadowed her moments in handcuffs

I listened
I listened intently
While biting my lip at the moments I heard my mother's voice escape
    my mouth
"¿Que estaba pensando en ese dia?"

This was different
This was spoken and unspoken
Not youth development
Not girl empowerment

This was real, not scripted in a curriculum
Not a moment to be measured by traditional tools
The method
Well, the method was about living
This was about living
And dying
This was about having something and someone to live for
This was about the truth
A Black girl's truth
A truth contained in letters
Letters to each other draped in love

That night
My field notes became journal secrets
My research inquiry became soft and not enough

I cried
I cried for the girls
I cried for myself
I cried out the reasons the truth needs to be told
On our terms

"A Black Girl's Truth" brilliantly expresses how it feels to listen to the very hard stories girls tell about fighting. The sentiment of this poem is honest. As much as SOLHOT is fun, it is also extremely hard work. We work at loving the girls and ourselves. We work at living so that we may do more than survive. A crucial part of the work is learning how to listen. Part of the work is learning how to teach (defined as dispelling myths about the state as protection rather than how the schools "educate them for status quo"). Part of the work is learning how to be in relationship so that when, for example, girls talk about fighting over dirt-old issues like family, honor, and love, we can also say how those same issues have provoked and continue to provoke us as well.

But this homegirl heard a girl say that she was arrested. And as objectively sad about that as this homegirl was, this girl was as equally happy to have won the fight. The homegirl was afraid for her, and this girl was bold in her declaration of life. As ethnographically documented in this poem, on the day in SOLHOT when her story about fighting was shared, SOLHOT concluded with the writing of love letters. We need more spaces that practice love as pedagogy. In SOLHOT we re-search love and practice loving. We want to love ourselves back to ourselves. As Toni Cade Bambara might say, we love so that the girl who fights and the girl who was fought are unafraid to look at themselves.

As the title of the poem suggests, truth telling is at the heart of this performance-poetry project. The art of telling the truth is poetry itself, and in SOLHOT it is one way connections endure among people who would otherwise remain known as simply labels. According to June Jordan, "poetry is a political action undertaken for the sake of information, the faith, the exorcism, and the lyrical invention that telling the truth makes possible" (Jordan and Mueller, 1995, p. 3). Alexis Gumbs (2010) wrote of Jordan's use of poetry to nurture young people as a productively queer intergenerational work that makes conversation possible (p. 248). The resulting conversations are, as Jordan (1995) theorized, "a foundation for true community: a fearless democratic society" (p. 3). Writing about the life of June Jordan, Valerie Kinloch (2006) insisted that among her hyphenated identities, Jordan identified as a poet first, fearlessly exposing her own vulnerabilities through writing, because she believed that such exposure could motivate others in their search for strength (p. 161). Homegirls write and sometimes perform poetry to tell their truth and because June Jordan provided a blueprint.

Bambara also connected truth telling to poetry. In an interview with Kalamu Ya Salaam (2008) about writing, Bambara said:

> I'm just trying to tell the truth, and I think in order to do that we will have to invent, in addition to new forms, new modes and new idioms. I think we will have to connect to language in that kind of way. I don't know yet what it is . . . I think most poets play with that. . . . I'm trying to break words open and get at the bones, deal with symbols as if they were atoms. I'm trying to find out not only how a word gains its meaning, but how a word gains its power. (p. 59)

Part of the power of all of the homegirls' poetry is in the performance of it. The way "A Black Girl's Truth" was performed translated the sorcery of many a homegirl and woman at the Center, like that of Dada Bibi. The power homegirls and girls are capable of making with the word is one of SOLHOT's greatest resources.

In further speculation of why homegirls write poetry and the function it serves in SOLHOT, Audre Lorde's insights are scriptural. In her oft-cited essay "Poetry Is Not a Luxury," Lorde (1984a) called out the work for what it was—mothering:

> The white fathers told us, I think therefore I am; and the Black mother in each of us—the poet—whispers in our dreams, I feel therefore I can be free. Poetry coins the language to express and charter this revolutionary awareness and demand, the implementation of that freedom. However, experience has taught us that the action in the now is also always necessary. Our children cannot dream unless they live, they cannot live unless they are nourished, and who else will feed them the real food without which their dreams will be no different from ours? (p. 38)

"A Black Girl's Truth" models the mothering work defined as necessary by Lorde. Like mothering, neither is the work of SOLHOT nor the poetry it produces done as a whimsical mistake, unintentional, or without radical care and courage. Poetry is as necessary to SOLHOT as clean floors are to a crawling baby. So long as it is honestly felt, good or bad evaluations are not meaningful criteria by which to judge the homegirls' poetic responses. But rather, with Bambara and Jordan as our guides, a better question would be, does it improve on use?

Does the poem feed us?
Does the poem make power?

TWELVE

12: Do you think it's hard being a Black girl at this school?

KEISHA: Sometimes, cuz sometimes I thought I got in trouble sometimes because I called the teachers racist. And I had think about it
and because when I had called her racist and didn't think that was
the right thing to do. I was on the bus, like I told you I'm in here, cuz
the boy was hittin' another student and he was standing up while the
bus was goin' and I'm in trouble for throwin' a piece of gum, but you
sittin' there watchin' him and not sayin' nothing. Then uhh, you sittin'
here watchin' him hit another student, uh you sittin' there watchin'
him hit another student but don't say nothing but the boys calm
down but they still hittin' each other. But okay even if they was playin'
you supposed to stop them cuz they said play fighting can turn into
real fightin', but she didn't say nothing to them. But I got in trouble
because I threw a piece of gum.

I: Mmmmmm. Was the boy Black or white?

KEISHA: White. And I'm not sayin' that was racist but to me it felt like,
either you doin' it cuz the color of my skin or you just doin' it because
you don't like me or that's how I sometimes feel. When I go places or
in my classes or get sent outta class.

THIRTEEN

TINA: Most of them think, "She's bad. She's got a bad attitude," but
sometimes they probably think that I'm a good girl, 'cause I'm capable
of doing good things and bad things too, sometimes.

FOURTEEN

I: Why is it hard being a Black girl here?

SHA'RHONDA: Because, in school everybody be makin' funny jokes and
stuff that aren't funny to me. And it's hard 'cause they like, they try to
make jokes that are funny about me, but they aren't funny to me. So, it
makes me mad and stuff, but I just walk away.

I: What kinda jokes do they make?

SHA'RHONDA: They, well really I can't remember but they were makin' fun of me 'cause I had glasses on and it really made me mad cuz I was sittin' there like other people have glasses, but you had to make fun of me. So, I just walk away.

12: What other things do Black girls get teased about here?

SHA'RHONDA: Well, they get teased about their color, like be like, "Don't get mad cuz I'm lighter than you." I know my friend Joy, well not Joy but Dara, she was walkin' around and we was just walkin', and people walked past us and were like, "Hey, what's your name?" Dara. And she was like, "You dark. Ugh, you ugly, you look like dark choc," and I was like mad them. I just wanted to hit them but I couldn't, so I walked away.

FIFTEEN

TIANA: I was playin' wit dis girl hair and they thought I was pullin' it cuz she kept walkin' away and my finger had got stuck. So, I told her to stop and she wouldn't, she was like, "Tiana let go a ma hair." So, I like grabbed her by the back of her chest and pulled her down, but I didn't mean to knock her hard. And, I knocked the wind outta her and she couldn't breathe. But I thought she was fakin' cuz any otha time I do it, she don't do that. But we had conflicts before because her mom doesn't like me—

12: How do you know?

TIANA: 'Cause, we were at the skating rink and me and her had gotten into a fight. It's a white girl and her mom came in there sayin, "I don't like you. I don't like you. Keep your hands off my daughter."

1: Hmmmm. So what happened? Who did you get in trouble by that you ended up at detention?

TIANA: Umm, the dean.

1: Uh-huh. She sent you to detention that day?

TIANA: Two days.

1: Oh, for two days?

TIANA: I got suspended. Umm, I had got suspended for six days and I came back on Wednesday and got suspended on Tuesday and they gave me in-school suspension.

12: What were you suspended for the first time?

TIANA: Uhhh fightin' on the bus.

12: How did that fight start?

TIANA: This girl she kept pushin' me an' stuff. So I told her to keep her hands off me. And I thought she was gon' swing on me, well she pretend she was, she said she was pretendin'. So then I pushed her head and then she got up and swung and I just start hittin' her back.

12: So how many times you been suspended?

TIANA: Twice.

⌒◇⌒

1: What is the top issue facing Black students at this school?

KEISHA: Fighting.

⌒◇⌒

THEORY VS. PRAXIS[6]

Theory in its simplest form is
an explanation,
speculation
or thoughts about the ways we exist in the world
and praxis
is how we go about getting things done.
So while we're at lunch she gets me.
She asks me the difference between theory and praxis when she says,

"Would you be mad at me if I got into a fight?"

Now theoretically I want to say to her,
"Baby girl by fighting another Black girl you would only
be buying into a rhetoric of racism,
sexism,
capitalism
and heteropatriarchy
that's more played out than auto-tune on Kanye tracks."

But in praxis,
I remember not wanting to be a punk.
When girls messed with me
running away was never an option!

6 Written by Chamara J. Kwakye.

I know how much courage it took
for her to even ask the question,
so I do what I do when I'm at a loss,
turn on the sarcasm,
"Yeah, I'd be mad, matter of fact I would fight you!"
She giggled, we giggled. She said,

"No, but for real I'm serious."

The way she looked in my eyes
I knew she was serious,
I knew it was grave.
See it's all good when we're hanging out at SOLHOT,
those 2 hours are safe, comfortable, pretty, heroic, CLEAN.
She comes through, I come through.
She leaves, I leave, never together.
I get to be the weekend parent, sister, friend.
But today she was asking me to step up.

We blurred the lines between theory and praxis.

So I said,
"Yes. I would be mad Baby Girl, but I wouldn't be upset
if you were defending yourself."
She shook her head up and down.
But I couldn't let it rest. I had to ask,
"Why are you fighting?
Who are you fighting ?
What are you fighting for?"
It all escapes my lips in a rush.

She told me how this girl told was bothering her and her cousins,

"Catching me in the hallways,
calling me FAT . . . BLACK . . . BITCH!"
I was angry. At this point, hell I wanted to fight her.
I felt like,
I felt all the years of teasing came back
and slapped me in the face,
revisited by bullies past who called me FAT . . .
BLACK . . .
and BITCH!

I felt like,
I felt like a mother seeing her child being hurt,
like I couldn't protect this girl child,
my girl child,
me.
Helpless.

We sat in silence.

I said,
"Well baby girl what is it?
Why doesn't she like y'all?"
I saw the look in her eyes
of wanting to know, why?
My spirit was searching for why
another Black girl could hate another Black girl?
There were thousands of reasons,
but neither of us came up with one.
She interrupted and declared,

"Well if she come at me again.
I'm going to fight her.
I can't have her out in the hallway
disrespecting me in front of people
and trying to fight my family. I ain't no scary chick."

In praxis,
I was right there with her.
I had already constructed the fight in my mind.
Ole girl would hit her and Baby Girl would BEAT HER DOWN . . .
but in theory
and in praxis,
no matter who came out looking the most beat down, they would both
    lose the fight . . . Black girl children whose bodies would officially
    marked as "Other" in an educational system that already told and
    expected of them mediocrity.

"Look Baby Girl, you have too much going on to lose it this way."

I reminded her that I had seen, heard and experienced her in the spaces
    that she claimed and used as her outlets, her spaces of freedom . . .

"I mean you don't want to get kicked out of basketball, dance, cheerleading, concert band, marching band, upward bound and school?"

"No. But I ain't no punk."

Praxis. I had to tell her, "And I hear that but, but you don't want to lose your chance to shine over something stupid."

In theory, I wanted to tell her that I loved her too much to lose her to something stupid like that. But what would that do for her in praxis . . . Theory, Praxis . . . So what is my theoretical framework? Right now Marxism, Critical Race Feminism, not even Black Feminist Thought could save me from the truth that she was telling and the truth that I was withholding . . .
Theory (Intangible)
Praxis (Tangible)

In a study on Black girls and fighting, the Ohio Department of Mental Health (Price, 2011) found that Black girls often feel trapped as both victims and aggressors. Fighting as a pervasive experience led the authors to conclude that Black girls live with daily trauma. The girls in the study are just as concerned as the authors by their findings, and are quoted as explicitly wanting to figure out how not to over-rely on physical violence as a solution to their every problem. The study concluded that prevention methods tailored to the "specific needs of Black girls" are important and significant. Even if girls in SOLHOT find themselves facing extreme uncertainty like Rae Ann, rarely do girls in SOLHOT ask us directly what to do, except in the case of fighting. When the subject is fighting, the girls are direct. They ask us, What should we do? What would you have done? Are we going to judge them based on the way they handle(d) the situation? What would you think of me, if I fight her?

In the face of Black girls' specific needs and questions, theory and praxis matter. Ideally, homegirls are ready when they ask, so that their responses may be of help and not taken as opportunities to provoke further trauma or retraumatize themselves. In work with young people, especially in response to their questions, "appropriate" responses are encouraged, though always debatable. Dishonesty is too often the result of being appropriate with youth. Radicalism, as in addressing the root of the problem, is all too often avoided. The inconclusive ending of "Theory vs. Praxis" signals that perhaps the better answer is one that invites dialogue and allows the conversation to go on.

Although not the primary framing of SOLHOT, the relationships created between the girls and the homegirls do the kind of preventative work often attributed to positive youth development. Being in relationship seems to ease the daily trauma of violence described by Jordan while also alleviating the uncertainty of traveling between girlhood and womanhood as indicated in Bambara's short story. As acknowledged in "Theory vs. Praxis"—"See it's all good when we're hanging out at SOLHOT, / those 2 hours are safe, comfortable, pretty, heroic, CLEAN"—SOLHOT is quintessentially positive. However, when SOLHOT colludes with positive youth development, it is not complex enough to address Black girls' daily realities. Exemplary youth-development missions such as "programs should encourage nonviolent attitudes and teach nonaggressive conflict resolution strategies to give children the tools they need to reduce aggressive behavior" (Cotten et al., 1994, p. 620) cancel the productive possibilities of "Theory vs. Praxis." Positive youth development calls for the homegirl to forget her own childhood experiences and deny the shared understanding that aggression is already a part of it. An uncritical embrace of positive youth development silences the experiences of volunteers, adults, and homegirls. It does not attend to the space needed for adults to own their privilege, to admit their complicity, or to address their vulnerabilities. It certainly does not allow for homegirls to be anything other than appropriate. As demonstrated in "Theory vs. Praxis," the homegirls' ability to be "right there with the girls" operates as underground currency against a conceptualization of positive youth development and as a distinguishing factor between homegirls who build relationships with girls with an ease assumed to be natural, typically attributed (though wrongly so) to some visible common marker of identity, and those homegirls who rely solely on their physical presence.

Dada Bibi was controversial. Even though Rae Ann suspected her brother, Horace, felt the same way about Dada Bibi as she did, he spoke just the opposite. Horace warned Rae Ann, "That ole plain-face bitch don't know nuthin" (Bambara, 1982, p. 156). Moreover, Rae Ann's caretaker, M'Dear, also shared a less glowing view of Dada Bibi, dismissing her by admitting, "She ain't studying them folks over there" (p. 161). M'Dear and her sister friend, Miz Gladys, were cool on Dada Bibi with all of her talk of Africa and being African. M'Dear said she was "one hundred percent American and proud of it" to disassociate herself from the woman at the Center (p. 162). Mentors as assumed outsiders are often (mis)read as different from, and therefore other and better than, those they mentor. "Mentor" and "college students" operate via the lens/logic of Progressive Era helperism that imposed class, racial, and gendered boundaries between the helpers and so-called helpless. Those who could "help" could do so only because they had the privilege to. In the wake of the nonprofit industrial complex, we understand SOLHOT to be about organizing rather than mentoring, because there seems to be this prevailing notion that working people don't do activism. A traditional mentoring discourse in relationship to current neoliberal arrangements of "youth engagement" is not politically productive. The ideology of positive youth development also reinforces this unhelpful othering.

Dada Bibi's lackluster reputation influenced Rae Ann, even though she enjoyed a different relationship with her than everyone else in the story. Ironically, according to Rae Ann, her assumed stupidity must have come from an assumed "perfect health" that allowed her to hug Rae Ann and "even the dirty kids from Mason Street" while also doing things like drinking "behind them too without even rinsing the cup" (Bambara, 1982, p. 165). To which Rae Ann declared, "Either Dada Bibi had a powerful health to combat germs, she thought, ripping open the packages, or the woman was crazy" (p. 165). Even still, it seemed to be Dada Bibi's outrageousness that comforted Rae Ann as she sat in her locked bathroom attempting to make sense of her period for the first time. To overcome fear, Rae Ann constantly invoked Dada Bibi:

> Rae Ann thought about Dada Bibi over at the Center. If the shiny-faced woman were here now with her, it wouldn't be so bad. She'd know exactly what to do. She would sit in the chair and examine Rae Ann's schoolbooks. Would talk calmly. Would help her. Would tell her there was nothing to worry about, that she was a good girl and was not being punished. Would give an explanation and make things right. But between the house and the Center she could bleed to death. (p. 153)

Youth development is too safe to address stories of girls' fights, violence, and becoming women. Youth development does not afford the opportunity to be outrageous. SOLHOT depends on the outrageousness of some very unconventional homegirls who are right there with the girls, but in theory . . .

In SOLHOT, the homegirls share stories and the girls also respond with poetry—though they are less likely than the typically-nervous-before-every-performance homegirls to want to share the public spotlight. In this way especially, the girls in SOLHOT are very reminiscent of Rae Ann. In the small yet vital moments of crossing into womanhood, Rae Ann could not do it herself, and she called on Dada Bibi. In SOLHOT the girls often call on the homegirls. Our hope is that the girls enjoy the way poetry is used to dialogue and to question. Rae Ann imagined that upon learning of her current situation, Dada Bibi would simply say,

"You're becoming a woman and that's no private thing. It concerns us all who love you. Let's talk sometimes?"

Rae Ann liked the way she always made it a question. (Bambara, 1982, p. 156)

SIXTEEN

KEISHA: Today, I'm in detention because of an incident that on the bus, cuz I threw a piece, a piece of gum at somebody. Because they threw it at me and I threw it back at them and got caught on the bus, on the school bus for a school trip to the theater to see a musical I think, or learn about Black history . . .

I: Uh-huh.

KEISHA: So, I had got in trouble and they sent me back to detention. And so now, today I'm in detention and I got another day on Monday because I was eatin' and I got caught. I told 'em I was hungry and I had a nutty bar in detention and I had asked him to take us to lunch and he said no, you gotta wait longer. And so I was hungry, I opened my nutty bar and I ate it and he told the dean and she said, "Personally I think she should have another day," and personally she gave me another day. She gave me another day and then, I was upset and I started cryin' and a teacher came and calmed me down and gave me somethin' to work on. Then the counselor called me down here to have an interview.

SEVENTEEN

I2: Wow. So, how many times have you been suspended out of school?

KEISHA: [smacks teeth] In the first quarter thirty-six times and second quarter forty-eight times. Third quarter . . . we went over this like two days ago . . .

I2: Uh-huh.

KEISHA: The third quarter it said something about me slowing down in going to detention. I can't remember the third quarter or the fourth quarter.

I: So the numbers are like when you went to detention or when you were suspended?

KEISHA: When I went to detention and when I was suspended.

I: Oh, ok.

KEISHA: But basically when I went to detention.

EIGHTEEN

I: Do you think, is it mostly Black kids in detention or is it pretty equal?

KEISHA: Hmmmm, mostly Black kids in detention. And then I don't
. . . cuz Black kids, I'm not sayin' like white kids didn't know how
to control things better than we do, and they know how to solve
problems because they was, they not [sighs] like they don't. What
I'm tryna say is the Black kids have more problems than white kids
because white kids it seem like they can get away with more stuff.
Well they don't get away with more stuff cuz it's some white kids in
there or white, everybody understand white kids more than they do
Black kids.

I: Why do you think a lot of adults don't understand Black kids?

KEISHA: Because I don't think adults don't understand Black kids as
much as they do whites because when the kids get all mad and stuff
and they just snap out and they don't understand, then what they say,
what the people tryna say to them and they don't know how to calm
down because they're too upset or to say anything to the teacher. So
they don't understand what they're tryna say or they don't get what
happened because they had to wait a minute for the Black kids to
calm down. So they can talk to them and then maybe they can give
'em another chance. But in my case, they didn't give me another
chance. They just sent me to detention.

I: Uh-huh. And is it mostly girls or boys in detention? Or is it . . .

KEISHA: Equal.

NINETEEN

TIANA: The passing period—they got us on lockdown so we can't go
nowhere.

TWENTY

1: So, can you talk about a time that you were in detention? Like, what happened, why you had to go, do you think it was worth it?

TINA: Awww yea. This was the first quarter. I threw a orange. I threw it real high in the cafeteria.

1: At somebody? Or . . .

TINA: Up.

12 AND TINA: "in the air."

1: Ahhh.

TINA: And, I threw it up 'bout two times and then after it dropped, I catched it. And then, the lunch lady had told me to come here, and she was like "go to detention," and I was like fa what? She was like fa throwin' the orange up. She was like, the dean was like, "go ahead." And then I got suspended.

1: Wait, you got suspended?

TINA: I was madddddd.

1: You got suspended 'cause you didn't go to detention, or?

TINA: I got suspended for throwin' the orange up.

1: So, you got suspended and had ta go to detention? For throwin' a orange in the air?

12: How many days did you get suspended?

TINA: Three.

1: For throwin' an orange in the air? It didn't hit anybody, you just threw an orange in the air? Ok.

TINA: It didn't hit nobody. I just, I threw it up high though.

1: Right.

12: What'd you think about that? Did you think that was fair?

TINA: No. I didn't think that was fair. Why would they suspend somebody, just for throwin' a orange up?

TWENTY-ONE

SHA'RHONDA: Well, it's because uhhh she, cuz I had threw a orange at somebody, I really wasn't aiming for, I was aiming for the trash. And so, she said, she was talkin' 'bout me and stuff. And I got mad, but I didn't wanna go hit her, and if I hit her I would be three days out. And then, I didn't wanna go tell, cuz I don't like tellin' on other people. So I threw the orange at her and I got in trouble. So I hadta go to detention the rest of the day and then, I had two days outta school, which is kinda fun.

I2: You got suspended?

SHA'RHONDA: Uh-huh.

I2: This is for the orange incident?

SHA'RHONDA: Yup. And really, we should do two days and school because like Saturday and Sunday, cuz if you get two outta school, all you do is stay home and you get to be free.

I: Mmmm. Uh-huh.

SHA'RHONDA: So, I'm wonderin' like why do you have a two-day out-of-school instead of, cuz like other people can just go home and stay home for two days. But on a suspension you stay home, which other people love to do. [I and I2 laugh]

SHA'RHONDA: So, after we get in trouble because you don't wanna be in school for two days. So you just go home and be you.

TWENTY-TWO

TIANA: 'Cause last year I went to detention like—how many times? I think it was equal to nine or ten times, cause I got suspended when I fought the girl on the bus. Then, I got three more days in-school suspension. I had an out-of-school suspension, and I came back and this girl—I pulled her hair, and I was kicking her around. Well, that's what they said. But I was really—I had my fingers in her hair. I put 'em in her hair, and she kind of snatched it away from me. Then, I just stopped so I could get my finger out. So, they—

I: Why'd you have your fingers in her hair the first time?

TIANA: 'Cause her hair was pretty. It was still nappy. But then they try to say I knocked the wind out of her, 'cause she fell. I didn't touch her. So, I got suspended three days more. I was on punishment for so long.

TWENTY-THREE

ALEIA: They could use a metal detector if they don't want any knives and stuff in the school. And they can really separate people from different things if they always get into fights and stuff. That's it.

I2: Is that a common problem—people bringing knives into school? Anybody ever use 'em?

ALEIA: Yeah, my friend did.

1: In school, or out of school?

ALEIA: In school, but she didn't get in trouble because didn't nobody
see it. Well, this boy was an asshole to her, so then they started fighting, and she put a knife on him. And she was telling him to let go of
her, and he wouldn't. And then this boy came and grabbed it and told
her to put it up, and then they tried to get her away from the boy.

TWENTY-FOUR

QUEEN: This grown lady had the nerve to walk in the school and tell me
she was gon' f— me up.

12: What?

1: She work here?

QUEEN: No. So, I laughed at her.

12: Did you know her?

QUEEN: Yeah.

12: She came to tell you this?

QUEEN: Yeah.

1: To your classroom?

QUEEN: Nah, we had just walked into the school building.

1: This is in the morning?

QUEEN: Yeah.

12: Somebody's parent? Somebody's mom?

QUEEN: Yup. School haven't even started yet.

12: What, what'd you say? What'd you do?

QUEEN: Laughed at her [laughing].

12: Hmmm, why did she say that?

QUEEN: Cuz I wanted to fight her daughter.

12: Why?

QUEEN: Cuz ah my brother.

12: Why?

QUEEN: Cuz she was stuntin' on ma brother name.

1: What?

12 AND QUEEN: "She was stuntin' on ma brother name . . ."
[Queen laughs]

QUEEN: Then, so her mom told her to get out the car. We don't know
why, she wasn't gon' do nothin'. So, I laughed. Then her mom called
me a b—. I laughed at her mom in her face. Her momma walked in

the school thinkin' she was gon' get information about where I live, what my momma name was, what was my phone. Haha, funny. She wasn't gonna get it though. Then she said, "Imma f— you up. I fight kids too. Go getcha mom." I laughed. She tried to get in my face. So I took my stuff off. I was gon' fight her. Then I called my mom. My mom told me, "Shut up," 'cause she already knowed that I was loud and obnoxious and being crazy. That was the worst day ever, but then it was funny at the same time.

12: Whatchu mean, "she was stuntin' on your brother"? What do that mean?

QUEEN: [*Laughing*] Because she said—this is the nastiest thing I ever in my life heard. Why would my brother kiss my sister?

12: That's what she said?

QUEEN: Yeah! And then she said that, cuz my brother had a cold sore on his lip and she said he got it from Sheri, which is my sister. Why in the world would he kiss my sister? That is so nasty. Cuz she wanted to go wit my brother and my brother said no. Then, she was on the alternative track last year when we went here and she said that when she was on the alternative track, she was punkin' everybody that was on the alternative track with her. Not me. So, she was just stuntin' from the whole ready/beginning.

I took to sleeping with a knife under my pillow. So when my father rumbled those mahogany doors open and started to beat me in the middle of the night, I pulled my knife and I asked him, "What do you want?" And I meant, "I'll kill you!" And soon after that my father stopped waking me up.
(Jordan, 2001, pp. 136–37)

Though Jordan was taught to fight by her father, she acknowledges in hindsight that her preparation was also useful for teaching her how defend herself at home, against her father. In Black girlhood, home becomes a signifier, not of safety, but as yet another premier battleground.

And I remember
Wondering if my family was a war
Going on
And if

There would soon be blood
Someplace in the house
And where
The blood of my family would come from. (Jordan, 2001, p. 76)

FOR A QUEEN[7]

In my heart, I'm ready on my way—window
cracked.
Calling to postpone my 9 p.m. get together with friends
I reread her text—
Terrified, I hold my head in my hands
Her blues in my heart.

If this were anybody else
If this was Niya
Who texts me every other day
    "Can you bring me lunch?"
    "Come pick me up?"
    "Good Morning!"
    "Hey, is SOLHOT today?"
I would have read and not replied.
A post-modern luxury to ignore and not deny.

But, this girl—
her disposition mostly hard.
Melancholy.
Texted me.
This girl—
feared for good reason.
Stoic with poetry passed in secret.
She speaks . . . brilliantly, intentionally, and never in your preferred
    tongue.
This girl—
of the kind typically underestimated.
Texted me.

7 Written by myself, Ruth Nicole Brown.

Making my response neither dilemma, nor a choice.
I've already, in my mind, decided:
   —a hotel room not more than $100.00 I can do.

In another thought, I'm ashamed to admit boys come to mind, and sex,
   and the possibility of another kid. A party gone awry at my expense.

In yet another, because I don't know the source of her pain, I foreshadow
   the possibility of suicide.

We've lost one Black girl too many.

Roshauwnna Winfrey transitioned on Tuesday, January 22, 2008.

She will stay with me, at my house, maybe a safer space. But then
   wait . . .

It's probably just better to call.
I speak. She speaks.
I listen:

   . . . he pulled a knife out on me . . . called
   me names in front of my baby . . .

I heard her:
In a brief moment of unexpected disruption to minding her business
A truth:
Today she faced death and threatened to kill her uncle.
I knew she meant it.
I know her.
Her words are few and always to the point.

The truth hurts.
& I want to say . . .
   "I'm not in the mood."

My truth:
I can't save anyone today.

& I heard her hear me:
strongBlackwoman self immolation to the nth degree, Demeter reaching
toward infinity/searching endlessly
her words echoed through my body/conjuring history.
So I ran (in my mind) to heal her with a hug

as I realized I'm paralyzed by a precise historicity of:
    "this is just what we do"
    "you don't deserve a break, anyway"
    "for the sake of the child"
    "kill yourself, die slow, you know, say yes"
    "if you don't, who will?"
    "I would want someone to help me and my daughter"
    "you can't refuse a Black woman girlchild who found the courage to
    ask for help, c'mon now"

Time passes at lightning speed
Usually it's someone you know who throws the first blow:
this time it was me
unknown
She needs out
Think of the baby
You need out
Think of the baby
Let it go
Think of the baby
There's no place to go
But down.

And I am Demeter pissed,
strolling, mourning, mothering, and thinking again.

This is how the saving *really* happens.
This is how the truth is *really* heard.

Baby girl, (I want to say)
I'm against suicide of any kind
Yours and mine.
You escaped death but want to die—
I'm addicted to a pain that causes death slowly,
not suicide but it's suicidal nonetheless: human sacrifice.
Of the Black woman brand
Throw your body in the way to intercede for
Any and everything including
All that we deserve.
Truth is:
You should have a place to go. And when you reach out to me

I should be here, healthy, and whole.
Clearly my feminist future includes
Community controlled institutions ran by, for, and with
Black girl genius at the helm;
A Black girl like Natasha who makes policies based on valid and reliable
    data she collected and analyzed,
quantitative of course, so it can't be denied, she cites stats,
"9 times out of 10 girls don't really wanna throw dem hands"
and make policy around that.
Not internal thoughts of just how much we give up
So that saving you doesn't
require the death of me.
There should be
the opportunity always to live—
A truth of a new kind, where self sacrifice does not become a
    requirement of
Black girlhood
Not for you
Nor Black womanhood
for me.
My freedom dream of a feminist future
Deletes the crisis (of why you text me)
    increases your possibility and your son's opportunities.

Baby girl, your truth showed up as a lesson
for us both,
& this time I get to say, "SOLHOT has changed my life."
Precious you are but not pink-bowed,
Loudly you come and loudly you go
& as you said the golden rule for us in SOLHOT remains,
"Don't be on bullshit"
& I smiled when you told me the revolution started
Yesterday.
Urgent and like SOLHOT, non-chalant
(unless provoked) this birth
clearly demands
our respect.

On a random Saturday afternoon, I received a text from one of the SOLHOT
girls and I did not have the strength, capacity, or resources to give her all that

she needed. To be fair, I don't think she fully expected me to do anything but be concerned and to listen. But because I listened, as a reflective and thinking person, I could not but lament the lack of a social structure that should have provided more. I also thought about my own very human limitations. Sometimes people seem to think that as the SOLHOT visionary, I am infallible. But I only have so much energy. Saying I was a working single mother at the time of the text and the poem does not even begin to explain why my attention, energies, and resources plateaued. Via text, her situation met mine, giving occasion to recognize not so much of what we were missing, but what was missing in our community and neighborhood, and how what was going on with us personally matters politically.

As is the case with girls' stories of fighting, my feelings too are structured, produced, and made meaning of within a specific set of conditions. What it feels like for me to do collective and creative work that foregrounds complexity from the location of the academy is not all good. No matter how fanciful and idealist images of working with girls may seem to others outside of the work, nothing should be taken for granted or reduced to an elementary simplicity because it is, in part, social and cultural work. When it is forgotten that SOLHOT is work, requiring labor, I feel abused. The ways we collude with and resist the logic of capitalism in SOLHOT must consistently be questioned. When we don't, feelings of being used and taken advantage of represent another kind of violence.

SOLHOT as an anticapitalist space has to be consistently concerned with fair labor. Particularly, as Black women working with Black girls, our collective marginalization often means that we all struggle. This matters for SOLHOT in every way, down to the logistics: Who's responsible for bringing what? Who will organize supplies, rides, etc.? Each SOLHOT session begins by playing a Black girl game that someone must start. Who will start it? These are labor issues. Many of us in SOLHOT have jobs outside of SOLHOT because our survival depends on it. During the time we set aside to organize SOLHOT, we often use it to vent our frustrations about those jobs, our feelings about having to work all the time, being underpaid, and the like. Most of us are already in situations where we are overworked and underpaid, so we must make sure that those dynamics don't get recapitulated in SOLHOT. If we become seduced into thinking that we have created a perfect place for Black girlhood celebration while forgetting or displacing our very real issues of having to pay bills (overdue), lack of access to affordable day care, and our need to be nourished, we have been seduced by fear, white supremacy, and the false promises of heteropatriarchy.

I was vulnerable. I had to own up to the fact that I was tired and of no help. This confession does not support the strong Black woman persona both foisted on me and the one I all too often enact, in spite of knowing better. She called me to save her, but at the time I was trying and not very well succeeding to save myself. I was worried about her survival and my own. She and I should have a place to go, together if we wanted. Multiple and contested fights in the home result in a kind of fatigue that leaves very little imaginative capacity to fight in struggles for freedom that exist outside of one's immediate circumstances. According to Ruth Wilson Gilmore (2007), premature death means dying at an early age, which is exactly how race, fatally coupled with gender and fatally coupled with class, accomplishes the most efficient disposal of Black girls' bodies.

Violence and militarization are endemic to our socialization, and as such I'm not surprised that injury shows up in SOLHOT. We all have plausible explanations for how violence was done to us based on our different experiences, but injury is neither absolute nor definitive. I wrote the poem days after I received the text and performed the poem much later after I wrote it because I did not want to remain any longer with the guilt of being not enough. I continued to worry about this place we found ourselves in, and I continued to envision a place that does not yet exist. When I wrote, "Clearly my feminist future includes community controlled institutions ran by, for, and with Black girl genius at the helm," I meant it. This was no concise futurism. Even as I wrote of the future as a short distance between the time of the text and the place I dreamed of where her problems and mine were resolved and forever abolished, I understood that the process and politics needed to make it happen were no express train.

Black girls' lives must become inextricably linked to institutional and personal visions of the future. Poetry gave me a way to be in the now of the moment and the future, simultaneously, with us both present and whole. Nikky Finney theorized poetry as a methodology of bringing people with us into the future. In an interview by Natalie Elliot (2011) in reference to the poem "Left" from her collection *Head Off & Split* (2011), Finney stated:

NF: As a person who creates, I don't know if I want to worry about doublebacking on what anybody has done. I saw a woman on a rooftop holding a sign P-L-E-A-S and I thought, this is very powerful, what can I do with this? How can I bring her into the future? Americans have such short memories about hard things and so I wanted to bring her forward. So she was the symbol for me. I wrote to her. I wrote around her. I wrote for her. Whenever I'm talking about that poem, "Left," I say, "Do you remember the woman standing with the homemade sign?" So many people remember her and haven't thought of her for a long time and then I read the poem and they are taken back in their memory to how much empathy they had at that moment.

I wonder how many people are familiar with the symbol of a Black girl in need. Probably a lot. I wonder how many people are familiar with the symbol of a fully human and capable Black girl resisting violence so that she may bring her child into the future with her, a future she undoubtedly needs to be better than the present moment. Probably a lot. How many of us remember getting that call from a loved one who needed help, and not having a way to help? Remember that feeling? How many of us as the perpetual helper, when called on, wished we had been the one who dared to ask for help? Well, let's access that empathetic space before we begin to listen and hear girls' stories about fighting and violence and dare to offer solutions. Toward that end, the distance between the then of the poem, the now of the discussion, and the future as poetically stated is up to each one of us. For now, sometimes that is all we have. Until later, we create spaces so that we will not be able to envision a future without them and us all, together.

But the sharing of stories has become big business. It matters how stories are told, hence ethnographers' fixation on issues of ethics and representation. Stories may be commoditized into feel-good narratives that change nothing, if not carefully handled. To avoid the misuse of power, even unintentionally, Joy James (1996) suggested that stories of pain and violence should reveal everyone's vulnerable proximity and culpability (p. 151). In the performance of our poetry, we aim to create spaces where we share our stories together, to acknowledge our own complicity in and relationship to violence.

When you let the girls tell it, there are reasons to fight.

Based on the girls' stories, it is clear that people in positions of authority fail to protect Black girls in particular, and youth of color more generally. Yet problems exist and have to be solved. Fighting requires using the body, which Black girls are expected to do from a very young age. Fighting provides an immediate result—someone wins and someone loses—and an answer. Fighting does not require permission, a hall pass, a signature, a fee payment, or transportation. It is a relatively accessible option, and given the social rewards of winning, like respect, attention, and honor, it's a big payoff for anyone who is typically marginalized on the daily. Moreover, when problems remain unresolved by people in positions of power, racism and carelessness are to blame. In the stories Black girls share about fighting, they bear the burden of punishment, regardless of fault. Listening to what they have to say when "caught" is a luxury of the privileged.

Fighting is on the hearts, minds, and bodies of all the girls I have worked with in SOLHOT. All of the girls. I too share the sentiment of Nikki Jones (2010) when she wrote, "These girls' lives are not contained in labels. These girls are good girls, pretty girls, sometimes violent girls, and fighters who are deeply involved in a struggle for survival" (p. 181). I am deeply concerned that so much of their everyday, particularly in school, revolves around fights. Moreover, the punishment they receive related to fights and disciplinary actions means that the girls we work with in SOLHOT spend a great deal of time outside of the formal school classroom. If suspension and detention worked, then I'd imagine they would not also become as routine to the girls as the fights themselves (or other encounters with violence).

Listening to the frequency with which girls talk about fighting and violence, I also wonder if SOLHOT works. This is not to assume that we function as a violence-prevention program at all, but even as I write of the power of the homegirls' poetry and the strengths of the relationships created in SOLHOT, I am also aware that our presence seems miniscule against the violent context of school fights and intimate violence that occur in the neighborhood and at home. As made clear in the homegirls' poems, we too are dealing with so much violence that the power of our relationships with the girls would seem to suggest that we would see some change in our daily lives as well—that we, for example, would not be too tired to organize and attend SOLHOT. But I'm convinced that our relationships with each other do make a significant impact on our lives. Subsequent rereadings of the stories and the poems make me wonder how much more dismal each of our everyday fights could have been, if there were no SOLHOT.

Based on the interviews and in my relationship with the girls in SOLHOT, Keisha comes the closest to identifying the more structural explanations of violence and fighting, yet she is also the one who has been in the most trouble in school. Keisha is a brilliant girl who has lacked sufficient opportunity to shine. I feel as if the more politically astute girls are punished by design. Keisha is a girl with presence. The other girls look up to her, in part out of fear and also in part because they too value her intellect. Keisha is a fighter, as capable as June Jordan. But even as I think of Keisha now, several years after these interviews, she is very much the same as a young June Jordan, more focused on changing who she is than on acting on her analysis of structural power dynamics. SOLHOT certainly presented Keisha with the space to practice her advanced analysis, but because she was often in and out of school due to behavioral discipline, she was also in and out of SOLHOT. When I think about fighters in SOLHOT, I think of Keisha, and wonder.

Both Bambara and Jordan wrote of Black girls' lives and were fierce advocates of children's voices. Abena Busia (2006) wrote of Bambara: "Her children are responsible, competent, efficient, and principled, and if they are not acting that way, the purpose of the story is to show them that they should be" (p. 188). Likewise, Kinloch (2006) acknowledged that Jordan used her writings to enter into conversations on the victimization of children, children's bodies, and childhood, as well as discussions of the value of cultural practices of Black children and the diverse language features and heritages of people of color in America (p. 109). Each on their own, and taken together, Jordan and Bambara's texts offer so much more insight on Black girlhood than I can cover here. However, for the sake of rethinking Black girls' relationships to fighting, there are several instructive insights that cannot be overlooked and in fact aid in the process of undoing fighting, war, and violence as the predominant lens through which Black girls understand their lives.

To overcome the conditions that create fighting Black girls, Jordan tells us a new kind of power is needed. Those who have power over Black girls typically train them in ways that make them available for service, and as dutiful daughters they take on the corresponding label of soldier. However, Bambara demonstrates that women like Dada Bibi can make a kind of power, through active relationship, that renders them permanently unavailable for servitude.[8] In a series of ritual-like invocations, Rae Ann "pictures" Dada Bibi as a liberating source capable of assisting her in the seriously definitive moment of being a girl and becoming a woman. In deciding between soldiering and herself, between survival and freedom, and being a whole girl and becoming a whole woman, Dada Bibi was pictured right there with Rae Ann.

Through fiction and memoir, June Jordan and Toni Cade Bambara characterize reasons why Black girls fight and endure violence without falling prey to carelessness, categorization, and oversimplification. Although their stories are

---

8 In the short story "The Seabirds Are Still Alive," Toni Cade Bambara wrote the phrase "unavailability for servitude" as a double entendre. In describing a military soldier's return home from war, she wrote of his unavailability to mean two things at once: His service requirement was over, and his return home alongside other soldiers meant collective freedom.

different, the similarities in their descriptions of Black girlhood are noteworthy. Rae Ann does not allude to being a soldier, yet for most of the story she remains confined in a locked bathroom. Both the bathroom as a carceral space and metaphors of soldiering implicate the criminalization of Black girlhood. Race, gender, age, and nationality mark Black girlhood and Black girls' bodies as deviant and devalued. Whether as soldiers or menstruating, Black girls wonder if all the bleeding represents a death sentence they must suffer alone. As both authors contend with meanings of "blood" in their home space resulting from the intricate and intimate workings of their own bodies, it is their relationships with others that make an urgent life-or-death difference.

The homegirls are culpable and intimately tied to the kinds of violence that make Black girls into soldiers. Poetry is our preferred means to strengthen our imaginative capacities in order to resist premature death, particularly the social and civic death Black girls experience daily. Relationally, homegirls do not know what to say, how to mean, or why they should immediately respond to girls' stories about fighting and violence. In our own time, while remaining in relationship with the girls in SOLHOT, we share what we honestly feel in poetic form, and sometimes we perform. The kind of power we are able to generate because of poetry does not change policy, nor does it result in the immediate liberation from the conditions that gave rise to the girls' stories and the homegirls' poetry. Rather, it is the type of power that makes it possible for us to hold thoughts that counter common sense and mainstream narratives of mentoring and rehearse actions that make freedom a closer felt and shared experience. This is healing work.

Violence is explained in the poetry of SOLHOT homegirls as a public and collective problem. In our performances, we use poetry to create a space to listen, act with courage, and dialogue in community. We aim to manifest the power girls told us we all deserve, where our lives are central and violence is neither the most accessible or acceptable option. When we perform our poetry in the presence of Black girls, we deprivatize our pain to border-cross into public activism, demonstrate vulnerability to bring the grief up close, and delight in our fragile idealized identities as homegirls (James, 1996, p. 153). As an act of solidarity, girls' stories about fighting in relation to homegirls' poetic responses trouble the conditions that make fighting synonymous with Black girlhood.

At the end of the day when a homegirl asked, what is the top issue facing Black students at this school? A girl in SOLHOT answered, fighting.

5 More than Sass or Silence
The Creative Potential of Black Girlhood

I have been asked at least one hundred times to travel and talk to young girls about the path of my own life. I have been honored to do so. But I have never been asked to travel and listen to any young girls talk about how they see the world or how they think the world sees them. Always while there, in the middle of whatever I have come to say, even if I look up and reach out in hopes of lifting up a two-way conversation into the air, most of the girls still look lost. What could I possibly want to hear from them? (Everything!) I'll admit, I didn't push hard enough, and SOLHOT makes me wish I had. . . . In every situation the stage was set for my having the answers for the girls I was about to meet, who had been carefully instructed to keep mostly silent and still. This pre-fabricated stage remains the set design for far too many of us who travel in the world, who call ourselves, "working with" young people.
—Nikky Finney (2009, xxii)

Listen to Black girls. What do you hear?

Silence.

The girls referenced by Nikky Finney and so many others have been wrongly instructed that their voices are unimportant. Taught to be unseen and unheard, their silence may be self-imposed or sanctioned. Silent Black girls have a lot to say; however, without time, good relationships, and patience, their voices remain a backdrop to conversations about them. Not to be confused with personality characteristics like shy or apathetic, silent Black girls may be willfully lost in fearful power struggles that position them as mute. Though Black women and girls have historically used illocutionary force to make their voices heard, more often than not, they were ignored and silenced (Pough, 2004, p. 45). Silent Black girls and speaking Black girls both have in common the all-too-usual response of misunderstanding all-things-theirs, spoken and unspoken. Too often, even when Black girls speak, no one hears them. We do not know.

~◇~

just because Black girls talk slang
just because I am me
just because I am a Black girl
just because I have a bad attitude

does not mean they're ghetto
does not mean I got attitude
does not mean that I'm mean
does not mean that I ain't nice

my name is Tasheka
my name is LaKisha Jackson
my name is Shalondra
my name is Angel

and I am not ghetto!
and I am me.
and I am 11 years old and I'm proud to be Black!
and I am the bomb!

Listen to Black girls. What do you hear?
Sass.

Teachers, parents, and community workers are quick to offer anecdotes about Black girls as in need of management, because of what they say and *how* they say it. Black girls have been acknowledged for a particular brand of sassiness or sass that always seems especially displeasing to those in positions of power and authority. Joyce Stevens (2002) defines *sassy* as "willful forthrightness in demeanor that expresses a spirited behavioral expressive style of boldness, independence, and courage, which Black adolescent girls learn early to deal with everyday hassles" (p. 189). In SOLHOT no one uses the term *sassy*. *Sassy*, as the choice pre–girl empowerment and pre–pink power descriptor of deviance, is more akin to recent monikers of *loud*, *ghetto*, and/or *reckless*. When used to categorize Black girls as a group, these terms erase intragroup differences and deny personhood. Yet willfulness remains the underlying foundation for Black girls' expressive behaviors. Whether it was previous generations of sassy girls, or more recent reports of having "flipped" or going "beast-mode," Black girls are all too often admonished for the memorable, stylistic, and always recognizable way they emphasize tonality with expressiveness. As a result, we remain clueless about what they said.

> *If we did not have a dime to our names SOLHOT would still exist. SOLHOT would exist if no one ever wrote down one thing about it. SOLHOT would exist without big grants and conferences. The only thing required in order for SOLHOT to exist and operate is the will of people to come celebrate Black girlhood, period. If there are two people or 200 people, if it happens in a middle school, a club, an alley, or Ethiopia, it will still exist and operate. The energy, beauty, knowledge, and overall dopeness that is created in that space is the only reason these papers, grants, conferences, trips out of town, books, and publishings are possible. And to be honest, I personally am not invested in any of those byproducts. If people think that second-hand accounts of what happens in the actual SOLHOT space are sufficient enough to experience it, then fine, write until you're blue in the face. But I can tell you that it's not the same.*
> —*A SOLHOT homegirl*

Listen to Black girls in relationship with Black women, what do you hear? Knowledge.

Making spaces for Black girls is extremely personal. Sometimes, like in the tone of this particular homegirl's message, what is at stake in the making of Black girl spaces sounds hardcore. But to focus only on tone would dismiss the larger, more theoretical concern that is raised. Like Conquergood (2002), this homegirl points our attention to the dangerous privileging of the written word as the definitive way to know. Moreover, this homegirl makes the same distinction as Diana Taylor between the archive and the repertoire. According to Taylor (2003, p. 20), the repertoire, as enactments of embodied memories, is usually thought of as ephemeral, nonreproducible knowledge and subsequently less valued than the archive, consisting of material texts and products that supposedly endure time and change. But because in SOLHOT we listen to raised eyebrows, side and rolled eyes, a particular intonation, a smack of the lips, out-of-turn talking, and shared hugs, we know better than many. There is also something about being in a space to celebrate Black girlhood that makes introspective thoughts sound louder. Hearts beat. Minds race. Blood moves. Then we become aware of what we do not know. What are we doing? Who's going to feed me? What is love and where is it? How does she know? Many are fond of the idea of SOLHOT, but fewer can be present, and even fewer people than that can develop a repertoire, a continuous practice of engaging Black girls that accounts for what they know and for uncertainty. This truth-telling, theorizing-from-practice, quoted homegirl knows that the way SOLHOT sounds is often more romantic than the practice, in spite of our blue-in-the-face writings that suggests otherwise. Listening is the archive. How to listen is the repertoire.

As a way to think through the more dominant categorizations of how Black girls are heard, as either sassy or silent, in this chapter I offer a new frame for working with Black girls that builds on the creative potential of a complex Black girl sound. Based on Black girls' expressive culture as ethnographically documented in SOLHOT in the form of original music, I think through and challenge dominant categorizations of how Black girls are heard. Sampling Andrea Smith's (2006) "Heteropatriarchy and the Three Pillars of White Supremacy: Rethinking Women of Color Organizing," representing hip-hop feminism, and troubling girls' studies, I present a new framework of Black girl organizing. This new frame accounts for differences among Black girls, amplifies Black girls' critical thought, documents the often overlooked creative process of Black girl music making, and, most importantly, moves those who do Black girl organizing toward a wider repertoire of actions and conversations that affirm differently sounding Black girls. In much the same way as Nikky Finney recounted, I aim to change the set design of Black girlhood by amplifying our sound, to foreground Black girlhood beyond identity, but as an organizing construct that makes radical movement possible. Black girls know a lot, and Black girls who organize Black women who organize through Black girlhood are profoundly productive when they know that they know and also when they know that Black girls know better.

THE CREATIVE POTENTIAL
OF BLACK GIRLHOOD

I use the phrase "creative potential of Black girlhood" to denote a frame of organizing dependent on the energetic charge of creativity to move ideas and people. In this framework, potential, as in energy, is invoked as a property of collectivity. This is important because too often, Black girls are seen as valuable for who they will become as presumable citizens in the making, not for who they are as people marginalized, without the protections and privileges of being defined as an adult. As previously mentioned, Black girls know a lot, and it is the potential of the collective—the entering into relationship—to build and create something beyond a self-serving good time that is Saving Our Lives Hear Our Truths. Creativity activates the coming together of individual people to make relationships sacred, to question and interrogate how we are seen, and to bring the complexity of issues, like fighting, to the surface. The creative potential of Black girlhood as a frame of organizing minimizes the distance between Black girls' critical thought, what they know, as a generative force of creativity that when critically engaged reveals how their personal lives, stories, and testimonies are structured by governing institutions and larger social, political, metaphysical, ecological, and economic systems. When creativity activates the potential of the group, as SOLHOT demonstrates in the naming, practicing, and remixing of certain organizing practices that are theoretically oriented toward abolishing structures predicated on the dismissal and disregard of Black girls' lives, potential abounds for movement that feels and seems more just. The creative potential of Black girlhood frame serves as a double referent for the articulation of Black girls' expressiveness, style, and sound to mean movement that accounts for difference and also highlights what is possible when Black girlhood operates as an organizing construct, not as a static category of identity.

The creative potential of Black girl organizing frame suggests a Black girlhood sound that nobody can organize. Stated differently—we must resist archiving the ways Black girls sound, as loud or quiet, as the most important things about them and instead embrace and begin to name a wider repertoire of how Black girls sound as a potentially creative source of knowledge that informs the kind of movement work made possible when Black girlhood is deployed as an organizing construct that moves and affirms Black girls' lives with justice. I theorize a Black girl sound for the purpose of movement based on an analysis of four musical tracks created in SOLHOT. This analysis articulates three specific logics—volume/oppression, swagg/surveillance, and booty/capitalism—of organizing that emphasize the creativity of differently sounding Black girls to inspire different (embodied) movements that can potentially come together and literally touch. More than a metaphor, the creative potential frame is a call for those who work with Black girls to move beyond binary categorizations of Black girls as sassy or silent and toward emancipatory organizing practices that offer us a way to acknowledge conflict about how Black girls sound, without being prescriptive.

This practice-to-theory, theory-to-practice, and back-again analysis samples Andrea Smith's (2006) "Heteropatriarchy and the Three Pillars of White Supremacy: Rethinking Women of Color Organizing." Smith (2006) provides an insightful argument about how women-of-color organizing may be framed more carefully so as to not succumb to smackdowns over who is the most oppressed. Smith pointed my attention to the ways binary thinking divides and conquers people who are otherwise inspired to do revolutionary work together. As a framework, Smith (2006, p. 67) proposes three interconnected pillars, slavery/capitalism, genocide/capitalism, and Orientalism/war, that assume racism and white supremacy are constituted by separate and distinct, but still interrelated, logics. This new frame unpacks how difference in "women of color" and "people of color" politics often leads to different (and at times contradictory) actions that implicate how we organize. Following Smith's activist-informed scholarship, I propose a new framework of Black girl organizing, the creative potential of Black girlhood, to clarify how binary categorizations like the loud versus quiet Black girls are encouraged because of white supremacy and heteropatriarchy but do not function as reliable organizing logics for moving toward greater collective visions of justice. For example, if we in SOLHOT invent Black girlhood only to operate as settler colonists, then not only do we rest easily on false binaries, but we also disappear those we do not like and, always as a rule, imagine the public school system as a permanent threat. By theorizing Black girlhood sound in relation to ethnographic music production in SOLHOT, which I am assuming is music most readers have not heard and do not know, I hope to *show* the complexity of a Black girl sound and how I sense the songs sound in order to reorganize toward greater cacophony that echoes Smith's call for a model of liberation based on community relationships and mutual respect (2006, p. 73). This analysis of the SOLHOT CD creates both a pull and push on the shoreline of Black girlhood organizing to experiment in a productive un/knowing that requires us to remain on our toes, catch the beat, blow our minds, and awaken our bodies so that leaning on each other becomes more familiar and acceptable—like in a slow dance.

The analytical insights presented in this chapter are highly circuitous, non-linear, and articulate parallel conversations about Black girlhood, music, movement, and organizing. Traveling from, between, and within practice to theory, and theory to practice, most specifically, this analysis is one of praxis. *Praxis* is defined by Swarr and Nagar (2010, p. 6) as a process of meditation through which theory and practice become deeply interwoven with one another. The documentation of music made in SOLHOT and the creative process of how it was made is the practice. I then theorize from this practice, to address how the creative process of Black girls' music production in context of SOLHOT represents hip-hop feminism and informs girls' studies.

Following the example of Andrea Smith (2006), I too invite readers to build on, interrogate, challenge and/or further explain the creative potential of Black girlhood organizing as presented in this chapter. Sound is but one axis from which to extend this frame; I hope others will suggest different sensory and culturally constructed fields from which to analyze the relationships among Black girlhood, girls of color, and organizing efforts.

Turn the music up.

LINER NOTES: THE CREATIVE PROCESS OF MAKING BLACK GIRL MUSIC

When I listen to Black girls, I am often moved to write. When SOLHOT homegirl Taylor listens to Black girls, she makes music. At one SOLHOT site, Taylor documented Black girlhood in musical form to create *The Official SOLHOT CD*, an ethnographic soundtrack of Black girlhood as performed in SOLHOT that consists of five tracks. Out of her own deliberate and creative genius, Taylor created each song based on our conversations in SOLHOT. After being present for the conversations and then listening to *The Official SOLHOT CD*, I memorized the words, sang along, recalled the exact moments captured by a lyric, processed and debriefed with Taylor in person and over email about the process of making the CD, distributed the CD to girls both in and out of SOLHOT, watched public performances of the title track, "Ms. Understood," and unabashedly bragged about its overall dopeness as an exemplary female-focused hip-hop feminist media-studies project with profound pedagogical implications for illustrating Black girlhood critical thought and circulating this new knowledge beyond SOLHOT (Brown, 2009; Durham, 2010).

As a value in SOLHOT, we recognize Black girlhood culture as a productive and generative site of artistic creativity and knowledge production. Drawing from our own Black girl "cultural well," what we voice through song may sound feminist if, as Kyra Gaunt (2006, p. 88) asserted, to not do so may very well be acknowledged as patriarchal. This is as much a political project as a pragmatic concern. As a way to counter the normative academic management of Black girls' voices as only objects of feminism, SOLHOT "privileges the in-betweenness of a Black girl epistemology or a Black feminist standpoint" (Durham, 2010, p. 122). So while it may seem at first glance a far stretch (or overreaching use of authorial authority), this analysis demonstrates how music made in SOLHOT makes possible an articulation of Black girls' thought, particularly a feminist critique of practice, as hip-hop feminists in particular have well begun to document and name.

According to Aisha Durham (2007), *hip-hop feminism* is defined as "a socio-cultural, intellectual and political movement grounded in the situated knowledge of women of color from the post-Civil Rights generation who recognized culture as a pivotal site for political intervention to challenge, resist, and mobilize collectives to dismantle systems of exploitation" (p. 306). I use the term *hip-hop feminist pedagogy* to name the ways hip-hop feminism engages younger people in the life-sustaining work of self-affirmation and determination, creates relationships to practice love, and works collectively to do culture, politics, and education (Brown, 2009). This work takes seriously the responsibility of those who grew up with hip hop to critique, rehearse, participate in, and transform the cultural terrain with those younger than us, to point out the obvious but necessary material and symbolic annihilation of young girls of color (Brown, 2009; Durham, 2010). Hip-hop feminist pedagogy as both a process and product is multidimensional and looks how the girls who are centered in the work need it to feel. Media is a key component of hip-hop feminism (Durham, 2010), and Black girls as media makers, especially as it relates to music, represent a kind of anomaly in academic literature. If not for the interventions of hip-hop feminism, we would know even less about the creative processes they engage.

Girls' studies gives too little attention to cultural media made by Black girls. Music as media is identified by Mary Celeste Kearney (2006) as less researchable than the more conventional girl-made zines, websites, and movies due to the hypermasculine and patriarchal culture of music production. Black girls' music making is posited as a kind of misanthropic reality, when really the sounds and rhythms of Black girlhood are ubiquitously musical. What can be made of this misdirected assumption? Kearney reviews existent literature on girls' music production and finds that patriarchy, sexism, economic inequality, accessibility, gender socialization, and gender barriers are the primary reasons for girls' historical lack of interest in making and recording music. Regarding the seeming impossibility of music-making girls, Kearney questioned,

> For if female young are discouraged from liking loud, hard music, playing electronic instruments, buying equipment, developing friendships with boys, joining bands and crews, and obtaining and exchanging music-based cultural capital, how in the world do they get up the nerve to perform publicly, much less make a record? (pp. 299–300)

Yet girls do make music even if they don't make a record—and this distinction is noteworthy. Girls perform, and it is their sounds that many have repurposed for capitalist consumption in the for-profit corporate music recording industry. Nerve, then, is not so much the issue as is the framing. Girls' studies, with its privileging of archival sounds, should also look to unincorporated cultural sites, for example, to learn more about Black girls' repertoire of musical production. Music, and specifically Black-girl-made music, is always present in SOLHOT (Brown, 2009), as the games Black girls play display an innovative soundscape of embodied musical knowledge (Gaunt, 2006). According to Kyra Gaunt (2004), "Black girls' musical games promote the skillful development of musical authority that reflects Blackness, gender, individual expressive ability, and the very musical styles and approaches that later contribute to adult African-American musical activities" (p. 251). Through games and everyday expressiveness, Black girls learn early on the particularities of a Black girl sound that many popular professional artists have capitalized on, to the point that all too often a Black girl sound is mistakenly attributed and credited to someone else and ignored in academic literatures that focus on music made for the purpose of an externally oriented gaze that validates Black girls' performances for others, not themselves. Hip-hop ambassador, emcee, and cultural worker Toni Blackmon acknowledged that her involvement in hip hop began as a girl: "So I came into Hip Hop as a dancer. Yeah, and then

I started rhymin when I was a cheerleader in high school. I was rhyming for fun at rallies cause I was in charge of the rallies for the basketball and football team, and I would make up rhymes for the games" (Richardson, 2007, p. 63). The creative process of making music is often developed by Black girls in forms of experimental play that engage a repertoire of Black girls' musical culture that may or may not later be archived. Furthermore, it cannot be assumed that Black girls are always credited, as the originators and innovators of music once archived sounds differently than how it was first played by Black girls.

Another important distinction about Black girl music making in context of girls' studies literature is that the privileging of the recorded voices also mirrors the focus of girls' studies on the individual, at the expense of Black girls' music making that is social, more often than not. Black girls play games and create rhymes that are performed in chorus, in collectives, among friends and sometimes against foes. In Aisha Durham's (2010) model of media literacy, the valuation of the self in relation to community is described as a component of a performance of praxis. Durham argues that the work of naming personal experiences, along with interpersonal dealings, is useful for inspiring collective action in much the same way as Joan Morgan's memoir led to hip-hop feminism, as a movement, pedagogy, and field of academic inquiry (*ibid.*). To advocate for self in relation to community means that the ways Black girls, in particular, make music informs and is informed by hip-hop feminism and challenges the erasure of Black girls' creative music-making process in girls' studies. Moreover, scholarship of Black women's creative traditions also speaks back to the individualism privileged in girls' studies. The creative process of Black women singer/songwriters as documented in LaShonda Barnett's (2007) *I Got Thunder: Black Women Songwriters on their Craft* is particularly instructive for how music is a form of documenting a self in relationship to community, in much the same way as Taylor wrote (and in a sense co-authored) the songs on the SOLHOT CD. Barnett interviewed twenty notable Black women singer/songwriters, devoting a chapter to each artist that features conversation about their personal background and upbringing, artistic process, social and political commentary, and musical muses and philosophy. In the introduction, Barnett (2007) echoes Durham's foregrounding of the self in relation to community and surmises,

> Black women's songs are a tool for deciphering the individual experiences, beliefs, and deepest feelings of their originators, and the African diaspora experience in general. For though they are usually informed by a personal

experience, these songs signify the ideas and values of the singer's community. (p. xv)

On this point, Abby Lincoln was particularly clear,

> I've always been concerned with the story I'm telling. This music is social. Our music is social. Nobody cares whether it sounds pretty or not. Can you tell the people what it's like to be here? To live here? That's what the people care about. Can you be honest in your singing? . . . So you see, we don't come from a tradition that worries about pretty singing. Good singing is in the way you use your voice. It's in what you are saying and how you say it. (Barnett, 2007, p. 8)

In Barnett's interview with Toshi Reagon, she also locates the significance of her music to her community:

> For me, ultimately my music is about creative documentation on my life and my community. You know, long after I'm gone, people should be able to listen to my records and hear a truthful story about what it was like to be here. And also, they should get validation for their experiences, whatever they may be. (Barnett, 2007, p. 302)

Barnett's interviews implicate ethnography as a method of "beingness" that may be translated creatively through music, art, performance, and other aesthetic ephemera. Discussions and reflections about the process of making music as revealed through Black girls' and women's experiences show the import and possibility of one voice to stand in for many, to note that the "I" spoken and sung can stand in for many beyond the singer/artist in view, to engage the complexity of a single sound. In making the SOLHOT CD, Taylor relied on the girls' individual experiences to make music about practicing Black girlhood in SOLHOT. The lyrics and my interpretation of the music represent a different kind of field note than typically written up in standard ethnography. Making sense of the process, and its affective production, means that the songs presented in this analysis sometimes reflect the sentiment of what was said and felt in SOLHOT and at other times are a direct transcription of our conversations. In the analysis that follows, my primary concern is to demonstrate how the artistic excellence and musical integrity of each song also contain knowledge that makes greater movement possible.

Who carries the girls' voices is important to consider, because it is also here that the creative process of music making in SOLHOT complicates understandings of the "girl" in girls' studies. On the CD, there are a total of three voices—that of Taylor, "Lo" (one of Taylor's artists who was also a student and later became a homegirl), and Jenny, a white girl friend they recruited to do a speaking part. In SOLHOT, we (Black girls) do not have the privilege of going at it alone—the CD would not exist without the girls, the homegirls, and our friends. I argue that the proverbial "girls' voices" are present and accounted for in the SOLHOT CD, though students of girls' studies may disagree. When I listen to the CD, I hear our SOLHOT conversations in the voices of Taylor, Lo, and Jenny (whom I have never personally met). I hear the voices of the girls in SOLHOT through Taylor and Lo, and this is characteristic of the kind of fluidity between Black girlhood and Black womanhood SOLHOT thrives on. There is no way to provide a "direct" transcription of the girls' conversation alongside the musical lyrics written by Taylor, as they are unapologetically interconnected. The CD exemplifies how listening to Black girls among Black women who are also listening to each other ignites possibilities of circulating different sounds and new narratives and, most importantly, conveys logics for improving our daily practice of SOLHOT by amplifying uncertainty and building on over-the-top expressed expressiveness. What is made known in and through the music moves sound, bodies, and ideas, in those usefully particular and aesthetic ways that only music can.

Taylor decided to be the voice on the CD when a few of the girls who can sing chose not to sing though they still liked the idea of making a SOLHOT CD. Barnett (2007) is clear that the gift of music making, singing, and song-writing for those she interviewed (primarily "secular" musicians) is spiritual, a calling, not a vocation or chosen work. It is completely plausible to me that the girls did not want to sing on the CD because, while they like music and some can very well hold a tune, they did not feel called to do so. Moreover, Taylor, a student of music and independent artist of her own, is called to do music—we all know this in SOLHOT. The lack of interest among the girls about being directly involved in all aspects of the process could be attributed to their respect for Taylor, a way to honor the call of music on her life. It is also completely plausible to me that the girls entrusted the CD music pro-duction to Taylor because they are in relationship with her and know her; they trust and love her, and see her as also like themselves. When I listen to Black girls talk about who should make what, certainly what one is called to do in life trumps age. Hip-hop feminism has been particularly helpful in thinking through Black girls' creative process as it relates to music, much more so than girls' studies scholarship. The process of making the SOLHOT CD, as a form of Black girl media, is instructive for scholars interested in Black girlhood and creative production and underscores the need for more research about the relationship between spirituality and girlhood, particularly in the way spirituality is invoked in communities of Black women and girls, the artistic possibilities and tensions of articulating self in community, and performance-based repertoires of embodied musicality and knowledge.

Track 1: The logic of volume/oppression

The identification of Black girls as loud and therefore threatening, especially when in a group rather than isolated, is predicated on a negative (de) valuation of Black girls in union and positively affirms Black girls alone. However, because Black girls need other Black girls, a negative devaluation of Black girls together functions as means of oppression. Seen as loud and therefore threatening, the logic of volume in context of oppression misrecognizes loudness as a sensible response to structures and institutions that seek to silence Black girls. Volume as a technology of control either works toward minimizing sound oppressively or creating spaces where loudness is punishable and therefore unintelligible as a (re)action or resistance to social inequalities and narrow identity politics. When force is applied to manage Black girls' volume in the direction of silence, the greater the potential becomes for violence, typically acknowledged and experienced by Black girls as a misunderstanding—or being misunderstood.

"MS. UNDERSTOOD"—3:41

Hook (x2)
I don't wanna be
but sometimes I will be
I speak real loudly
but you don't really hear me

I don't wanna be
but sometimes I will be

Verse
When I speak my voice no one's listening
I trya tell my story but they keep on questioning
how I've made it *this* far
I say I don't know
I guess faith
brought me this far
Some folks tryna trap me

media tryna brainwash me
but I confide in a group
I know that will support me

SOLHOT GIVES
a reason for my swaggg
and for the ones that really
don't understand
being a Black girl
is more than poppin'
gum and rolling necks
'cause even at my worse
I'm still the best

Hook
I don't wanna be
but sometimes I will be
I speak real loudly
but you don't really hear me
I don't wanna be

Verse
When I grow up
Imma have a terrace
Even though at times
you look at me like I'm a terrorist
Please believe
Imma stay real real true to dis
rocking a trendy fashion
that you don't really wanna miss
Sometimes I go to school
not because it's cool
but because there's food
that might be the only thing that I get to
speaking my slang,
having crazy ass names,
snappin' my fingers
and playing what you call ghettofied games
Holding my head up and
sticking my chest out

but even still,
Imma be
misunderstood

Hook
I don't wanna be
but sometimes I will be
I speak real loudly
but you don't really hear me
I don't wanna be

Bridge
I'm misunderstood
You run from my hood
you say that I up to no good
even if I'm trying
you just walk right by me
and I don't know
what I can do
to keep from being
misunderstood

"Ms. Understood" swings, like a 1990s Aaliyah cut/jam. A hip-hop R&B-infused anthem of Black girlhood, the everydayness of Black girlhood sonically portrays the various ways that the oppressive ism's show up in a Black girl's life. Soulful in the ways that our parents may prefer but to which we also easily cling, this track quintessentially speaks back to how Black girls are misunderstood while producing rock-steady agreement. The first voice on the CD is a sampled hook from Nina Simone's "Please Don't Let Me Be Misunderstood." Lo comes in next with the hook from "Ms. Understood," creating instant dialogue that spans generations, lamenting the same plight—the denial of Black girl genius. When Lo sings the hook, her voice is higher in register but is also reminiscent of Mary J. Blige—real, relatable, and experienced. Demonstrative of second-generation hip hop, the catchy hook is followed by a dope verse. Taylor is the emcee of the second verse; her voice is already familiar because throughout the song she provides synthesized background ad libs as Lo sings. Taylor's alto commands attention with full authority.

"Ms. Understood" also documents Black girls' cultural style and particular racialized, gendered misunderstandings. Inspired by two girls in SOLHOT who shared their sense of frustration and annoyance with people in positions of power and authority who were unwilling to listen to them but quick to pass judgment, leading to punishment (in-school detention), this song draws on culture as a form of resistance. In SOLHOT, the reality that we know how to say something in a very culturally specific way is not a source of shame or reason for punishment; it is an inspiration to create, a way to express what we know. That we know how to give a glance or perform a gesture to mean a life-or-death difference is something that we recognize as potentially resistive and artistic. We perfected the eye roll to which one might reply, "I heard that!" That Black girls' being misunderstood is often an a priori reason for punishment with carceral consequences implicates a particular racialized, gendered formation of violence that often results in the institutional surveillance of Black girls, whose weaponry is body-specific and is punishable as a threatening yet nonviolent technology of terror.

Listening to "Ms. Understood" means imagining a world where it is possible for those in positions of power and those in relationship with Black girls to admit to not knowing. In spite of institutional documentation, official policies, common sense, and popular reports of who Black girls are, in the tune of this song is an ad-libbed truth that adults do not always know. That knowing is not predicated on always being right. That understanding does not mean peace, as much as misunderstanding does not always mean defeat. To "linger in the music," as suggested by Fred Moten (2003, p. 192), is to acknowledge the distance between the whole and impartial, or, for the purpose of this song, the distance between Black girls and those who attempt to understand them. Just as the Black girl in the song sings, "I don't know what I can do," uncertainty proves productive for cultivating a repertoire of listening that accounts for what misunderstanding opens up and for what it excludes.

Tracks 2 and 3: The logic of swagg/surveillance

Black girls' swagger may be defined as a culturally gendered and racialized performance of confidence, style, and expressiveness. In essence, Black girl cool as a particular kind of embodied knowledge enables a triumphant negotiation of public and private spaces against an archivable and resistant history of desirability, sexuality, and entertainment. As much as swagg depends on being seen, Black girls recognize that they cannot be seen apart from surveillance strategies that have only intensified for post-9/11 youth of color (Maira, 2009). While surveillance has become a normal part of everyday life, swagg and particularly a Black girl's swagg as a resistant performance of intersubjectivity reminds those looking at them that they too are looking back, watching you watch them. That they can negotiate and carve out an intersubjective gaze that remains hidden and out of view, while keeping the gaze on them in view, means that even while everyone thinks they know Black girls because they see them, resistant Black girls remain in some ways and in some spaces unknowable. Their shape-shifting transformative gaze means a good time is always possible in their line of sight, so long as they are able to articulate the terms of engagement. This is SOLHOT, and, while admittedly possible though arguably unsustainable, it does mean that once the system is undone, at the moment a revelatory vision is enacted, they will know freedom because they've had some practice.

"JUKE"—1:30

Intro [Speaking]:
Aye You
Yeah You
Bet you weren't ready for this one
Naw you weren't ready for this one
Bring that beat back

Hook
We rowdy
sometimes we be naughty
We dance til the mornin'
til sweat be a drippin' bae

Verse
We walk into the boys and girls club
'bout to get our party on
These boys grabbin' on my arm
and we 'bout to get our juke, juke on

Hook
We rowdy
sometimes we be naughty
We dance til the mornin'
til sweat be a drippin' bae

Verse
When you're an amateur
you hold on to someone else,

but a pro like me can do it by
herself
Count eight beats
then I gotta let 'em free,
'cause I got the boys lined up,
who wanna juke with me

Hook (x3)
We rowdy
sometimes we be naughty. We dance til the
mornin' til sweat be a drippin' bae

"Juke" opens with Taylor and Lo telling us we are not ready, and when the beat drops, they prove correct. It's a slow, sexy, steamy beat set to Lo's spicy rendition. They set a familiar scene: two girls, probably long time best friends, have planned all week to go out, and the night of the party has finally arrived. They carefully picked out their outfits, not matching of course, but both equally fly. The hair is done, nails outrageously painted, and body accessorized with good smells. The beat, like the girls, mesmerizes. They are ready to kick it and get it in. The hook hypnotizes. Blood-red gels provide steamy nighttime lighting that seduces. These girls, of course, are not the bad girls, but tonight they have pinky sworn to take off the good-girl masks and turn heads, purposefully. The planning pays off. They have fun, feel good, and enjoy every minute. They are in control, and while we may have doubted it at first, by the song's end, we are fully convinced.

Jukin' refers to a popular dance among young people during the early 2000s. It is a bold dance that requires at least two people. One way to juke is to stand in front of someone (in this song, it is a boy) with your back turned to them and grind and wind your hips to the music. Of course, when it gets really good, it's customary to bend over at the waist sticking your butt toward the other person's crotch. Bodies touch. It is often necessary to lean against a wall or comrade for greater support. It sounds pretty much how it looks if you are an adult, two people grinding to sexually arouse. For the girls who juke, it's a playful dance. The physical experience of the dance is intimately connected to the music, but the sound provides no consensus.

According to Katrina Hazzard-Gordon's (1990) classic study on Black secular dance, the term *jook* connotes a place where lower-class African Americans drink, dance, eat, and gamble (p. 80). In jook joints, musical styles and aesthetic preferences originated, birthing elements of currently recognizable genres such as blues, jazz, and hip hop. Citing Zora Neale Hurston's ethnographic fieldwork on music, "the jook" is a definitive Black style (Hazzard-Gordon, 1990, p. 83). For Hazzard-Gordon, Black sound and movement contain historical retentions traced from the Middle Passage to the northern urban 1960s United States. That the "jook," now spelled "juke" in SOLHOT, transmuted into a "new" popular dance among youth in the north midwestern United States who came of age in the 2000s brings with it historical traces of the possibilities of juke spaces to transgress assumed norms, while also providing temporary relief for those who endure marginalization. The juke, then, as a nighttime spot and dance of deviant ingenuity also means that a certain suspension of what is believable makes it possible for the protagonist in "Juke" to be free. This freedom is neither a form of false consciousness nor predicated on violence, but a form of power that makes an expressively good time possible in a Black girl body to sound like fun.

In SOLHOT it is possible to sustain a full conversation about a girl enjoying her body through dance and music. In SOLHOT the potential to experience freedom abounds: the girls who jukes well creates space for Black girl expertise to be demonstrated outside of the norms of what might be considered proper femininity. Gwendolyn Pough (2007, p. 94) rightfully acknowledged the need for hip-hop feminists to be engaged with *all* aspects of Black girls' lives so as to not be accused of being irrelevant to young Black women in the ways that some of us have categorized academic Black feminism. Likewise, Whitney Peoples (2000) mindfully suggested,

> While I might agree that Black women are in danger of losing ourselves if left to see our reflection only via the images presented in pop culture, I suggest that whatever the plan is formulated must bear in mind that the young women whom "we" purport to save have agency in their own ways, and by their own means, do exercise that agency. (p. 29)

As told to us in SOLHOT, and sung out loud by Taylor and Lo, for some girls, jukin' represents one such form of creative expression. SOLHOT is a space where Black girls themselves may author what feels so exciting to them in company of others who will not only listen, but invigorate their testimony with a tight music remix that then serves as a remembered sound of potential resistance they can (re)play and share at will. Differently sounding Black girls inspire different (embodied) movements that can and do in SOLHOT come together metaphorically and literally touch.

"WE ARE WOW"—3:00

Verse
Step up to the club.
The bouncer dere won't let me in the door.
He look at my ID,
then he tell me,
that I need to be a little olda.
But that's okay
'cause Imma go to the back door.
My man back dere,
he gon' let me on the floor.
That's why
it's good to have connections.
When I come through
no need for elections.
'Cause I've already been selected
the President of Swagg.
And when I come through
oh baby don't be mad.
I know you like flow
and I know you like my style.
When you see me,
go 'head and just smile.

Hook
Betcha thought I couldn't change my sound.
I keep my flow stacked up by the pounds
and every time you see me now,
you betta know that I mean
business and say wow.

Verse
So now,
I'm all up in the club
and all the dudes,
from me, want a hug.
'Cause I'm looking good
in my Dereon.
When dey play my song
den it's gon' be on.

Now dis dude
steppin' up in my face.
He tryna spit that game to me,
but he looking like a lame to me.
He said is there a drink I can order.
I said no, just get me some water.
Then another guy came to take his place,
and I looked up, he grabbed me by the waist.
Pulled me to the floor and time he didn't waste.
This dude must be a baker
'cause we standing up here, now we cakin'.

Hook
Betcha thought I couldn't change my sound.
I keep my flow stacked up by the pounds
and every time you see me now,
you betta know that I
business and say wow.

Bridge
When you're with me,
expect the unexpected,
'cause you might get something up my sleeve.
Just let me know when you're ready to leave
and you can walk me to my ol' skool Chevy.
Just make sure the bouncer don't see us,
'cause then he might try to treat us.
I will be Bonnie and you will be Clyde,
and out this club we will slide.
I keep a low profile.
I don't never try to hide.
I just be incognito.
It's my style that they want so bad!

Hook
Betcha thought I couldn't change my sound.
I keep my flow stacked up by the pounds
and every time you see me now,
you betta know that I
business and say wow.

"We Are WOW" is a reggae song with mad riddem, sung and rapped in Taylor's best patois. Different than the other songs, Taylor's lead vocals channel Patra, Lady Saw, Rita Marley, Tanya Stevens, and Grace Jones all wrapped up into one. The dance-hall sound of "We Are WOW" immediately inspires movement, the pepper seed (leading with the shoulder) to be exact. This song represents an instant classic diasporic anthem of Black girlhood. In "We Are WOW," recognition is demanded in context of dominant narratives that otherwise misunderstand and ignore/erase Black girls. Penned as the ultimate superheroines, the currency of Black girl style is in the ability of Black girls to be and be hidden in diverse experiences, systems, and institutions.

When Black girls create their own stories and set their fantasies, desires, and playful whims to a beat and challenge dominant narratives of Black women and girls as props, property, and perpetual victims, then we may see Black girls *differently*. Sapphire, mammy, Jezebel, ho, chickenhead, and video vixen are a few dominant stereotypes of Black woman/girlhood that are primarily defined through sex and sexuality (Collins, 2008; Harris-Perry, 2011) that Black girls understand themselves to be measured against. They also know that hypersexualized images of girls generally do not cause such a stir on an everyday basis, as they have been subject to explicit surveillance strategies for most if not all of their lives. From music and videos to commercials and television shows, that Black girls' bodies are often in service to everyone's desires but their own is mocked by Black girls' swagg that knows everyone is looking at them. The line "betcha thought I couldn't change my style" sounds so pointedly about a Black girl's own power, her own decision-making ability, and a full awareness of her sexuality as her own, which together demonstrate a kind of swagg that wows.

I would like to suggest that "dis dude" in the song represents more than a man, but systemic inequality. Black girl swagg wows, as signified by an ability to morph from silent Black girls to be talked to, to loud Black girls to be heard. The directive to "expect the unexpected" is but one such warning to surveillance strategies that knowing comes solely by sight. For example, listening to who and what Black girls desire must occur outside of the very familiar narrative of Black girls' desirability as predictable, presumably within heteropatriarchal norms, and legible only from the point of view of a single sound. "We Are WOW" bets on Black girls having also watched those institutions and individuals charged with investigating them to then juke those who so often and so predictably reduce Black girls to a single sound. Swagg wows in the intersubjective knowledge embedded in the nuanced niche of difference between loud and invisible, empowered and in servitude, in need of management and controllable, investigation and love. Swagg signified here as the ability to change it up sonically sounds like either a technology of resistance that enables survival or all-out liberation, depending on the circumstances.

Track 4: The logic of booty/capitalism

Booty abounds in the capitalist underpinnings of the United States as it currently exists. White supremacy and heteropatriarchy, mediated by popular culture, sell an ideal body type: the big-booty Black girl. The premise is fairly simple: the bigger the booty, the more patriarchal protection and privilege one is promised to receive via heterosexual conquest. To be bootylicious, then, is to be read as sexually attractive and marriageable. The irony is Black girls are expected to have big butts yet reap none of the constructed and imagined benefits. Fully aware of the farce and mythical quality associated with big-booty Black girls, in SOLHOT, girls articulate full well how traveling in Black girls' bodies does not make life better, does not guarantee fairness and equity, does not get one paid. They recognize how no one really measures up and they resist commodification by playfully engaging in a fake commercialization of a new kind of magic-pill cure-all—the SOL Thirsty energy drink—a drink that promises junk in the trunk. A playful engagement in hip-hop neoliberal hustlerism (Spence, 2011), "SOL Thirsty" allows them for a moment to ponder what it would be like to secure the full promissory benefit of a racist and heterosexist trope literally propagated on their backs.

"SOL THIRSTY"—2:46

Intro [Speaking]:
The Girl: Hi! My name is Jenny and I'm from Lombard and I want a big booty! My jeans are always falling off of me. I wish I had more junk to keep 'em up.
The SOL Thirsty Fairy: Well don't you worry honey, 'cause I got something for you. We got this drink called SOL Thirsty and I bet you get that big ol' booty you been lookin' for. Fit all ya jeans.
The Girl: Are you sure?
The SOL Thirsty Fairy: Oh I'm sure! Just trust me. Now you drink up so you can get that big ol' booty.
The Girl: Thanks SOL Thirsty!

Hook
SOL Thirsty
not just an energy drink
SOL Thirsty
keep your mind so in sync

SOL Thirsty
drink all of this
SOL Thirsty
Your flat booty they won't miss

SOL Thirsty
not just an energy drink
SOL Thirsty
Your flat booty they won't miss

Verse
when u drink this drink
u gon get some pep in yo step
when u drink this drink
it's yo swagg it's gon really help
when u drink this drink
it's gon' put some junk in your trunk
and every time that you hear music
u gon' make your trunk jump

Hook
SOL Thirsty
not just an energy drink
SOL Thirsty
keep ur mind so in sync
SOL Thirsty

Verse
Kayne got the workout plan
but SOLHOT got the booty booster
not only in bottles but in aluminum cans

Hook
SOL Thirsty
drink all of this
SOL Thirsty
Your flat booty they won't miss
SOL Thirsty

Verse
Drink-Drink-Drink it up
Girl don't take sips, take big gulps
'Cause when you done
You gon' be like
Oh My Gosh!
That's What's UP!

The Girl: My name is Jenny and my booty is soo big yay
The SOL Thirsty Fairy:
I told u it was gonna work, but no one ever listens to me
so until next time, you keep gulpin' this miracle drink
And I promise you'll live
Happily SOL Thirsty

Verse
When u drink this drink
u gon get some pep in yo step
when u drink this drink
it's yo swagg it's gon' really help
when u drink this drink
it's gon' put some junk in your trunk
and every time that you hear music
u gon' make your trunk jump

Hook
SOL Thirsty
drink all of this
SOL Thirsty
Your flat booty they won't miss
SOL Thirsty

The Girl: Thanks SOL Thirsty! Now I have a booty!

"SOL Thirsty" sounds like an infomercial set to music. Jenny's "suburban voice" creates an image of "the white girl with the big booty," set in contrast to Lo's Black girl assumed booty expertise. The concept of this song is gimmicky in much the same way as Jenny's speaking voice. A superficial listening sounds like they are just perpetuating the stereotype that the bigger the butt, the better (and of course, if you don't have a big butt, it's your responsibility to change it, by purchasing a quick fix). But "SOL Thirsty" is not a cheap trick, as the undercurrent of the song conveys critical thought. Between the lyrics and the music, what exactly is being sold, to whom and for what purpose, is never really identified. Who or what is the commodity in "SOL Thirsty"? Who or what is capital? The commercial sound of the song works because it is contrasted against a Black girl stance that cannot be purchased, at least in SOLHOT. "SOL Thirsty," as play and protest, questions Black girl/woman stereotypes and the current capitalist configurations of the United States, where one drink is advertised as the great booty equalizer.

White-supremacist imaginations about Black women's sexuality have historically fixated on the buttocks and continue to fuel racist beauty standards for women and girls of color (Durham and Baez, 2007; Hobson, 2005; Sharpley-Whiting, 1999). Andrea Smith (2006) instructs, "The capitalist system ultimately commodifies all workers—one's own person becomes a commodity that one must sell in the labor market while the profits of one's work are taken by someone else" (p. 67). In spite of child labor laws, the youngest Black girls in SOLHOT nonetheless are scripted within current capitalist formations as producers of a cultural "look," always for the perpetual benefit of others. In this way, the butt literally and potentially holds "an especially charged place in the history of both Black sexual expression and white classification of it as a sight of sexual perversity and inferiority" (Rose, 1994b, p. 167). In this song, girls in SOLHOT give attention to the well-worn message sold to Black girls that they then creatively thrift back to those who attempted to sell them out. As an unique kind of hip-hop revenge fantasy, "SOL Thirsty" positions Black girls against capitalism to bring wreck to stereotyped images sold to them, but which they refuse to buy (Pough, 2004, p. 74). The joke of quick cure-alls and fixes of the supposedly inferior body is not at their expense.

Admittedly, I did not, at first, get the joke. The idea of "SOL Thirsty" seemed hilarious to everyone except me. I did not think the discussion and conceptual development of "SOL Thirsty" was humorous. I heard them compare backsides, admit with woe to having flat butts, affirm juicy booties as better, and then think up this supposed drink that would solve every highly problematized booty. I remember the laughter, the giggles, the wiping of joyfully teary eyes that day in SOLHOT, and I did not say much of anything, but I continued to listen because everyone else seemed so committed to the idea. In hindsight, perhaps I was being too literal. I thought SOLHOT had declared itself liberal capitalist, with politics of survival that colluded with white-supremacist notions of exploitation. I could have imagined myself as the lone dissenter, and been okay with it, except that in all of my years of doing SOLHOT I rarely, if ever, witness the girls who participate arguing uncritically for system maintenance. Actually, it was not until I reheard the conversation in the form of the song that I understood how they used humor as a form of critique. "SOL Thirsty" adamantly disproves the stereotype that Black girl equals big butt. When one of the girls in SOLHOT said, "Sometimes I wish I could just drink something and make it [her behind] grow just a little bit!" and another girl playfully replied, "We'll get you some SOL Thirsty," lyrics, music, and humor intersected in the form of a song called "SOL Thirsty" to reimagine and un-brand ourselves anew.

DISCUSSION: A BLACK GIRL SOUND NOBODY CAN ORGANIZE

> Developing a style nobody can deal with—a style that cannot be easily understood or erased, a style that has the reflexivity to create coun-terdominant narratives against a mobile and shifting enemy—may be one of the most effective ways to fortify communities of resistance and simultaneously reserve the right to communal pleasure.
> (Tricia Rose, 1994a, p. 85)

Black girlhood sound is style nobody can organize but is often colonized to the detriment of Black girls and women. The truth that Black girlhood sounds implicate how we move with Black girls and women holds collective possibility and creative potential. Black girls' repertoire for being in spaces marked deviant, criminalized as illegal—spaces in which they were not meant to survive but may still triumph—is a sound nobody can organize. For those of us interested in creating and sharing power as an emancipatory project of self- and collective transformation, not programming ourselves to be enter-tained, or worse, to be the entertainment, is incredibly insightful. The full repertoire of what Black girls know to resist white-supremacist, capitalist, heteropatriarchal impulses is unarchivable, but its unintelligibility, especially in the form of state-sanctioned and disciplined behaviors, should not sug-gest that they do not know and that we do not know ourselves. Black girls in relationship with Black women in relationship with Black girls do know, but that also does not mean that we may be known without trust, outside of relationship, in our own time.

Increasing state-surveillance strategies, distorted popular media, pre- and post-9/11 anti-Black terrorist anxieties, poverty, increased criminalization of youth, fear, privatization of public goods, limited spaces of youth control, restricted social spaces, and the undeniable and historical theft of Black girl-hood (style) informed my reading, listening, and dancing to the music of the official SOLHOT CD. This may sound insufficient, if not preposterous, but SOLHOT as space of naming—ourselves and the work—has moved many to something more lovely for Black girls. Black girls, armed with a repertoire of wisdom to navigate social contexts that result in Black girl silent-versus-loud binaries, may be musically documented as an archive of rhythm that allows for movement beyond existing material conditions to invoke through song a future where it is their lives, not their sound, that stand for them.

Ultimately, I am interested in how this analysis of sound makes it possible to frame Black girlhood organizing in a way that accounts for listening be-yond superficial categorizes of a Black girl identity. When identity is premised on sameness and Black girlhood premised on shared oppression, organizing Black girls' spaces may surely replicate the same kind of disciplinary measures of control and surveillance strategies that Black girls have long since manipu-lated and outsmarted, foreclosing the kind of solidarity SOLHOT depends on. These spaces where security is assumed based on shared phenotype also often compel conformity to certain types of performance of Black female identity (Reid-Brinkley, 2008, p. 242). Sameness premised on a concept of safety, where violence occurs "out there" (meaning outside of the space) by "those" people (who do not share our experiences and look like us), is an illusion (Anzaldua, 2002, p. 4). White supremacy is maintained by structural inequalities that op-press Black women and Black girls differently, and so we must remain careful in our theorizing to refuse wholly oppressed and marginalized Black girls and women (Nash, 2008) and always be critical resisters (Edell, 2010; Stokes, 2007; Ward, 1996). In our practice, we must resist managing the unique articulation of Black girlhood sounds that particularly make the organizers uncomfortable. More important is that Black girlhood as an organizing framework allows for a repertoire of self-determined Black girl knowledge that may be used to improve practice inside of the very spaces that organize Black girls. Black girlhood as an organizing framework is sound that moves us closer toward interrogating how the state works in and through us, challenging institutions that do not see us even when we are present, and practicing love.

For the last five-plus years I have had the privilege and honor to listen to girls in SOLHOT. When I listen to a girl in SOLHOT tell me she was suspended for something bogus and outrageous, even though she was in a terrible situation, and enjoyed it, I hear complexity, honesty, and conflict. When I have been away from SOLHOT (to write, to profess, to mother) and return after missed activity, and I hear a girl share her story of losing something valuable (of personal significance to her), I can recognize and appreciate how she is flippant while telling her story and also sincere when she ends with a question: "Do you believe me?" When the homegirl who primarily organizes the space in my presence and absence promptly responds, "I believe you because you said it," I hear compassion. I have enjoyed working with the other homegirls as we tried to catch up to what we heard. Out of SOLHOT time, we reflect on our interpretations. Were we listening? How did we hear each other? SOLHOT is layers upon layers of interpretation.

More than sass and silence, I listen for a wide(r) range of expression, affect, sense, meanings, nonsense, truths, sincerity, and fear than we ever seem to admit publically when organizing SOLHOT. As an organizing concept, Black girlhood brings more than those who travel in Black girls' bodies together and surfaces Black girl knowledge so often devalued in non-SOLHOT spaces. Valuing Black girls' expressiveness offers a strong foundation from which to reevaluate organizing efforts. Forbidden Black girls' expressiveness contains wisdom that, when checked and rechecked against dominant stories, marginalized retellings, and counter- to the counter-narratives, contains teachable moments for all, not least among them those organizing on behalf of Black girlhood. This may very well be an insider lesson, but it is one whose potential resounds.

How we sound is critical, and who listens to us is crucial. In many youth-centered programs, gatekeepers, decision makers, politicians, and those in positions of power are assumed to the primary audience for the group's work. While these folks are important, in SOLHOT our first and most valuable audience is ourselves. Once we learn how we all matter, once we name the truths we live and share with others, once we call SOLHOT a way of moving through the world, what we produce becomes significant only because of what it demonstrates about how we listen(ed) to the girls, and to each other (or not). In SOLHOT we are known, unknown, uncertain, and dangerous. Externally funded or not, we are determined. Influenced by our own (un) voice(ed) embodied biographies, we are also not absolute in our opposition; we are sometimes conflicted. It is often questioned which girl—the girl who is loud, or the one who is silent—we are most attentive to. Some of us in

SOLHOT love the loud Black girls, because we were once and proudly remain loud Black girls, or we are silent Black women who want to be loud Black girls. Some of us in SOLHOT love the silent girls, because we were told to shut up and we did so forever. The girls who never speak are often invoked as the primary signifier of what is wrong with our practice, as an obvious symbol of marginalization. The girls who speak are accused of dominating the space, imagined as colonizers who mean no good. I listen to us talk about who we are in SOLHOT as Black girls and Black women, and this is what it sounds like. I listen to who is heard in SOLHOT and who is not. I hear us theorize from our personal experiences and become paralyzed. I hear us do the same thing and move to action. I hear us call out the ways oppression keeps us tired, distrustful, and isolated. I hear some of us betrayed by our experience of yearning to be upgraded by the shine of someone else yet remaining fearful of change. Complexity has a sound, and it sounds like all of us in SOLHOT.

As a both/and kind of visionary, I am too often in the middle to satisfy those on either end of the silent-versus-beast-mode continuum. I listen to challenge commonsense understandings and to resist white-supremacist, capitalist, heteropatriarchal norms that position Black girls as subjects to be worked with, worked over, and overworked, which is why I foreground the SOLHOT CD in this analysis as archived telling that hopefully inspires a repertoire of more just movement and listening even though its circulation in and out of SOLHOT, among homegirls in particular, is limited. The CD is not without controversy, in and out of SOLHOT. It is often dismissed, perhaps because we made it, maybe as a sign that we sometimes collude with white supremacy by attempting to disappear certain ideas that critique our own sense of righteous action. That the CD is banned or, as was reported to me, not allowed to be played in one of the youth nonprofits that many of the girls in SOLHOT frequent, was unexpected yet completely ironic, in the sense that it is in the same youth space where girls explicitly talk about honing their wowing and juking skills. But again, being misunderstood is a Black girl trope that reigns supreme, a sign that there is always work to be done.

Loud Black girl and quiet Black girl binaries position Black girls against each other, mask complexity, and stall (if not foreclose) solidarity. In practice, we who claim to listen may unwittingly collude with white supremacy when we rely on language like *loud* and *quiet* girls as dominant categories from which we then ascribe meaning on the bodies of certain girls and ourselves, all in hierarchical relationship to the other based primarily on the way we sound (loud) or not (silent). The ease with which sound becomes fodder for equations of personhood and privilege is especially relevant to organizing

Black girls. In non-SOLHOT spaces, how Black girls sound is the way they are seen, and how they are seen is the way they are known. Less rarely interrogated is how Black women and Black girls listen to each other and are heard. Listening to improve practice means engaging what I hear and, more than equating with a firm knowing, provides impetus for reflection about how I move as an honest account of praxis.

CONCLUSION

At the end of the day, after the program, and in the self-determined spaces Black girls navigate, the relationships created in SOLHOT and the practices enacted in that space matter most. In SOLHOT we do hip-hop feminist pedagogy and media studies; outside of SOLHOT, we enact a repertoire of a wider range of actions that we have already named and identified as valuable. When we listen for what Black girls know, the music, movement, ideas, and relationships produced recontextualize our sound in a different time and space, to listen and hear what is perhaps otherwise inaudible. We are more than how we sound, and within our knowledge are logics, influences, and collective possibilities that provoke uncommon actions and enforce our creative potential.

Sound overdetermines Black girlhood. To emphasize how someone sounds at the expense of reflecting on the subsequent movement results in unproductive binaries that reverberate our voices back to us, in unfamiliar and irrelevant hauntings that dominate the space and paralyze courageous practice. Organizing SOLHOT means to coming to value a complex Black girlhood sound like how misunderstanding, juking, wowing, and thirst sound in SOLHOT. Black girlhood as an organizing construct must remain concerned about the bodies of those who travel as Black girls to affirm how differently sounding bodies make different knowledges possible.

Organizers of gender-specific spaces for girls must assume girls know, rather than relying on how they sound to determine that organizers know better. It is already the case that the spaces, public and private, that do not boast radical care for Black girls whereby how they sound are simply providing excuses to not listen or to only hear only one way as correct. While many of the spaces they navigate are penned as attempting to hold them down, girl-centered spaces that attempt to lift them up are sometimes just as culpable. By proposing a new frame of organizing Black girls in context of ethnographic music production in SOLHOT, I outlined a creative potential of Black girlhood that no one can organize. Though I have often relied on the visual to describe sound, my aim is not to be reductive, but rather to emphasize how the phonic matters materially in the organizational efforts of moving people (in and beyond SOLHOT), particularly toward an amplification of a complex Black girlhood sound that requires a repertoire of listening that may include dance and certainly implicates every/bodies. Especially in discourses of the body, disease and disorder are much more frequently invoked than freedom (desire) and difference, but, as the music sounds, confiding in a group like SOLHOT means sustaining complex conversations that in turn make spaces like SOLHOT both different and emancipatory.

Track 5: "The Director's Cut"—6:42, by Ruth Nicole Brown

Saving Our Lives Hear Our Truths

I am in praise of you.

I thank you for who you are and all that you gave.

For the uncertain, critical, quiet, and critique . . . it all inspires.

Because you had work to do, came, did not come, suggested an idea, got a hug, and were hurt. That is SOLHOT.

Because at one point in time I suggested that we leave campus to commune. You did. We are. Here. Still standing. Then

It was poetry in motion.
We cried as we learned.
We danced with each other.
Talked and debated politics.
Discovered new excuses.
Held my baby as I tried.
The secret, we learned, again. Was us. Nobody else could do what we did. No longer in search of that which would make us whole. Within we went, joined by new young girls who
Took up a smile, and called it SOLHOT.
Noun, verb, adjective, past and dangling participle, gerund, preposition, adverb, conjunction, modifier

We were present perfect tense.

Four Years later

we are still here.

He.

is still here.

She.

is recalled back—fist in the air.

They.

reasons SOLHOT must continue to grow & change & find new ways younger ones,

If I did not move out of my own room to write

If I did not think our collective swagg was doper than my individual singular self

If I assumed that as the professor, older, published I knew better

If I was the kind of person that denied and denigrated low-end scholarship, abstinent virgins, bad biotches, second chances, and absent presences

would we know what we know now?
Which is when you decide your own education, school becomes irrelevant because learning and teaching become necessary.

We, "flaws and all," healed, hurt, and grieving, have when WE decided come together and time traveled, overcome giants, & created magic.

When we feeling really grown we put on knowledge in action and words and send it out to the world because we know:

"If your friends don't know it, then you don't know it, and if you don't know that, then you don't know nothing."

And so we make OURSELVES KNOWN.

We know how to create ciphers where Black girls and Black boys are remembered in the same breath.

We know how to translate the meaning of a lip smack, and a silent voice.

We are NOT afraid of volume.

We are NOT afraid of volume.

We are NOT afraid of volume.

Because we KNOW this is OUR chance to batty dance

First we JUKE IT. Then we JERK IT

Then we look at each other and now, LISTEN.

Because as we fully own up to our own shine we also own up to our faults, because we are not perfect, because we have made mistakes, because we were afraid, because we have disappeared people.

We remember.

We Black woman, Black man, strong, straight, queer, curious, younger, older, student, master teacher, tired, quiet, loud, exhausted, unimpressed, overqualified, Black girls have moved to the end of our rainbows . . . and find it necessary to get a witness.

Of a moment, never taken for granted, where some of us came together and fell apart, at least nearly one hundred times only to do it all over again and have found a hand still reaching out, at every beginning and at every end.

This is why I do it.

Conclusion

Dear C—,

When I was told that one of the students at the jail took an interest in my research on Black girlhood, I was immediately humbled. I had no idea that my work would penetrate those segregated concrete walls topped with spiraling barbed wire that swirled endlessly. But it did. Secondly, I felt immediately humiliated, because honestly, when writing about Black girls, never once did it occur to me—the visionary—to imagine you as an audience for my book, my research, or my passion. This shortsighted omission was a lesson you taught me as soon as you said something about celebrating Black girlhood and feminism to the student who generously shared with me your enthusiasm and critique. A few of the girls in SOL-HOT have a parent or two, and certainly many loved ones, who are locked up, and I know that when we check in, we sometimes hear stories about visiting family members in jail. But the letter you sent to me invited me to rethink this Black girl work that I do in SOLHOT with you standing with us. I mean, we invoke so many to our space—our ancestors, beloved grandmas, celebrity icons, the thugs we love, the street intellectuals, our crushes, and our nemeses—that it seems only more just to intentionally include you in our cipher, as well, and the millions more who celebrate Black girls from the inside.

I wrote you back and promised that after you read my next book, you would not again have to wonder or muse over what you, as a Black man, can do to support Black girls. Since I received your letter, about midway through this book, I've been thinking about you as a potential reader and would like to offer a few practical suggestions for ways Black men can support SOLHOT and celebrate Black girls.

First of all, you told me you were a father to Black girls, and I do believe that as parents we have a divine responsibility to show our children what love is. In SOLHOT, I hear many stories about what fathers mean in Black girls' lives, and, regardless of the circumstances, they want to know. Black men, fathers and father-like, are often looked to as models of what it means to be masculine, of what it means to be human, of how love can look when expressed via a Black man's heart, strong and true. Policies and institutions that separate Black fathers from their daughters do us all a disservice and sometimes unnecessarily extend a deep searching for that which is love. Fathering daughters is an exceptionally rewarding gift, and we must honor the love we can share with them every day.

As you taught me, Black men can remain compassionate and loving when it comes to conversations about feminism, gender, and organizing. Your letter was a part of a gift that came in threes. That same week I received your letter, a young man set up a meeting to share with me his desire to be a leader in his community—that he wanted to rise to the feedback of his friends who told him he had something special they respected. He didn't know what to do with this information, but he heard about SOLHOT and wondered if he could learn from it. The third Black man that led by example in that same week I meditated on your letter and personal well-being made a sacrificial financial donation to SOLHOT. Black men who give out of their hearts inspire me to do the same and return to SOLHOT with lessons for us all. Compassion is what you offered to me—a sincerely initiated conversation about us—together, living, learning, and organizing on behalf of communities we want made better. Compassion is then what I extended to others. You can do, Black man, what you've done: Read and share. Reach out to those who do feminism, write about Black girls, and interrogate what gender means for us all so that we cannot continue to write without you present and accounted for. Your witness means that I can tell a different story about Black men—who are not threatened by feminism because it includes them, too, who do not look at SOLHOT as something against them or Black boys, whose incredible insight allows us to keep open a necessary conversation about a collective vision of Black girlhood.

You asked me what Black men could do to support Black girls. I would encourage Black men to love their daughters and to remain teachable. Black men should hold the thought that Black girls' experiences are different and may be harder than their own. Black men should hold the thought that Black girls can lead us to something better than we've determined for them. Black men can be nonviolent and teach compassion just as well as anyone else. These things we can all do, that we attempt to do in SOLHOT, and because you asked specifically about Black men, I wanted to address Black men, as you asked me to do.

I am very thankful for your letter and the lesson you taught me in a few short words and very powerful actions: There is an education in humiliation, a spiritual development by way of getting it wrong. I want you to know and remember SOLHOT, and together we will keep shining, keep going, and keep on.

In solidarity,
Ruth Nicole Brown

Dear Black Woman Who Came to My Office and Broke Down,

You are rightfully tired. Mother, sister, daughter, organizer, freedom fighter, wife, lover, partner, luminary, friend—the world thrives on your selflessness, and my request that you have a self and be present invited a reflection you did not like and brought you tears. I get it. I get it good. Sister, writer, artist, people mover, and instigator of togetherness, it's okay to admit that you don't know if you are coming or going and already feel guilty for taking up my time with your tears and feeling bad that you're late for your next appointment. I will stand with you and extend a touch because I know that, before we can heal anyone, tears are often the first sign that the love we most desire is our own. You saw me, and us in SOLHOT together, engaged in work you deem important, and that image of us enthralled by our own laughter, the sight of us on purpose, sent a shiver past your to-do list and next appointment to contemplate about yourself, the senselessness of running on empty for everybody else, and missing the joy of your own somebodyness.

I say to you, take more than a minute to speculate on freedom. Fill the auditorium where we were with thoughts of what kind of Black girlhood you deserve, affirm your nieces, nephews, and mentees, express gratitude for every Black woman who has been telling you that ain't no love like the love you give to yourself.

I do know something about that moment—where you are—that special mix of self-pity and fragmented thoughts of shoulda, coulda, woulda, and didn't. I recognize the subtle surprise of being so snappy—spitfire words of condemnation escaped your tongue before you blinked an eye. Oh, I know too well the fifteen minutes before SOLHOT where you contemplate raising the covers above your head—silencing the cell phone and regretting that you said you would be there. No food cooked, children to pick up directly after, surely the one million requests you would receive to do something for somebody else, before you started your car that is need of an oil change, to the work that awaits at the close of the incense circle—I get it good. Disengagement only seems like the right thing to do, to be, since bringing your tired, sleepy, grumpy, grieving, unfulfilled self would only bring the group down—you rationalize. You decided to deny us, then, the pleasure of your company, and stay at home in the name of self-care. Only problem is, after you've slept those two hours of doing SOLHOT away, after you've watched back-to-back episodes of reality television to numb your mind, after you checked and responded to email in order to catch up, you do not feel any better. So of course when you run into us unexpectedly, when we come knocking on your door to see what is really going on, when we greet you in class to lecture on the work, the tears start as a twinkling of the toes until after the speeches are over, in which they fall with Katrina-like force out of your eyelids, you find yourself in the embrace of someone willing to love you back to yourself.

Come to SOLHOT.

I wonder why the girls are so much more skilled in this than the oldest of us in SOLHOT. I mean, over the years, they are certain: "Dr. B, me and so-and-so got a problem and we need to solve it right now, in SOLHOT." "I was waiting all week to get my hug in SOLHOT." "I feel so much better now." "Hey y'all, I didn't think I was going to make it, but ain't God good, play some gospel, then follow that up with Drake." "I want you to know and remember that I love y'all." "Is SOLHOT today?" "Just because I didn't come last week doesn't mean I wasn't thinking about y'all." "Yeah, I got suspended, but I'm trying to do better." "What is love?"

And forgive my skepticism when after you've excused yourself for crying in my presence and declared that I should never mind the moment so we can get to the business at hand, which you announce is doing something about the real problem that is the Black boy crisis, I sit back in myself and beg you to finish because I want to confirm that you, Black woman who just broke down, actually think you can do something to help save someone else. Especially in a state where if I were to breathe on you, as if to blow a dandelion, you too would actually disintegrate into pieces. I know you are on autopilot, Black woman, and can't hear me at this time, but I will still say to you, breathe. I will testify that yes, racism will take us out, won't it. Sexism always underestimates our ability, and ain't nothing micro about aggression, right . . . and for those reasons and so many more, we owe it to those coming after us, all those looking back at us, to live and to live fully.

By this time, you've already wiped your eyes and checked our meeting off your to-do list. I see you, Black woman, because I see us in SOLHOT, too tired to do the batty dance, too afraid to speak our truth, too ashamed of who we are to play a lead role. I stop. I meditate. I breathe. In the what-was-that-moment-that-now-feels-all-too-familiar, I express gratitude for SOLHOT. I affirm us all living with our lives. I refuse to play the "who is worse off" game, Black girls versus Black boys, because it will certainly not produce a winner, and if by Monopoly logics it does, the winner will only be at the expense of someone else. This work is not a game.

We are so good at being miserable; this system makes sure of that. But envision Black girlhood anew. Organize freedom, and find out, like so many before us, there is joy in the struggle. And struggle ain't mandatory.

Love you,
Ruth Nicole Brown

Dear Dr. Maparyan,

You asked with the courage of a mother-womanist-warrior, "What if Jesus came back in the body of a middle-class Black girl from urban America?" (Maparyan, 2012, p. 303). Would we recognize and embrace her? I am here to answer you that that yes, we would recognize and embrace her. I am here to tell you that in SOLHOT we would be healed by her coat worn indoors, that we would learn to love because she never spoke but kept coming back, we would be better off because she gave us the side eye and made us think again. In SOLHOT we make the space for Black girls and those who love them to return, and especially to return in ways that illumine the power, for example, of a sunset or sunrise in a sound of a Black girl's voice, in her rhythm, in her absence, in her resistance, in her ideas. Yes, we absolutely would, I am certain, in SOLHOT recognize and embrace all that she knows that defies the official story because only then do we ask the right questions, the forbidden questions, questions once thought inappropriate, the kinds of questions you name as "womanist what if's" (Maparyan, 2012; pg. 303). Somebody in SOLHOT would ask that girl to write a poem and perform it for us just so she could show off her disorderly conduct, and we could all clap and offer snaps because we all knew her Black girl performance was really right on, and not outside of nothing, but only at the intersection of genius and style. The laughter in this space would be palatable and palpable to all those who have once been called crazy and Black, or loud Black girl, or bad girl, or otherwise labeled goody-goody with the intent to reduce our power because we know how much fun it is to sharpen our wit, perfect our glances, practice our theology, and share our knowledge.

SOLHOT is a space, for now a small one, with big effects that honors what Black girls bring to us and to the world. We have seen it all and have not turned away. We who have done SOLHOT once or since the beginning know that no academic analysis can capture, let alone predict, the power of Black girls from the city, from small cities, from the suburbs, and from the rural farmlands. Absolutely diasporic, as I believe you would agree it is exactly, how we enter a double-dutch rope, how we come up with a move that cannot be replicated (which is why we made it up), how we interact Black girl to Black girl in ways that travel underwater, on water, over water, through water, and how we recognize other Black girls who divinely reveal themselves to us, having grown up in the city of Addis Ababa, Capetown, or Accra, or in broadbandless remote villages. In SOL-HOT we welcome Black girls in Black girl bodies and those transgressive bodies who perform something like Black girlhood but name it differently. We acknowledge Black girls whose premature deaths have rendered them body-free. At the close of every SOLHOT, it is possible to honor our baby ancestors and our baby angels so that we never forget. After reading your courageous witnessing and learning of your beautiful daughter—I answer you with a sincere yes.

I will remember Aliyah Phillips. May every good thing in SOLHOT recall her marvelous gifts and honor the so many, many, many others she now divines with to open our hearts to what they already know.

You, dear womanist, fierce mother intellectual, are purple; I am lavender. There is indeed an idea that pushes us to create what will one day no longer be needed—and though it is available to all, as you say, and not everyone accepts, I am honored to be in your sacred company.

In great respect and sincere admiration,
    Ruth Nicole Brown

Dearest SOLHOT girls and homegirls,

What's up??!! I love you all so much, and I'm so thankful. We have created this thing called SOLHOT that functions for each and every one of us differently but, for those who keep coming, means exactly what we need it to mean. I'm so incredibility excited that SOLHOT still exists, even though I know it won't always and I believe that it really should not have to. But to each of us, who show up with the expectation that something is going to happen today in SOLHOT that is needed, necessary, and allows us to be better people, I am so grateful.

Depending on what you know to be SOLHOT, I wonder if you know me at all. Given that I've sometimes been away from SOLHOT to mother, to give life, or to do work at the university that makes it impossible to be in SOLHOT at the same time, some of you who do SOLHOT or have done SOLHOT may not even know who I am. That's more than fine. I just ask that whoever you do know as the visionary in SOLHOT, the girls or homegirls who you see as responsible for making it happen, send her a special whisper of love. Encourage her and let her know that SOLHOT is appreciated. If you go to SOLHOT and don't know why you keep going, just do it. I promise you will know in time.

To those who have sacrificed, and I know you know who you are, I am so proud of us! I mean, we did this thing and are continuing to do it. People may look at us weird, but do not be bothered by the haters. This work of organizing, this work of researching, this work of changing the world should be fun, and don't we make it look good?! Remember what you learned and who taught you, reminisce about the smackdowns and grown-up revelations, keep in touch with those who have moved on, and give a hug to those who are still here. You all inspire me to turn the music up and rap along with Invincible's (2008) "Keep Goin" because, like them, I really mean it:

> And I keep keep on
> Even when my hand tires
> No labels or vampires
> No funders or grantwriters
> Inspired by freedom fighters
> Before us and coming after us
> To the present survivors of human massacres—If you "considered
>   suicide when rainbows were not enough"
> And bank rolls were clotted up
> It's painful I brought it up
> the truth gotta come out from different angles it's bottled up
> Serve it with a ladle from the cradle til my body's dust
> Nothin else synonymous to the feeling i get from demanding respect
> And knowing that i'm earning all my papes (I keep goin)
> Stay persistent you determining your faith (I keep goin)
> Always changing cuz I learn from my mistakes (I keep goin)

Even when I wanna stop . . . Let me just say this: We are improbable. We are ahead of our time. We keep the traditions we choose alive and are unafraid of our blues. We are too fantastic to doubt ourselves, but we do anyway because we are human and need a break—Queen Jessica is so right about that. We are bigger than the university and bigger than the public school. We are the poets' muse. We are charting our own course and adding stars to the sky when we shine. We are the formula to the scientific equation for how to do what is now in vogue as "civic engagement" plus recognition minus ego subtracting the funding that should have been yours anyway plus every single judgment, admonishment, and idea (and there have been too many) that suggested we were wrong, not wronged. But we are well. We know that we need to know so that we can share it with Black girls in and out of SOLHOT. We are so underground that those looking for Black girls will miss us because *he* showed up. We will get it back because we wanted it done right and so used our own resources, money and beyond. Armed with the love of those who raised us and given our ability to share what they taught us, we organize, educate, question, and move. At the end of the day, we are freedom personified, and that is enough for us all.

Free Black girls, free us all!

Love,

Dr. B

Dear Maya Sanaa and Addis,

The people want to know how motherhood changed me. Since SOLHOT and you, Maya Sanaa, grew up together, many wrongly assumed that because you are a girl, SOLHOT was for girls only. My dedication and passion for working with girls predated your birth, Maya Sanaa, but was certainly more corrected and informed by your being. Now you are six, and you tell me to drop you off at SOLHOT, and they will bring you home. Now you are six and tell me you want to perform with us. Now you are six, and I am changing how I hear the girls because of what I learn from you. Now you are six, and I am feeling like maybe I am too old for SOLHOT. Now you are six and say that your mom's work is SOLHOT and writing. You tell me I am an author, we are famous, and SOLHOT is for you and Black girls. Now you are six and SOLHOT, and growing.

Addis, you are my baby boy that everyone expected would be responsible for my SOLHOT program for boys. This supposed SOLHOT for boys hasn't happened yet because it's called SOLHOT that I fully expect you too will shape and know as a space of celebration and freedom. You won't be the first boy in SOLHOT, and you won't be the last. Your being and birth was assumed to awaken me to the "bigger plight" that is the Black boy crisis.

My son, you are enough all by yourself and are not responsible for any of my professional or personal epiphanies. And this of course you already know, the way you came into the world showing off your power to upstage me with a kick from the inside, how you take up space so sure of your voice and your reason for being—the way you make mommy walk the SOLHOT I talk about means that you are nine months of a leader, fully capable of rising beyond any and all crises that existed, with the assurance that it may have awaited your presence only to be solved and, because of SOLHOT, will not be yours to be solved alone.

So far both of you have only known life with SOLHOT, and I know life because of you both. Motherhood and SOLHOT sometimes seem oppositional to the other, but that is only because I work in a system that denigrates motherhood and makes it hard, especially on Black mothers. But really, I guess if the people had to know how you all changed the work I do, I would say that Black mothering and SOLHOT is like womanism to Black feminism to hip-hop feminism—until you all say otherwise. Mommy loves you!

Love, hugs, and kisses,
Ma

AT THE END OF THE DAY TRUTHS WE CAN USE

"At the end of the day" is a turn of phrase used by many a Black girl to preface truth-telling. In the spirit of Black girl talk, plain, honest, and from the heart, at the end of the day the big idea in this book is that Black girlhood envisioned as a space of freedom makes it possible to create and share new knowledge, as we currently do not recognize the full genius of many a Black girl. Saving Our Lives Hear Our Truths (SOLHOT), as one particular site of making this vision a material reality, offers an array of usable truths from which we, as scholars/artists/activists, may rethink Black girlhood for the purpose of affirming Black girls' lives. SOLHOT does not claim to have it all figured out, nor is it always all good, but those who labor to make the space of Black girlhood through time, in a Black girlhood organizing framework, have witnessed a Black girlhood genius that absolutely would border on romanticism if it wasn't so adept at making it possible to do as the name implies—save lives and facilitate the hearing of truths.

As I contemplated writing about the policy solutions, the anecdotes about where we are now, the tangible action steps that could be taken, I instead offered letters that I hope articulate in a very real way what needs to change, who can do it, and how. I first received a letter from C—, then I wrote him back, and later I was presented with an opportunity to teach in prison because he, along with a few other students, wanted to take a course on Black feminism and organized my visit. Essentially, we did SOLHOT, and it reconfirmed that SOLHOT is not "only for Black girls"—as many commonly and wrongly assume. My letter to C— shows that the principles and methods of doing SOLHOT are particular yet universal and that the practice of SOLHOT, in all kinds of spaces, particularly those where carceral borders make freedom seem less attainable, offers the possibility of transformation.

The letter to the woman who came to my office is meant to invoke the very real issue of Black women's health in relation to labor. Future research has to give attention to the personal and health costs of doing work like SOLHOT, often from institutional locations that value neither Black women's bodies nor their intellect. I too have very much known what it is to write and work from a place of fatigue. The typical response to feeling tired is to withdraw from the work, often using the rhetoric of self-care as an excuse from being held responsible and accountable to others. My invitation to the woman and to those who are a part of something like SOLHOT is not isolation, but the prioritizing of community building and participation. This may seem counterintuitive. However, if the work is worth doing, then restorative energy is necessarily a part of it, and if it is not, then the work is not worth doing.

The letter to Dr. Maparyan commends her brilliant and courageous research and writing while also demonstrating my desire to bring SOLHOT and Black girlhood into womanist conversations and theories. In this book, I have privileged hip-hop feminism and feminism-of-color terminology while recognizing that much of what I am concerned with is also addressed by womanism. Black girls, homegirls of various generations, and mothers who identify with and break from numerous intellectual traditions have much to learn from each other with the hope that our collective vision of a liberatory Black girlhood is more just than any singular lens. Likewise, scholars in the fields of girls' studies, youth culture, hip-hop studies, and cultural and ethnic studies would do well by centrally taking up questions that critically examine Black girlhood.

This book would not seem complete without a letter to the SOLHOT girls and homegirls—those in SOLHOT who intentionally make the space for Black girls and beyond to gather and attempt to celebrate our complexity. I am grateful for those who, for no matter how short of a time, give their time, energy, creativity, and intellect to make SOLHOT happen. Especially because SOLHOT turns out to be much more work than expected, I am deeply appreciative of those who grow the practice and contribute toward knowing and doing better.

The last letter, to my children, flowed unexpectedly in the writing. I do give a lot of mothering energy to SOLHOT itself, the girls, and the homegirls, and in turn SOLHOT is very giving to my children as well. I suppose it is because I do work with young people that many listen to my research on SOLHOT and solicit parenting advice, though I typically refrain from answering because I do not claim to be an expert on parenting nor am I a researcher of parenting. Motherhood and SOLHOT do not exist in a one-to-one comparison or opposition. They both feed each other; they both take from each other. The lack of institutional support makes both more difficult, as a huge understatement, and I only mean to suggest through my letter that I have found imperfect ways to do both. The labor of mothering too often remains hidden in the shadows of professionalism, and my love letter to my children is an intentional break in subject and tone—a graffiti-inspired tag on an otherwise clean and neat surface. All of the letters are profoundly personal and grounded in the insights and ideas that emerged from writing this book, yet as a means of conclusion I have also meant for them to point toward necessary conversations and areas of future research that deserve greater scholarly attention that should also result in policy change and political transformation.

As a whole, this book has demonstrated the significance of listening to Black girls, valuing complexity, questioning the primacy of sight as the way to know, abolishing state-sanctioned and interpersonal racialized and gendered forms of surveillance that punish and imprison Black girls, and rethinking how and for what purpose Black girls experience programming, organizations, and activist collectives. SOLHOT as a space of celebrating Black girlhood in all of its complexity has enabled documentation and analysis of creative methodologies and engagements that include transformative collective work that is sacred, affirmed intersubjective insights between Black girls and Black girls and also between Black girls and Black women, created and advanced relational solutions to the issue of violence and fighting, and made music that moves people to practice collective actions and dreams of justice and freedom for Black girls everywhere.

Academically, this work urges scholars to centralize Black girlhood for the purpose of theorizing and documenting the necessity of Black girls' critical thought and how it often challenges both the institutions that govern their lives and also the academic constructs and ideas so often implicated in policy making, which abuse what they know, how they know, and the sometimes contested ways they say it. In this research I have found various genealogies of feminisms, girls'-studies discourses (in spite of the narrowness of that field), and performance epistemologies, methods, and analytical distinctions useful for advancing how SOLHOT, or the various ways love is enacted and performed to affirm Black girls and those who love them, can make possible new questions, offer alternative explanations, and provide usable knowledge that improves upon Black girls' freedom and the greater emancipatory possibility their lives hold for us all.

This book is made possible because of SOLHOT, but it is not SOLHOT. While at all times I am careful to name and to credit SOLHOT as responsible for some of the ideas shared in this book, my hope is that the analysis presented reads as more than a case study of SOLHOT. I resisted the case-study approach because I did not want this book to be read as the definitive story. There are multiple stories of SOLHOT that are all valuable and as valid as mine. In fact, many people have written about and are writing about SOLHOT, and their writing, along with this book, should add to the overall picture—enlivening greater discussion, pointing to contradictions, and highlighting paradoxes that should minimize the distance between Black girlhood as we now know it and Black girlhood as we want it to be. Other scholars, including Stephanie Sears (2010) and the Girls Empowerment Project, Maisha Winn (2011) and Girl Time, Shawn Ginwright (2010) and Camp Akili, Korina Jocson (2008) and Poetry 4 the People, Aimee Cox (2011) and BlackLight, Alexis Gumbs and BrokenBeautiful Press (2012), Bettina Love (2012) and hip-hop education and social-justice praxis, and so many inspiring others are writing about how working with youth changes them, resulting in new ideas that challenge what is currently known about youth, programming, identity, politics, and education. Our tomorrow will certainly be brighter than today.

Creative scholars/artists/activists are needed because the system is broken. At this particular historical moment, public schools are disintegrating, public spaces like parks are dilapidated and disappearing, media is also very isolating in spite of its claim to the contrary, and the prison-industrial complex is ever expanding. The premature deaths of Black youth in the United States happen violently fast and, when gendered feminine, is violently slow—begging the question "Where is the love?" while also beckoning more creative responses in the forms of collective, interpersonal relationships, national policies, face-to-face and virtual instances, and sustainable meetings that show love is right here between us (Jordan, 1981, p. 140). Performances of Black youth should not give rise to moral panics but rather inspire us to creatively follow the wisdom of how a fourteen-year-old Black girl, for example, responds to circumstances that are arguably harsher than those of her parents' generation. Clearly, so shows the girl who claims she doesn't sing but has a beautiful voice. So clearly shows the girl who remains suspended from school because she did not start any trouble but was the one that got caught. Clearly, the Black girl who knows she is going to Howard to prepare to be a first of something great, as well as the Black girl who hopes you don't ask her about her dreams because she doesn't have any. Creativity and what we have not yet thought of together will prove useful for ensuring that the youngest of us live with their lives, and we with ours.

Creativity was necessary to suggest and start something like SOLHOT; it was invaluable in theorizing our practice and absolutely indispensable to improve our practice, save ourselves, and allow our truths to be heard. We created together and collectively imagined what we wanted for ourselves and made it so. It was the creative source so often quoted, remembered, and celebrated in women-of-color feminisms that allowed me to speak in my own poet/playwright/scholar voice and teach others how to do the same. Creativity allowed me to name what I have witnessed in SOLHOT and to explain a bit of what is possible because specific people have found use in coming together and organizing themselves as Black girls and beyond. Admittedly, I delved deep into Black girlhood, specifically Black girlhood reimagined. I started with Black girls and end with them as well. I envision Black girlhood as a space of freedom to give homage, as did Lucille Clifton to our hips, as did Nikky Finney to our bare arms, as did Nikki Giovanni to our errors, as did Alice Walker to our Shug, as did June Jordan to our right against suicide, as did Sonia Sanchez to our freedom, as did Audre Lorde to our voice. To name, claim, organize, and perform, as did bell hooks on behalf of our feminism, Angela Davis on behalf of abolition, as did Robbie McCauley on behalf of our suga. I want a Black girlhood that gives homage to my mama's mantra "Do your best." I want a Black girlhood that gives homage as does Mrs. Regina to our spirit, as does Mrs. Angela to our abilities, as The One With The Camera Glued To Her Hand does to our feelings, as L.A. Bound does to our stories, as Chi-city does to our loudness, as The Praise Dancer does to our bodies, as Humility and Wellness does in our individual and collective quest to know that which love is so that it may be shared. This very specific kind of attention to detail was presented throughout this retelling and re-search of Black girls' lives to make this story about SOLHOT Black girls (and not even other groups of Black girls) into a story about us all.

Works Cited

Alexander, M. J. (2005). *Pedagogies of crossing: Meditations of feminism, sexual politics, memory, and the sacred.* Durham, NC: Duke University Press.

Alexander, M. J. (2007). Danger and desire: Crossings are never undertaken all at once or once and for all. *Small Axe,* 24(11), 154–66.

Anderson, L. (2008). *Black feminism in contemporary drama.* Urbana: University of Illinois Press.

Anzaldúa, G. (2002). Preface: (Un)natural bridges, (un)safe spaces. In G. Anzaldúa & A. Keating (Eds.), *This bridge we call home: Radical visions for transformation* (pp. 1–5). New York: Routledge.

Anzaldúa, G., & Moraga, C. (Eds.). (2002). *This bridge called my back: Radical writings by women of color.* Berkeley, CA: Third Woman Press.

Bambara, T. C. (1980). *The salt eaters.* New York: Random House.

Bambara, T. C. (1982). "A girl's story." In *The sea birds are still alive.* New York : First Vintage Books.

Bambara, T. C. (1982). *The sea birds are still alive.* New York: First Vintage Books.

Barnett, L. (2007). *I got thunder: Black women songwriters on their craft.* New York: Thunder's Mouth Press.

Beauboeuf-Lafontant, T. (2009). *Behind the mask of the strong Black woman voice and the embodiment of a costly performance.* Philadelphia, PA: Temple University Press.

Behar, R. (2007). *An island called home: Returning to Jewish Cuba.* New Brunswick, NJ: Rutgers University Press.

Berger, J. (1977). *Ways of seeing: Based on the BBC television series.* London: British Broadcasting Corporation. New York, NY: Penguin Books.

Bolles, A. L. (2001). Seeking the ancestors: Forging a Black feminist tradition in anthropology. In I. McClaurin (Ed.), *Black feminist anthropology theory, politics, praxis, and poetics* (pp. 24–48). New Brunswick, NJ: Rutgers University Press.

Bourdieu, P. (1981). *The logic of practice* (P. Nice, Trans.). Stanford, CA: Stanford University Press.

Boyd, V. (2003). *Wrapped in rainbows: The life of Zora Neale Hurston.* New York: Scribner.

Brown, L. M. (2003). *Girlfighting: Betrayal and rejection among girls.* New York: New York University Press.

Brown, R. N. (2009). *Black girlhood celebration: Toward a hip-hop feminist pedagogy.* New York: Peter Lang Press.

Busia, A. (2008). Teaching Toni Cade Bambara teaching: Learning with the children in Toni Cade Bambara's "The Lesson." In L. J. Holmes & C. Wall (Eds.), *Savoring the salt: The legacy of Toni Cade Bambara* (pp. 181–94). Philadelphia, PA: Temple University Press.

Chesney-Lind, M. & Jones, N. (Eds.). (2010). *Fighting for girls: New perspectives on gender and violence.* Albany: State University of New York Press.

Christian, B. (2007). *New Black feminist criticism, 1985–2000.* G. Bowles, M. G. Fabi, & A. Keizer (Eds.). Urbana: University of Illinois Press.

Cohen, C. (1999). *The boundaries of Blackness: AIDS and the breakdown of Black politics.* Chicago, IL: The University of Chicago Press.

Collin, L. (2012, January 30). Teacher accused of racial discrimination on paid leave. *CBS Minnesota.* Retrieved May 17, 2013, from http://minnesota.cbslocal .com/2012/01/30/st-paul-teacher-accused-of-racial-discrimination-on-paid-leave/

Collins, P. (1991). *Black feminist thought: Knowledge, consciousness, and the politics of empowerment.* New York: Routledge.

Collins, P. (2008). *Black feminist thought: Knowledge, consciousness, and the politics of empowerment.* New York: Routledge.

The Combahee River Collective (1995). A Black feminist statement. In B. Guy-Sheftall (Ed.), *Words of fire: An anthology of African American feminist thought* (pp. 231–40). New York: The New Press.

Conquergood, D. (2002). Performance studies: Interventions and radical research. *The Drama Review,* 46(2), 145–56.

Cotton, N., Resnick, J., Browne, D., Martin, S., McCarraher, D., & Woods, J. (1994). Aggression and fighting behavior among African-American adolescents: Individual and family factors. *American Journal of Public Health,* 84(4), 618–22.

Cox, A. (2008). Thugs, Black divas, and gendered aspirations. *Souls: A Critical Journal of Black Politics, Culture, and Society,* 11(2), 113–141.

Cox, A. (2009). The Blacklight Project and public scholarship: Young Black women perform against and through the boundaries of anthropology. *Transforming Anthropology,* 17(1), 51–64.

Cox, A. (2011, September 21). Dunham in the air: A reflection on radical choreographies and programming social justice. *The Feminist Wire.* Retrieved May 15, 2013, from http://thefeministwire.com/2011/09/dunham-in-the-air-a-reflection -on-radical-choreographies-and-programming-social-justice/

Davies, C. B. (1994). *Black women writing and identity migrations of the subject.* New York, NY: Routledge.

Dawson, M. (1994). *Behind the mule: Race and class in African-American politics.* Princeton, NJ: Princeton University Press.

Deck, A. (1990). Autoethnography: Zora Neale Hurston, Noni Jabavu, and cross disciplinary discourse. *Black American Literature Forum,* 24(2), 237–56.

Denzin, N. (1994). The art and politics of interpretation. In N. Denzin & Y. Lincoln (Eds.), *Handbook of qualitative research* (pp. 500–515). Thousand Oaks, CA: Sage Publications.

Dillard, C., Abdur-Rashid, D., & Tyson, C. (2000). My soul is a witness: Affirming pedagogies of the spirit. *Qualitative Studies in Education,* 13(5), 447–62.

Dillard, C., & Okpalaoka, C. (2011). The sacred and spiritual nature of endarkened transnational feminist praxis in qualitative research. In N. K. Denzin & Y. S. Lincoln (Eds.), *The Sage handbook of qualitative research* (pp. 147–62). Thousand Oaks, CA: Sage.

Dolinar, B. (2009, October 9). Champaign police fatally shoot unarmed 15 year-old African American youth. *Urbana-Champaign Independent Media Center.* Retrieved on October 17, 2011, from http://www.ucimc.org/content/champaign-police-fatally -shoot-unarmed-15-year-old-african-american-youth/|FCO|Hyperlink

Durham, A. (2010). Hip hop feminist media studies. *International Journal of Africana Studies, 16*(1), 117–40.

Durham, A., & Baez, J. (2007). A tail of two women: Exploring the contours of difference in popular culture. In S. Springgay & D. Freeman (Eds.), *Curriculum and the cultural body* (pp. 130–45). New York: Peter Lang Press.

Edell, D. (2010). *"Say it how it is": Urban teenage girls challenge and perpetuate cultural narratives through writing and performing theater* (Doctoral dissertation). Available from ProQuest dissertations and theses. (AAT 3427007)

Elliot, N. (2011, April 6). Interview with Nikky Finney. *Oxford American.* Retrieved on October 17, 2011, from http://www.oxfordamerican.org/interviews/2011/apr/06/ featured-poet-month/

Evans-Winters, V. E. (2005). *Teaching Black girls: Resiliency in urban classrooms.* New York, NY: Peter Lang Press.

Feldman, M. (2008). Why Performance? Why Not? Presentation at the Rackham Interdisciplinary Workshop on Narrative Theory and Methods. University of Michigan Ann Arbor.

Finney, N. (2009). Foreword: Pinky swear: SOLHOT & Dr. Ruth Nicole Brown, pioneer. In R. N. Brown, *Black girlhood celebration: Toward a hip-hop feminist pedagogy* (pp. xiii–xxii). New York: Peter Lang Press.

Fisher, M. (2011). *Girl time: Literacy, justice, and the school-to-prison pipeline.* New York: Teachers College Press.

Flynn, R. (2002). "Affirmative acts": Language, childhood, and power in June Jordan's crosswriting. *Children's Literature, 30,* 159–185.

Flynn, K., & Marrast, E. (2008). Spoken word from the North: Contesting nation, politics and identity. *Wadabagei: A Journal of the Carribean and Its Diasporas, 11*(2), 3–24.

Gaunt, K. (2004). Translating double-dutch to hip hop: The musical vernacular of Black girls' play. In M. Forman & M. A. Neal (Eds.), *That's the joint: The hip hop studies reader* (pp. 288–304). New York: Taylor & Francis.

Gaunt, K. (2006). *The games Black girls play: Learning the ropes from double-dutch to hip hop.* New York: New York University Press.

Gbowee, L. (Speaker). (2012, March). *Unlock the intelligence, passion, greatness of girls* [Video webcast]. Available from http://www.ted.com/talks/leymah_ gbowee_unlock_the_intelligence_passion_greatness_of_girls.html

Gilmore, R. (2007). *Golden gulag: Prisons, surplus, crisis and opposition in globalizing California.* Berkeley: University of California Press.

Ginwright, S. (2010). *Black youth rising: Activism and radical healing in urban America*. New York: Teachers College Press.

Giroux, H. (2002). Neoliberalism, corporate culture, and the promise of higher education: The university as a democratic public sphere. *Harvard Education Review*, 72(4), 425–64.

Goddard, L. (2007). *Staging Black feminisms: Identity, politics, performance*. New York: Palgrave Macmillan.

Golden-Biddle, K., & Locke, K. (1993). Appealing work: An investigation of how ethnographic texts convince. *Organization Science*, 4(4), 595–616. doi:|FCO|slug-doi10.1287/orsc.4.4.595

Gordon, A. (2008). Something more powerful than skepticism. In L. J. Holmes & C. Wall (Eds.), *Savoring the salt: The legacy of Toni Cade Bambara* (pp. 256–266). Philadelphia, PA: Temple University Press.

Gossett, H. (2002). who told you anybody wants to hear from you? you ain't nothing but a Black woman! In C. Moraga & G. Anzaldúa (Eds.), *This bridge called my back: Writings by radical women of color* (pp. 119–22). Berkeley, CA: Third Woman Press.

Greene, M. (1995). *Releasing the imagination: Essays on education, the arts, and social change*. San Francisco, CA: Jossey Bass.

Gumbs, A. (2012). *brokenbeautiful press*, at http://brokenbeautiful.wordpress.com/

Gumbs, A. (2010). *"We can learn to mother ourselves": The queer survival of Black feminism 1968–1996*. (Unpublished doctoral dissertation). Duke University, Durham, NC.

Hamera, J. (2011). Performance ethnography. In N. Denzin and Y. S. Lincoln (Eds.), *The SAGE handbook of qualitative research 4th edition* (pp. 317–29). Thousand Oaks, CA: Sage.

Hansberry, L. (1969). *To be young, gifted and Black: an informal autobiography of Lorraine Hansberry*. Adapted by Robert Nemiroff. New York: New American Library.

Harper, D. (1994). On the authority of the image. In N. Denzin & Y. Lincoln (Eds.), *Handbook of qualitative research* (pp. 403–12). Thousand Oaks, CA: Sage.

Harris, A. (2003). *Future girl: Young women in the twenty-first century*. New York: Routledge.

Harris-Perry, M. (2011). *Sister citizen: Shame, stereotypes, and Black women in America*. New Haven, CT: Yale University Press.

Hazzard-Gordon, K. (1990). *Jookin': The rise of social dance formations in African-American culture*. Philadelphia, PA: Temple University Press.

Hemenway, R. (1977). *Zora Neale Hurston: A literary biography*. Urbana: University of Illinois Press.

Hobson, J. (2005). *Venus in the dark: Blackness and beauty in popular culture*. New York: Routledge.

Holmes, L. J., & Wall, C. (Eds.) (2008). *Savoring the salt: The legacy of Toni Cade Bambara*. Philadelphia, PA: Temple University Press.

hooks, b. (2009). *Belonging: A culture of place*. New York: Routledge.

Invincible. (2008). Keep goin. On *ShapeShifters* [CD]. Detroit, MI: Emergence.

James, J. (1996). *Resisting state violence: Radicalism, gender, and race in U.S. Culture.* Minneapolis: University of Minnesota Press.

Jocson, K. (2008). *Youth poets: Empowering literacies in and out of schools.* New York: Peter Lang Press.

Jones, N. (2010). *Between good and ghetto: African American girls and inner-city violence.* New Brunswick, NJ: Rutgers University Press.

Jones, V., Bradshaw, C., Haynie, D., Simons-Morton, B., Gielen, A., & Cheng, T. (2009). A glimpse into urban middle schools on probation for "persistently dangerous" status: Identifying malleable predictors of fighting. *Journal of School Violence,* 8(4), 284–300.

Jordan, J. (1969). *Who Look at Me.* New York, NY: Thomas Y. Crowell.

Jordan, J. (1981). *Civil wars.* New York: Touchstone Simon & Schuster.

Jordan, J. (1985). *On call: Political essays.* Cambridge, MA: South End Press.

Jordan, J. (2000). *Soldier: A poet's childhood.* New York: Basic Civitas Books.

Jordan, J. (2002). *But some of us did not die: New and selected essays of June Jordan.* New York: Basic/Civitas Books.

Jordan, J., & Mueller, L. (Eds.) (1995). *Poetry for the people: A revolutionary blueprint.* New York: Routledge.

Kearney, M. C. (2006). *Girls make media.* New York: Routledge.

King, W. (2005). *African American childhood: Historical perspectives from slavery to civil rights.* New York: Palgrave McMillan.

Kinloch, V. (2006). *June Jordan: Her life and letters.* Westport, CT: Praeger Press.

Kinloch, V., & Grebowicz, M. (Eds.). (2004). *Still seeking an attitude: Critical reflections on the work of June Jordan.* Lanham, MD: Lexington Books.

Ladner, J. (1971). *Tomorrow's tomorrow: The Black woman.* New York: Doubleday Anchor.

Ladner, J. (1995). *Tomorrow's tomorrow: The Black woman.* Lincoln: University of Nebraska Press.

Locke, K., Golden-Biddle, K., & Feldman, M. (2008). Making doubt generative: Rethinking the role of doubt in the research process. *Organization Science,* 19(6), 907–18.

Lorde, A. (1984a). *Sister outsider: Essays and speeches.* Berkeley, CA: Crossing Press.

Lorde, A. (1984b). The transformation of silence into language and action. In *Sister outsider: Essays and speeches* (pp. 40–44). Berkeley, CA: Crossing Press.

Lorde, A. (1995). *The black unicorn: Poems.* New York: W. W. Norton.

Love, B. (2012). *Hip hop's lil' sistas speak: Negotiating hip hop identities and politics in the New South.* New York: Peter Lang Press.

Madison, D. S. (2010). *Acts of activism: Human rights as radical performance.* Cambridge, UK: Cambridge University Press.

Madison, D. S., & Hamera, J. (Eds.). (2006). *The Sage handbook of performance studies.* Thousand Oaks, CA: Sage.

Maira, S. (2009). *Missing: Youth, citizenship, and empire after 9/11.* Durham, NC: Duke University Press.

Maparyan, L. (2012). *The womanist idea.* New York: Routledge Press.

Mazina, D., & DiBrienza, R. (2008). Sakia Gunn. *Outhistory.org*. Retrieved May 14, 2013, from http://outhistory.org/wiki/Sakia_Gunn

McCauley, R. (2009, October). Sugar [Performance piece]. In M. Shea (Chair), *Strong in the broken places: Performance, perception, and public policy*. Panel presented at Imagining America: Artists and Scholars in Public Life National Conference, New Orleans, LA.

Miller, J. (2008). *Getting played: African American girls, urban inequality, and gendered violence*. New York: New York University Press.

Miller, V. (2011, October 20). Why "Amber Cole" video is a cautionary tale. *The Grio*. Retrieved May 14, 2013, from http://www.thegrio.com/opinion/why-amber -cole-video-is-a-cautionary-tale.php

Mohanty, C. (2003). *Feminism without borders: Decolonizing theory, practicing solidarity*. Durham, NC: Duke University Press.

Morrell, C. (Ed.). (1994). *Grammar of dissent: Poetry and prose by Claire Harris, M. Nourbese Philip, Dionne Brand*. Fredericton, New Brunswick, Canada: Goose Lane Editions.

Morris, E. W. (2007). "Ladies" or "loudies"?: Perceptions and experiences of Black girls in classrooms. *Youth & Society*, 38(4), 490–515.

Moten, F. (2003). *In the break: The aesthetics of the Black radical tradition*. Minneapolis: University of Minnesota Press.

Nash, J. C. (2000). Rethinking intersectionality. *Feminist Review*, 89, 1–15.

Nelson, C. (2010). *Representing the Black female subject in western art: Routledge studies on African and Black diaspora* (Vol. 2). New York, NY: Routledge.

Ness, C. (2010). *Why girls fight: Female youth violence in the inner city*. New York: New York University Press.

Ngô, F. (2011). Sense and Subjectivity. *Camera Obscura 76*, 26(1), 95–29.

Oyewùmí, O. (2005). *African gender studies: A reader* (1st ed.). New York, NY: Palgrave.

Peoples, W. (2007). "Under construction": Identifying foundations of hip-hop feminism and exploring bridges between Black second-wave and hip-hop feminisms. *Meridians, 8*(1), 19–52.

Peoples, W. (2008). "Under construction": Identifying foundations of hip-hop feminism and exploring bridges between Black second-wave and hip-hop feminisms. *Meridans: Representin': Women, Hip-Hop, and Popular Music, 8*(1), 19–52. Retrieved May 14, 2013, from http://www.jstor.org/stable/40338910

Perkins, K., & Uno, R. (1996). *Contemporary plays by women of color: An anthology*. New York: Routledge.

Philip, M. N. (2008). *Zong!* Middletown, CT: Wesleyan University Press.

Phillips, L. (Ed.). (2006). *The womanist reader*. New York: Routledge.

Pough, G. (2004). *Check it while I wreck it: Black womanhood, hip-hop culture, and the public sphere*. Boston, MA: Northeastern University Press.

Pough, G. (2007). "What it do, Shorty?": Women, hip-hop, and a feminist agenda. *Black Women, Gender, and Families*, 1(2), pp. 78–99.

Pough, G., Richardson, E., Durham, A., & Ramist, R. (Eds.). (2007). *Home girls make some noise!: Hip-hop feminism anthology*. Mira Loma, CA: Parker Publishing.

Pough, G. D. (2007). *Home girls make some noise: Hip-hop feminism anthology* (1st ed.). Mira Loma, CA: Parker Publishing.

Price, R. (2011, July 7). Ohio's black girls fighting daily traumas. *The Columbus Dispatch*. Retrieved October 17, 2011, from http://www.dispatch.com/content/stories/local/2011/07/07/ohios-Black-girls-fighting-daily-traumas.html

Reid-Brinkley, S. (2008). The essence of res(ex)pectability: Black women's negotiation of Black femininity in rap music and music video. *Meridians: Feminism, Race, Transnationalism*, 8(1), 236–60.

Rhodes, J. E., Bogat, J., Roffman, J., Edelman, P., & Gallasso, L. (2002). Youth mentoring in perspective: Introduction to the special issue. *American Journal of Community Psychology*, 30(2), 149–55.

Richardson, E. (2007). It's on the women: An interview with Toni Blackman. In G. Pough, E. Richardson, A. Durham, & R. Ramist (Eds.), *Home girls make some noise!: Hip-hop feminism anthology* (pp. 58–61). Mira Loma, CA: Parker Publishing.

Rose, T. (1994a). A style nobody can deal with: Politics, style and the postindustrial city in hip hop. In A. Ross & T. Rose (Eds.), *Microphone fiends: Youth music and youth culture* (pp. 71–88). New York: Routledge.

Rose, T. (1994b). *Black noise: Rap music and Black culture in contemporary America*. Hanover, NH: Wesleyan University Press.

Salaam, K. (2007). Searching for the mother tongue: An interview with Toni Cade Bambara. In L. J. Holmes & C. Wall (Eds.), *Savoring the salt: The legacy of Toni Cade Bambara* (pp. 58–69). Philadelphia, PA: Temple University Press.

Scobey, D. (2002). Putting the academy in its place. *Places*, 14(3), 50–55.

Scott, K., Muhanji, C. & High, E. . (1999). *Tight spaces*. Iowa City: University of Iowa Press.

Search for remains of 5-year-old Jhessye Shockley begins today (2012, February 6). *NewsOne*. Retrieved May 14, 2013, from http://newsone.com/nation/kirstensavali/search-for-remains-of-5-year-old-jhessye-shockley-begins-today/

Sears, S. (2010). *Imagining Black womanhood: The negotiation of power and identity within the Girls Empowerment Project*. Albany: State University of New York Press.

Sharpley-Whiting, T. D. (2007). *Pimps up, ho's down: Hip hop's hold on young Black women*. New York: New York University Press.

Shohat, E. (2006). *Taboo memories, diasporic voices*. Durham, NC: Duke University Press.

Smith, A. (2006). Heteropatriarchy and the three pillars of white supremacy: Rethinking women of color organizing. In *Color of Violence: The Incite! Anthology* (pp. 66–73). Cambridge, MA: South End Press.

Smith, B. (Ed.) (1983). *Home girls: A Black feminist anthology*. New Brunswick, NJ: Rutgers University Press.

Smith, L. (1999). *Decolonizing methodologies: Research and indigenous peoples.* London: Zed Books.

Spence, L. (2011). *Stare in the darkness: The limits of hip hop and Black politics.* Minneapolis, MN: University of Minnesota Press.

Stevens, J. (2002). *Smart and sassy: The strengths of inner-city Black girls.* New York: Oxford University Press.

Stokes, C. (2007). Representin' in cyberspace: Sexual scripts, self-definition, and hip hop culture in Black American adolescent girls' home pages. *Culture, Health & Sexuality, 9*(2), 169–84.

Swarr, A. L., & Nagar, R. (Eds.) (2010). *Critical transnational feminist praxis.* Albany, NY: State University of New York Press.

Talbott, E., Celinska, D., Simpson, J., & Coe, M. (2002). "Somebody else making somebody else fight": Aggression and the social context among urban adolescent girls. *Exceptionality, 10*(3), 203–20.

Taylor, D. (2003). *The archive and the repertoire: Performing cultural memory in the Americas.* Durham, NC: Duke University Press.

Trinh, M. (1989). *Woman, native, other: Writing postcoloniality and feminism.* Bloomington: Indiana University Press.

Walker, A. (Ed). (1979). *I love myself when I am laughing . . . And then again when I am looking mean and impressive: A Zora Neale Hurston reader.* Old Westbury, NY: The Feminist Press.

Wang, C., & Burris, M. A. (1997). Photovoice: Concept, methodology, and use for participatory needs assessment. *Health Education & Behavior, 24,* 369–387.

Ward, J. (1996). Raising resisters: The role of truth telling in the psychological development of African American girls. In B. Leadbeater & N. Way (Eds.), *Urban girls: Resisting stereotypes, creating identities* (pp. 85–99). New York: New York University Press.

Weems, M. (2003). *Public education and the imagination-intellect: I speak from the wound in my mouth.* New York: Peter Lang Press.

Weems, R. (2000). "Artists without art form": A look at one Black woman's world of unrevered Black women. In B. Smith (Ed.), *Home girls: A Black feminist anthology* (pp. 94–105). New Brunswick, NJ: Rutgers University Press.

Williams, S. (2012, January 14). Suffering in silence: Black women, suicide and depression. *Backbone.* Retrieved May 14, 2013, from http://www.backbonewomenonline.com/2012/01/suffering-in-silence-black-women.html

Willis, P. (2000). *The ethnographic imagination.* Chicago, IL: University of Chicago Press.

Winn, M. T. (2011). *Girl time: Literacy, justice, and the school-to-prison pipeline.* New York: Teachers College Press.

Index

RUTH NICOLE BROWN is an assistant professor of gender and women's studies at the
University of Illinois at Urbana-Champaign.
She is the author of *Black Girlhood Celebration: Toward a Hip-Hop Feminist Pedagogy*
and coeditor of *Wish to Live: The Hip-Hop
Feminism Pedagogy Reader.*

The University of Illinois Press
is a founding member of the
Association of American University Presses.

Composed in 10.25/13.25 Minion Pro
by Celia Shapland
at the University of Illinois Press
Manufactured by Sheridan Books, Inc.

University of Illinois Press
1325 South Oak Street
Champaign, IL 61820-6903
www.press.uillinois.edu